Latin American
Popular Culture

Latin American Popular Culture

ARTHUR ARISTIDES NATELLA, JR.

McFarland & Company, Inc., Publishers
Jefferson, North Carolina, and London

LIBRARY OF CONGRESS CATALOGUING-IN-PUBLICATION DATA

Natella, Arthur A., 1941–
    Latin American popular culture / Arthur Aristides Natella, Jr.
        p.   cm.
    Includes bibliographical references and index.

    ISBN 978-0-7864-3511-1
    softcover : 50# alkaline paper ∞

    1. National characteristics, Latin American.   I. Title.
    F1408.3.N38 2008
    306.098 — dc22
                                                2008012761

British Library cataloguing data are available

Cover photographs ©2008 Shutterstock

Manufactured in the United States of America

*McFarland & Company, Inc., Publishers
    Box 611, Jefferson, North Carolina 28640
        www.mcfarlandpub.com*

To all those tourists to Latin America
who may have experienced
undue culture shock or confusion

AND

To all those businessmen and -women
who have tried to conclude a deal in Latin America
and have failed:

READ THIS BOOK AND TRY AGAIN.

Acknowledgments

I would like to thank fellow researchers who have shared their wisdom and learning with me. This would include Prof. Erminio Neglia of the University of Toronto, Canada; Mexican writer and artist Yolanda Salido Arriola; Colombian researcher Jennifer Cardozo; Peruvian Gonzalo Chacón; and Mrs. Ana Paula Trulín of Rio de Janeiro, Brazil; as well as Eve Taylor and Leonardo Santos of Belo Horizonte, Brazil.

I wish to thank the students who have used selected chapters of this manuscript as a text in our class in Latin American Popular Culture at the American International College in Springfield, Massachusetts, since we could not find any comparable text. Their comments, which have included many kind words of encouragement, have been most welcome and most helpful.

Lastly I would like to thank many of the Latin American colleagues I have worked with over the years in the teaching field. Little did I realize it at the time, although I do realize it now, that the casual conversations that we have had in the office, often over a simple cup of coffee, have offered me a better understanding of the Latin American mind and Latin American perspectives on a wide array of topics than I ever gained from a professional lifetime of teaching and research.

Contents

Preface

Books on the subject of culture of any given society do exist, yet they may not always be easy to find. Perhaps this is true because the very word "culture," which the dictionary defines as patterns of living, is a very broad, even abstract, term that does very little to fire up the imagination. All too often the study of this subject has been limited to a description of clothing styles, food or other aspects of life in exotic parts of the world which at first glance may appear to be of interest mainly to travelers or scholars.

College courses on the culture and civilization of a particular nation or part of the world have traditionally been largely limited to covering historical events and works that might be considered so-called "high culture," namely symphonic music, ballet, classics of literature, and the kind of art that we usually find in museums or important private collections. Rarely do published studies present the idea that daily life as it is lived by millions of people everywhere and anywhere actually reflects social patterns in a remarkable way. However, an increased academic interest in the study of popular culture has developed in recent years. Just in the area of music, college courses are now given in jazz and musical theatre. Academic research has even extended into the field of comic books.[1]

Still, little attention has been paid to the lives of millions of people as they go about the business of living. Many people either attend school or teach in an educational institution; they may work in an office, private or public, or they may have their own business, and traditional studies of the cultural patterns of any place in the world have often given little attention to these aspects of life — how is business conducted differently in other nations? What is home and family life like? What do people talk about in

1

their casual conversations, and are these topics at least sometimes influenced by the cultural patterns that form their lives? These are just some of the issues that this study attempts to investigate.

These topics are too important to be left in abstract terms, and every effort has been made to investigate these issues from a hands-on, down- to-earth view. The implications are immensely practical. Just in the areas of business and foreign policy alone, differences in attitudes and problems in communication often arise, not because of basic problems themselves, but from a lack of understanding of how these issues are perceived from a differing cultural perspective.

But even on a more personal level, questions such as whether or not it is true that in the Hispanic world people work to live while in a country like the United States people live to work are important to us all. After all, we all wish to get as much out of life as possible, and if there is at least some truth in this old adage we may wonder if we should consider relocating to another part of this world. If that is not possible, we might also wonder how we could acquire the Latin American positive approach to life.

These are hardly academic questions. Rather they go to the core of our existence as do a whole host of other values which we try to consider from a comparative point of view. This is not to imply that anyone should or might necessarily want to reject his or her own set of living principles and ways of thinking just because other viewpoints are possible. However the acquisition of a broader understanding of possible ways of thinking and living can lead to greater understanding among different segments of the world, and it offers all of us alternative ways of viewing the events of our own daily lives.

Our purview of course includes the whole continent of South America, including Portuguese-speaking Brazil and the three Guyanas — British, French and Surinam, the nation formerly known as Dutch Guyana. Our study extends into Central America, including Belize, formerly known as British Honduras, as well as the Caribbean political entities — Cuba, Puerto Rico, the Dominican Republic and Haiti.

Though the very phrase "Latin America," which implies a solid cultural unity among all these nations, is a vast and a politically dangerous oversimplification, yet a consideration of a study such as this one may suggest that there are certain cultural patterns that pervade the social fabric of these nations which constitute one of the most important sections of this world — an area that has the potential to form one of the most vital cultural and commercial parts of the planet.

I

How Latin Is Latin America?

The term "Latin America" used to refer to the land mass south of the United States border, is familiar to us all, yet there still exists some confusion about its meaning. On a very elementary level it usually refers to countries that speak languages that are derived from ancient Latin such as French, Portuguese, Italian and Spanish. These are called Romance languages since they are descended from the language of the Roman Empire. In a very real sense they *are* Latin since at no point in the last two thousand years did the inhabitants of the southern European countries that speak these languages stop speaking Latin. There were no silent days in their history. On the contrary, people kept on speaking Latin until the changes in that language become so great that new names were given to various dialects of local speech. For example, the Latin spoken in France was called French while the Latin spoken in Spain was and still is called Spanish. Therefore anyone who finds a remarkable similarity between these languages can be sure that it is not the product of an accident, for most of the languages now spoken in Latin America are truly branches of the same tree; or to look at it in another way, these languages are related to each other just as people are related to each other. They might be considered to be siblings or at least first cousins.

Still, even on this linguistic level, the adscription of a singular identity to Latin America escapes our facile generalizations, for there are many other languages which are spoken there besides those which are directly derived from Latin. There have always been and still are innumerable Indian languages. Paraguay, for example, is still considered to be a bilingual country with both Spanish and the indigenous language, Guaraní, of almost equal importance. In addition and contrary to popular opinion, there are countries which were colonized by Europeans who spoke languages from very different historical traditions. Such is the case of the Guyanas — British and Dutch Guyana, now known as Surinam. British Guyana has its own claim to fame as the place of origin of the world's rarest postage stamp, while Surinam is probably the least known of the Guyanas, yet the Dutch character of its settlement in terms of picturesque architecture and language cannot be denied.

Likewise the country known as Belize, or *Bélice* in Spanish, was known not very long ago as British Honduras. This exotic locale still boasts a melange of languages and cultures, not only English, but the language of Mennonite settlers, migrants from various parts of India and China, as well as Spanish-speaking inhabitants who have come from neighboring Mexico.[1]

Off the coast of Argentina is a group of islands known as the Falkland Islands, or Islas Malvinas to the Argentines. These have been a source of political controversy between Argentina and England, since both countries have claimed these lands as their own. The result was a short lived war between these two nations several decades ago with England emerging as the victor and the eventual owner of these relatively obscure territories.

Confusion exists on other levels as well when we invoke the name "Latin America." In the popular mind there exists much confusion between the names "Latin America" and "South America," since many people believe that both terms are synonymous. Actually, of course, Latin America refers to the entire geographical area south of the U.S. border while "South America" refers to the land mass which comprises the southernmost continent in the Western Hemisphere. The entirety of Latin America naturally includes Central America and Mexico as well as areas in the Caribbean.

The matter becomes even more complicated when we begin to consider the reality of a place known as North America. As someone said in the classic *Alice in Wonderland*, it all becomes "curiouser and curiouser."

A visitor from the United States in Latin America is likely to describe himself or herself as being an American. This title is as interesting as it is noteworthy, since some Latin Americans take umbrage at such a name. They believe that residents of the U.S. may be implying that they alone are the important citizens in this vast hemisphere and that all others do not have the right to call themselves "Americans."

Of course such is rarely if ever what is intended in such a description of nationality, yet the reaction mentioned above can and does sometimes take place. Therefore we might ask what alternative term might be used. One could describe oneself as being "North American," and that would seem to settle the issue, yet that is far from being the case. After all, North America includes not only the United States, but Canada and Mexico. To imply, then, that the term "North America" only refers to the United States is to also suggest in the minds of some listeners that only the United States is a significant part of this continent and that other countries are not even worth mentioning. This is generally not what is at issue when the name "North American" is used, but conceivably its lack of precision in describing national origin could give rise to such an interpretation.

But this does not even answer whether the name "Latin America" is valid in the first place. After all, it was not used by Spain or Portugal when those countries tried to establish their colonies in the New World, rather it is a concept of relatively modern origin. As we have learned, not all of the nations south of the U.S. border speak languages which derive from Latin, nor do they all share to an equal degree social characteristics which are usually connected with the European countries which speak those languages — the countries of mostly southern Europe — Spain, Portugal, Belgium, France, Italy, Switzerland and Romania. To lump all the land mass of Latin America together is to suggest that all the nations there are identical to some degree or other and they all share the same attitudes and cultural patterns.

Whether or not this may be the case is hardly of academic importance. On the contrary, it is of vital interest to such fields as international business and foreign policy. Can we adopt one political or commercial strategy that will solve all potential problems in all of these areas, or do we have to take a closer look to scrutinize the culture and civilizations in each and every nation, and tailor our approach to each nation state?

The problem presented here is analogous to that proposed by political strategists and business leaders who want to capitalize on the Hispanic vote or the Hispanic market in the United States. When dealing with popular culture and general attitudes it is tempting to believe that all Spanish-speaking people are in lock step with each other as far as their buying habits or their political leanings. Unfortunately, for those who wish to capitalize on the growing influence of Hispanics in the United States, reality is by no means as simple as that.

The same may be said of Latin America itself. Though most of the countries south of the U.S. border may indeed be "Latin," and we will continue to attempt to define that term more precisely as our study continues, there exist vast differences among them in terms of economy, popular culture, language, political realities, historical traditions and many other issues. To lump all of these countries together as identical would constitute a gross oversimplification.

This reality exists not only on a national level, but it reaches down to each and every individual's concept of self-identity. In the United States, Latin Americans and Spanish-speaking citizens within the United States are often called "Latinos" or "Hispanics," and there is certainly nothing incorrect nor misleading in either term. But these designations, like the term "Latin America" itself, imply that all people that would fit into such categories regard themselves in a generic way as being "Hispanic" or "Latino." The oversimplification of this reality was very evident when a policeman arrested a Spanish-speaking citizen in a U.S. city and asked, "You're Latino. Isn't that true?"

The policeman was very surprised when this man who came from Latin America was offended by the question. The policeman wondered, if this person is from Latin America, what is the problem in saying so?

To this officer's great surprise, the individual did not really understand nor recognize the term "Latino," and he resented his own nationality being grouped together with that of persons of different national origin. As far as he was concerned, these identities were as different as night and day, and should never be lumped together in one such generic term.[2]

The concept here is an important and basic one since what might be true for the popular mind of one Latin American may be true for the whole of Latin America itself. Far from this man feeling a kinship with the hundreds of millions of people known generally as "Latins" or "Hispanics," he simply regarded himself as a national coming from one specific Latin American country, and he deeply resented having his nationality generalized.

Making the very same mistake, decades ago, when the United States was having negotiations with Panama, a political pundit theorized that it was in the interest of the United States to hurry to return the canal to Panama; not doing so might severely hurt our relations with all of the nations south of the border.

Such mistaken thinking is surely prevalent among our politicians and our so-called political experts who try to devise "Latin American policies" that will appeal to every corner of the southern continent. The truth of the matter is that far from seeing themselves as one geographic, cultural or political entity, countries in that part of the world have historic rivalries. Chile and Peru have endured disputes of their borders and have engaged in what has been called the War of the Pacific. The same is true in the cultural sense between Guatemala and Mexico, inasmuch as the former nation has expressed a resentment of the invasion of Mexican culture through television, music and the arts in general.

Lifestyles

Although we may look at the heritage of the Latin language in the linguistic formation of countries, still more is implied in the use of the term. "Latin" also refers to the lifestyles of countless millions of people both in southern Europe and in Latin America. These characteristics run the gamut of preferences in daily living. In effect they determine popular culture on the most immediate level. Some of these supposed Latin characteristics may be almost commonplaces of "Latinity," while others may be less known. At the risk of forming oversimplifications, which always exists when we make generalizations about vast numbers of people, we will venture to list some of these differences. We will do so in terms of the origin of these living styles as they have existed for centuries in the parts of Europe from which they most likely have come — Central and Northern Europe as opposed to the Latin countries of southern Europe. These characteristics can include:

Northern and Central Europe	*Southern Europe*
Indoor culture	Street or outdoor culture
Individualist cultures	Group-family cultures
Present-future oriented	Tradition-oriented
Highly industrial	Less industrialized
Religion	Religion and religiosity
Greater respect for punctuality	Less importance given to punctuality
Respect for technical-based knowledge and high technology	Respect for traditional wisdom
Less superstitious	More superstitious
More direct in conversation	Less direct, less blunt in conversation
Greater pragmatism	Less concern with what is pragmatic or practical

Of course these generalizations may be too broad and too conclusive, since numerous exceptions must and will always exist. Other objections will arise to the stereotypical nature of at least some of these comments, which may appear to be little more than often-repeated clichés. However it may be helpful to remember that clichés and stereotypes become such because many people believe that they contain at least a basis in fact. Furthermore, while these generalizations are much too broad for everyone to agree with them all, they may at least serve as a springboard for further speculation about "Latinity" and about the Latin nature of Latin America.

Other Cultures

Once while giving a college lecture about Latin America, this author mentioned the name of the great patriot of Chilean history, Bernardo O'Higgins, at which point the students in the class laughed. "This is not the name of a Latin American," they all proclaimed. "This is the name of an Irishman."

This instructor then asked why people from Ireland could not have left their native country to settle in Chile? After all, millions of Irish families have come to the United States over the past centuries. Why not could they also go to Latin America?[3]

This student reaction highlighted a common misunderstanding relating to Latin America — that *all* of it directly reflects Hispanic or Portuguese culture only, and that everyone living there is of Spanish or Portuguese descent. Names in that part of the world always have to sound like typical Hispanic or Portuguese names. There never could be a Jones or a Smith living in Latin America.

This ridiculous stereotype is compounded by the U.S. government, which frequently on forms asks an applicant to identify his or her racial or ethnic background. The question in relation to people of Hispanic background is not are you or your family of Spanish or Latin American origin, but rather do you have a Hispanic surname? The implication clearly being that unless you have a "Hispanic" last name you could never actually be Hispanic or Latin American.

Of course the idea is absurd and many people such as the Latin American patriot O'Higgins would never qualify as a Latin American according to our government bureaucrats, who combine ignorance with what some might consider an invasion of privacy in the first place.

By the very same logic which they display in such questionnaires, the former president of Mexico, Vicente Fox, who of course has a typically Anglo-Saxon last name, should never have been president of that important nation because he does not really qualify as a Latin American.

The same could be said then for other Latin American presidents such as Carlos Menem, a recent president of Argentina, who is of Middle Eastern descent, as well as Alberto Fujimori, former president of Peru, who is of Japanese descent.

All of the above considerations may be seen as a perfect example of the ignorance regarding the reality of the Latin American world. Awareness often is based on entirely inaccurate stereotypes which are often not only mistaken, but woefully out-of-date as well.

The analysis of all of such stereotypical notions is beyond the scope of our study, however we can state that such ideas are themselves based on more pervasive concepts, often piling one mistaken idea on top of another.

The idea that the United States is and has been a melting pot of cultures, races and nationalities, but that all the dozens of countries of Latin America are strictly Latin, and no other groups other than those which have their origin in Spain or Portugal have any representation there at all, is a false one.

It is useful to bear in mind that many individuals commonly refer to Latin American cuisine as "Spanish" food, or Latin American music as "Spanish" music, not only implying that these and other aspects of the popular culture of that part of the world are identical to those found in Spain, but that all of Latin America is identical in these and in other respects. Nothing could be further from the truth, and this whole study will try to explain that Latin America, although it is Latin indeed, shares a rich and very varied series of cultures which are often markedly different from those found in the mother countries.

Not only is this true in the abstract, but on a geographical and political level. We have at least one country founded by Dutch settlers and others founded by English and French-speaking colonists, as well as a large number of immigrants who have come to Latin America from literally all other parts of the world.

Indeed one of the most remarkable aspects of Latin American immigration was the mass movement of millions of citizens from Italy, Russia and Eastern Europe at the turn of the twentieth century. Few observers outside of Argentina may be aware that, just as countless Italian immigrants came to the United States at that time, the population of Argentina doubled as many Italians sought their fortune there. The result, of course, was that the influence of Italy on the popular culture of Argentina was so great that at one point in its history a vote was taken in the national legislature to change the official language from Spanish to Italian. Surprisingly, the measure lost by only one vote. In addition, at that time, vast numbers of other immigrants arrived in the port of Buenos Aires from Russia and Eastern Europe and other nations as well. One of the classic works of Argentine literature is the novel *The Jewish Gauchos* (*Los gauchos judíos*) by Alberto Gerchunoff.

Even today the Italian lexicon has left its mark in the Spanish language of Argentina, including such words as *laburar* from the Italian *laborare*, meaning "to work," instead of the traditional Spanish word *trabajar*; or *mangar* instead of the Spanish term *comer* (to eat) coming from the Italian *mangare*.

Just to mention a few names of important contributors to the culture of Latin America of non–Latin descent is impressive. The list includes the Argentine authors Benito Lynch, author of *The Englishman of the Bones* (*El Inglés de los güesos*), Rodolfo Wash, author of such works as *Stories for Gamblers* (*Cuentos para tahures*); dramatist Samuel Eichelbaum; the French-born author Paul Groussac, the creator of the novel *Forbidden Fruit* (*Fruto vedado*); the Cuban Alejo Carpentier, who was of French family origin and who wrote the classic novel *The Lost Steps* (*Los pasos perdidos*) among many other works;

Mexican writer Justo Sierra O'Reilly; president of Paraguay whose Germanic sounding name, Stroessner, clearly indicates his descent.

Likewise we may mention the Mexican artists Frida Khalo, and Leonora Carrington as well as the well-known Mexican writer whose family is of Polish origin, Elena Poniatowska.[4]

There are often many nations within one nation in Latin America from the point of view of popular attitudes and culture. just as great cultural disparities exist among many of the nations themselves. This simple truth is well illustrated in the delightful Argentine novel, *Mashimón* by Liliana Najdorf, a story in which a middle-aged Argentine woman who takes a trip to Guatemala is so astonished by the exotic culture of that nation she almost feels that she is visiting a strange new planet.

In one section of the novel the protagonist reacts with great surprise. "Magda looked out of the window, now incredulous, taking advantage of the fact that her car had slowed down. She began to notice that there were no trees in the street. She commented on this without expecting an answer, only as a way of saying words to express her astonishment."[5]

In the aforementioned Cuban novel, *The Lost Steps* by Alejo Carpentier, the protagonist travels from New York into the Amazon jungle, realizing that he is really traveling through time, walking backwards through history as he experiences radically different cultures existing at the same time within the Latin American reality. At one point he reflects that he has journeyed from the twentieth-century world back to societies that literally still exist in the Stone Age.

In fact, far from this being a merely fictional reflection, Carpentier has commented in his essays that Latin America is very fascinating because these multiple layers of temporal development actually do exist side-by-side in the modern world.

Such a realization has not only national and hemispheric repercussions, but actually worldwide implications. In recent studies of so-called globalization and the formation of what has been called a flat world, at the same a "round world" is being developed; as technology advances, the "round," or more distinct differences between indigenous and technological-based cultures, actually become more pronounced.

The paradox is worthy of being noticed since it is infrequently mentioned in the mad rush of many pundits to proclaim the gospel of the seemingly newly found globalism.

Furthermore, if the Spanish-speaking parts of Latin America were actually just a carbon copy of the culture of the mother country, one would expect that the Hispanic elements in these societies would be carbon copies of the hallmarks of the ethos of Spain itself.

According to Ramón Menéndez Pidal, often considered to be the greatest hispanist of the twentieth century and author of more than one hundred books on Spanish studies, realism is a hallmark of the Spanish character. This can be seen as early as one thousand years ago in the classic of Spanish literature, *The Poem of the Cid*, a literary work which details the exploits of the national hero of Spain, Rodrigo Díaz de Vivar, better known as the Cid. This was a real historical figure who led Spain's wars against the invading Arabs in the Middle Ages. According to literary critics like Menéndez Pidal, this early epic poem does not show the flights of fancy which characterize similar poems of epic heroes like Roland in French literature or the knights in the Arthurian cycle in English literature. As a matter of fact the exaggerations of the knightly deeds of these bold adventurers were so outlandish in the literature of the period that they became the basis for Miguel de Cervantes's satire of the novels of chivalry, *Don Quixote*, one of the greatest classics of world literature.[6]

Spanish scholar Dámaso Alonso has reiterated this view in his study of realism in Spanish literature (not all literature in the Spanish language, but rather the literature of Spain itself) when he states that although the Spanish taste alternates between extreme realism and a taste for fantasy, it is very possible that the realistic vein in the classics of Spanish literature of the Renaissance may have become the basis for modern-day realism in literature and perhaps in cinema.[7]

The relevance of these observations about the Latin or southern European nature of Latin America is that this same realism does not characterize the history of Latin American literature. On the contrary, the magic and the fantastic views of the world around us which have become world famous represent a vastly different perspective on life which may be more in keeping with the heritage of African and indigenous cultures than with the possible cultural influence of Spain itself.

A Different Melting Pot

Realizing that Latin America does constitute a kind of melting pot and that it does not automatically imitate nor reproduce the "Latin" culture, however that may be defined, of the mother countries of Spain and Portugal, it is important to realize that the melting pot formed itself in different ways in different areas. In terms of indigenous societies, it is abundantly clear that one difference between the United States and many Latin American countries is that the United States tried its best to subordinate or even wipe out the influence of Indian cultures to prevent them from entering the mainstream of society. In Latin America this has hardly been the case. In Central America as well as in nations like Mexico, Brazil, and Ecuador among others, the indigenous native cultures continue to flow into the mainstream.

In the case of Mexico, the most prominent sign of the importance and recognition of that country's indigenous culture is to be found in the national flag, which proudly shows the figure of an eagle with a serpent in its mouth. This is a direct reference to the ancient Aztec Indian belief that their gods told them to continue to be a nomadic people until they should find a large bird eating a serpent. At this spot they should stop wandering and found a permanent civilization. This place turned out to be Mexico City, now considered to be the largest city in the world.

In other countries such as Chile, Argentina and Uruguay, traditional societies have not had the same degree of impact. Many Latin Americans believe that citizens of what is sometimes referred to as the southern cone may well have felt superiority over other Latin American nations, because they claim to have been the heirs to the cultural traditions of Europe without the concurrent influences of as many indigenous societies.

No study of the basic makeup of the popular cultures of Latin America would be complete without mentioning the impact of African-based societal norms. The great extent of the slave trade in that part of the world is a historical fact. Indeed the record indicates that some 60,000 slaves were brought into Cuba alone between 1830 and 1850.[8]

In addition, both Cuba and Brazil were the last countries in the Western Hemisphere to outlaw slavery, this occurring some twenty years after the banning of slavery in the United States. Just as a reminder of how prevalent slavery was in colonial Latin America, we might do well to note that in the days of the great Mexican author, Sor Juana Inés de la Cruz, a nun in seventeenth-century Mexico was permitted to bring her slave to live with her in the convent.

Colonial Latin America was indeed a racist society, with those who could boast of pure Spanish blood forming the cream of the crop of the social order according to the values of the time. In seventeenth-century Mexico alone there were some sixteen different social classes largely based on racial characteristics. Indians and slaves as well as people of mixed racial heritage were at the bottom of the social scale.

Of course the countries south of the U.S. border that have coastlines closest to Africa show perhaps the greatest influence of African social customs. This would include Venezuela and Brazil, as well areas in the Caribbean including French-speaking Haiti. Yet no amount of prejudice has been able to blot out the contributions that have been made by these groups to popular culture, including literature, music, religion, and medicine as well as other components of modern life. In the case of Brazil, the novel *Macunaima* by Mario de Andrade communicates the exotic charm of the culture of Africa in its very title, along with its fantastic vision of the world.[9] This also can be seen in the stories of Cuban writer Lydia Cabrera, among many other examples.[10]

The question then of exactly how "Latin" Latin America is remains to be answered, for it cannot be established in an absolute fashion since that definition of Latinity will change from place to place. Once again we must state that there does not exist, contrary to popular opinion, one Latin America, but many separate nations, each one with its own historical and contemporary identity.

To make matters even more complex, in another part of our study we will consider the very sizeable eastern and especially the Middle Eastern cultural influence in Latin America which has come down through the centuries as a heritage of the Arab influence in the history of Spain. This influence persisted for some seven hundred years, from 711 until 1492, the same year in which Columbus made his first voyage to the new world.

This is a heady mix of cultural patterns to be sure, and to it we would have to add the great influence of the United States, not only politically and economically, but socially as well. The list of foreign influences could go on forever as we come to realize that Latin America is and has been a melting pot, but it is not the same "crisol humano" found in Spain, nor is it the same racial and cultural mixture found in Latin America's neighbor to the north, the United States.

Yet there is much that is similar in the social formation of Latin America. The idea that once one goes over the border into Mexico one is entering a completely different world akin to a different planet is a false. This viewpoint, based largely on the monumental ignorance of the other part of our continental realities, is contrasted by Peruvian scholar Luis Alberto Sánchez in his book *¿Existe Latinoamérica?* (*Does Latin America Exist?*) where he rightly points out that many of the geographical features of the United States continue into Latin America. These include the Sonoran Desert, and the mountain chains which run throughout our hemisphere called the Rocky Mountains in the west of the U.S. and Canada. In Mexico they are called the Sierra Madre and in South America they form the Andes, all part of a range of mountains that help form our hemisphere from Alaska down to the tip of the Tierra del Fuego.

We can speak of geography and history, but perhaps it is in the mind and heart of the average citizen, those who live popular culture each and every day, that these realities are most important. The challenge of defining these qualities and attitudes will be the challenge of this study. But as we begin to do that we might well remember the words of American writer Carlos Castañeda as he reflects on the new reality to which he was introduced in his travels in Mexico. In his book *Journey to Ixtlán* he speaks, as in his other works, of his apprenticeship with the Yaqui Indian magician Don Juan, saying "I must first explain the basic premise of sorcery as Don Juan presented it to me. He said that for a sorcerer, the world of everyday life is not real, or out there, as we believe it is. For a sorcerer, reality, the world we all know is only a description."[11]

Latin America, then, is composed of many realities. On studying its culture one finds that it is like entering a hall of mirrors, a gallery of shifting images. On the one hand we see a reflection of ourselves, and we believe we are not seeing much that is radically different, then we continue down the hall and see new images and new reflections which surprise, perhaps even startle us. We cannot recognize nor understand them all at first glance. They are worth a second and a third look. These images are sometimes clear, sometimes cloudy. Perhaps they are even mysterious, but they are always a challenge to our ability to understand them. They may at times be unsettling, and they certainly are complex, but they never fail to expand our minds with their intrinsic fascination.

II

A Latin American View of Itself and the World

We all believe that we know the difference between what happens in the real world and what is sheer fantasy. Therefore it may come as a surprise to consider that the view of what is real and what is not, and where the fine line between the two concepts really exists, is more a product of one's culture that may be generally realized.

It is the thesis of this study that the Latin American vision of the real world is often different than that which exists elsewhere. The well known tendency towards depicting magical realism in modern Latin American literature has provided a world-wide audience for authors that portray such views of human life — authors such as Gabriel García Márquez, Juan Rulfo and many others. All too rarely, however, has the question been posed as to why this type of literature is found in the fiction of Latin America and not in many other national narrative traditions.

Perhaps the first Latin American author to try to define the "fantastic" nature of the Latin American reality was the Cuban author Alejo Carpentier, who in his essay on what he called the marvelous nature of Latin America, stated that the continent itself was frequently unbelievable. The geography, the flora and fauna and other aspects of this part of the world appeared to be so outlandish as to be almost impossible to comprehend with our logical mind. In effect, it was unbelievable, and he goes on to state that while in Haiti he realized that "the presence and authority of the real marvelous was not a privilege unique to Haiti but the patrimony of all the Americas."[1]

Historically speaking, Latin America is a combination of the indigenous Indian cultures, the African culture and the cultures brought over by the European settlers mainly those of Spain and Portugal. While American and African cultures based their belief systems on legend, myth and what might be best called a magical concept of reality, ostensibly the Europeans of the sixteenth and seventeenth centuries brought a scientifically based way of viewing the universe.

On taking a closer look at the colonization of Latin America we should keep in mind the observations of Irving Leonard in his introduction to Mariano Picón-Salas's *A Cultural History of Spanish America from Conquest to Independence*." He states, "In the one hundred and fifteen years from the first voyage of Columbus to the settlements at Jamestown, knowledge of the physical and intellectual world of Europe had expanded enormously."[2]

The English settlers, according to Leonard, were much more the heirs to the influence of the growing scientific revolution. As Picón-Salas has expressed it, many of the basic philosophical and psychological differences between North and South America were cast in a mold that was already formed in the era of colonial expansion. "There was in our beginning a kind of underdeveloped economic sense and a disdain for the pragmatic and utilitarian currents rising in northern Europe and destined to reach a high point in nineteenth-century industrialization and its machine culture."[3]

Because of this, the colonization of Latin America was based on myth and legend; for the early Spanish explorers were motivated by their belief in such fantasies as the Fountain of Youth, The Man Made of Gold, "El Dorado," and the Seven Cities of Gold, as well as the paradise of Adam and Eve, which they believed still existed on the other side of the Atlantic. Furthermore not only the *conquistadores* but their sailors harbored outlandish fantasies in their minds.

This in turn mixed with the myths and legends of indigenous populations among which the best known have been the Mayans and Aztecs in Mexico and the Incas in Peru. Added to this are the legends and myths brought to America by the slaves that came from Africa. To this day the culture includes so-called "magical religions" such as the Macumba religion of Brazil, and Santería and Voodoo, most notably in the Caribbean.

When the slaves were brought to America by force from Africa, they were forbidden to practice their traditional African religions. Under threat of severe punishment they were obliged to worship Catholic saints. Using popular Catholic imagery such as traditional statues of religious figures, they often outwardly prayed to those saints but inwardly considered those religious images to be those reminding them of their African gods. Thus began a complex system of worship in which it is has been said that African saints

or deities became mixed up in the popular imagination with Christian supernatural personages.

Far from being religions which are practiced today only in certain parts
of Latin America, immigrants from these parts of the world have naturally
brought their beliefs with them and now Voodoo and Santería are commonly
practiced in a number of parts of the United States. In the case of Santería,
the priests or practitioners of this religion are known as *santeros* in the case
of men, and *santeras* in the case of women.

These *santeros* and *santeras* give out objects such as ointments, herbs,
candles, and advice on many topics, all of which may accompany the worship of such deities as Olofi, the god of the universe, and Obatla, another
holy figure in the Santería pantheon of gods.[6]

According to Himilce Novás, at one time Cuban President Carlos Prío
Socarras was reported to have given government money to the Catholic
Church and to followers of the Santería religion.[7]

As in the case of the much more well known religion called Voodoo,
Santería is rumored to have its dark side in which spells or *trabajitos* are performed on hapless victims.

On one occasion this author asked a native of the Dominican Republic what a person from his country would do if he wanted to put a spell on
someone. He answered that the Dominican would probably cross over into
Haiti to find a witch doctor that would make a doll in the image of the person supposed to be the victim of a spell. Then the witch doctor would begin
to stick pins into the doll, indicating the areas where the victim would be
oppressed by pain or some unfortunate occurrence. Stores which carry statues of religious figures and other artifacts of significance to followers of such
magical religions, known as *botánicas*, can be found in a number of areas of
the United States that host high concentrations of people of Latin American origin.

The significance of such beliefs comes in the realization that here we can
clearly see that the Latin American vision of reality commonly intertwines
with we might call the paranormal or even the supernatural, not in extremely
rare occasions such as in the case of miracles which are claimed to have been
performed by Catholic saints, but almost on a daily basis. It may be possible
to claim that traditionally the Latin American view of what is possible can
be seen as being much wider than that of the Anglo-Saxon world.

Of course literature is an important aspect of any culture and literature
is also an important reflection or by-product of any culture. Therefore the
existence of a magical sense of what is and can be, as in the tendency to
employ scenes of what has been called "magical realism," is one of the most
intriguing aspects of modern Latin American prose.

In Latin America such belief in the common meeting of the real and the paranormal is not limited to persons of little education; rather it is widespread through the cultures. American writer David St. Clair, who spent years living in Brazil, states in his book on that country, *Drum and Candle*, that the big cars and limousines of major political figures can be seen parked outside the emotionally charged meetings and ceremonies of the Brazilian *macumba*.

Another Mexican who worked with high level figures of the Mexican government has stated that the lines of professionals including government figures waiting in line to ask to have spells cast on political rivals sometimes appear to be endless.[8]

Accordingly to this wider view of what is real and what can be real, psychic phenomena enjoy a well-established, well respected place in Latin America life. Indeed many ways of foretelling the future are common, not just traditional tarot cards and palm readings. This includes the reading of the lines of the feet and hands and tea leaves as well as coffee grain readings. In this latter form of divination, a person will drink a cup of coffee which leaves a sediment of grains. The psychic will turn the cup over so that the granules will fall on the saucer or similar object and then he or she will attempt to interpret the designs made or implied by the coffee in the bottom of the saucer.

The reading of crystals and crystal balls is popular as are the reading of a variety of types of decks of cards, including what is known as the "Spanish deck," as well as Tarot cards in many forms and in a variety of designs.

In Latin America it is not considered shocking that a president of a country or other major political figure would consult with a psychic. In the case of the former president of Peru, for example, Alberto Fujimori, this former mathematics professor is said to have consulted a psychic who told him to leave teaching and go into politics since he would be very successful in that field. He did just that and eventually became president.

While it was considered shocking that first lady of the United States, Nancy Reagan, frequently consulted an astrologer, one gifted psychic in Latin America informed the author that she had read coffee grains for the first lady of her country, indicating that such readings were not to be kept secret but could easily be public knowledge without causing a scandal.[9]

Even before the Mexican revolution of 1910, spiritualist president of Mexico Francisco Madero believed that his dead brother predicted to him, by way of the sometimes occult practice of automatic writing, that he would one day become president. David St. Clair has even stated, "Magic as a way of life is nothing new to the Mexicans. They've heard about it all their lives [and] have seen it in practice."[10]

In some parts of Latin America there are cafes which boast the name of *café turco* or Turkish café. Customers are given a menu not for food but for a variety of psychic readings, such as readings of the palm of the hand, tarot cards, crystal balls, tea leaves, or coffee leaves. After choosing, the client is directed to the table of a psychic that specializes in that particular type of reading.

This is not to suggest that all Latin Americans have an interest in or even believe in the validity of such predictions, or an interest in the paranormal. Still it may be fair to say that such psychic events have traditionally been much more in the mainstream of Latin American life than they have been in other cultures. Only recently have such activities become popular with large numbers of people in the United States, since the beginning of the New Age movement. Some observers believe that this movement is not so much "new" as it is a return of an industrialized society to the roots of traditional civilization.

It has been stated that reporting of the news is not so much a reporting of what goes on in the world as it is a reporting of only those events which conveniently fit within our somewhat arbitrary view of what is real and what is possible.

This is true both for individuals and for whole societies. It may therefore surprise many readers that accounts of paranormal events, or supposed paranormal events, often are given more importance in Latin American news reporting than is the case in other cultures. Reports of the sighting of flying saucers, for example, have frequently appeared on the front page of major Latin American newspapers, while this rarely if ever occurs in the United States. This may appear to be positive or negative depending on one's point of view; however it would appear to be an extension of an historical reality rather than simply the reaction of individual journalists.

Different Levels of Reality

Also part of the Latin American tradition is the exploration of what may best be called different levels of reality or different states of consciousness.

The first association with this elevation of the human psyche brings us into contact with the shamanistic tradition derived from the Spanish word *chamán*. Shamanistic practices not only relate to the practice of healing, they also derive from the belief that there exist other levels of reality or dimensions that the human mind can perceive under certain circumstances.

The shaman claims to have access to paranormal levels of knowledge which can be used in a variety of ways. He usually goes into a trance during which he believes that he is making contact with a higher level of consciousness. One special belief is that the shaman may come into contact with the spirit of one or more protective animals that can give special knowledge and special powers to the medicine man.

Another way of gaining a higher level of consciousness is through the use of hallucinogens such as the famed magic mushroom which is found in Mexico. This substance, which has been the subject of serious scientific study, reputedly allows the shaman not only to experience special visions, but also to bring him to a paranormal level of knowledge. In some rural villages where traditional beliefs are very strong, a shaman may be asked to solve a crime such as a robbery by going into a special state of enlightenment by way of a plant such as the mushroom.

Indeed the effects of this substance are reported to be so profound that Mexican writer Antonio Vázquez Alba has claimed that one person testified after using the mushroom that "if there somewhere existed a paradise, that biblical paradise, it was there in that place at that moment."[11]

The shaman's special knowledge may even extend into a paranormal awareness of plants, herbs and other items that may bring speedy relief to sufferers of various medical conditions.

But such beliefs go beyond mere aspirations to special powers and special knowledge. They lead us into a world of an alternate vision of what might be called a magical conception of existence itself. Such a mythic, if not magical, conception of reality has had a profound effect on both the high and popular culture of Latin America since time immemorial. In recent times, the art and literature of Latin America has broken away from a slavish imitation of European models to the incorporation of the popular indigenous view of the cosmos into its aesthetic essence. The new, non-rationalistic impulses behind the creation of the new novel or the narrative of the Latin American "boom" from such authors as Mario Vargas Llosa, Alejo Carpentier, and Juan Carlos Onetti among many others often portray the cyclic nature of time. This contrasts with the western chronological sense of time, which is the foundation for modern literature of the western world, while the art of the Mexican muralist school of such talented creators as Diego Rivera and others directly reflects the influence and respect for the influence of the Indian cultural heritage.

Latin Americans' View of Their World

The influence of Spain and Portugal has been basic in the development of most of Latin America, however, as noted, it includes nations outside of this historical sphere of influence such as French-speaking Haiti, Belize, which was formerly known as British Honduras, and British, French and Dutch Guyana, now known as Surinam. In addition, the Falkland Islands off the coast of Argentina belong to England.

Nevertheless while Spain held sway over the political fortunes of most of Latin America for centuries before the movement for independence from the mother country, France has always had a major cultural influence on Latin America. For centuries wealthy families have had the tradition of sending their children to study in France, and the ideas of the rationalist French thinkers of the 18th century such as Voltaire, Rousseau, and others were the true intellectual inspiration for the hemispheric revolution of political independence that took place at the beginning of the nineteenth century.

Even to this day the furniture styles of many upper middle- and upper-class Latin Americans betray the strong influence of the décor of the French furniture styles of Louis XIV or the Empire styles of Napoleon III, in contrast with the British decorative styles which have had a greater influence in the United States. At the same time French literature has had a major influence on the direction that the literature of Latin America has taken for at least the last two centuries.

We must also take into account the great cultural influence of the United States in fashion, popular music, television, movies and the like. Still there is the deep sense that Spain is the mother country for most of the Latin American world, just as England is the mother country for the United States.

These inherited or traditional modes of cultural indebtedness have led some observers to theorize that the influence of great European powers may have caused a lurking sense of cultural inferiority or lack of national and personal identity that may well have lingered up to modern times. Such an idea was succinctly expressed by the Mexican essayist Leopoldo Zea. "The man of America feels himself to be European in origin, but inferior to the European account of his dwelling place." He adds, "Anyone feeling inferior as a man of America also feels inferior as a national, as a member of one of the nations of the American continent."[12]

At the same time, the well-known Mexican man of letters, Alfonso Reyes, has expressed a similar idea in the following terms: "On top of the misfortune of being human and being modern, [there is] the very specific misfortune of being American, that is born and rooted in a soil that was not the present focus of civilization, but a branch office of the world."[13] Such a statement may remind the reader of a similar claim by the American author, H.L. Menken, to the effect that to be American is to be second-rate.

Yet the task of trying to understand the Latin American view of its place in the world goes to the national as well as the hemispheric level. Here we must recognize the best known attempt to understand the national character of a Latin American nation — the study of the Mexican national character, *The Labyrinth of Solitude*, written by the Mexican Nobel Prize winner Octavio Paz.

Going back to the days of the first Spanish invasion, Paz sees the Mexican as having developed a national sense of inferiority as being a member of a conquered nation. In this approach the Mexican author turns to the psychological theories of Alfred Adler by way of the influence of a previous Mexican thinker, Samuel Ramos. Just as Adler claimed that human beings inherently grow up with an inferiority complex, Paz expressed the view that Mexicans, as conquered people, harbor an even deeper sense of their own inferiority.

A contrasting view of national character is given by Argentine author Jorge Luís Borges when he explains the nature of his countrymen. "Unlike North Americans and almost all Europeans, the Argentine does not identify himself with the State. That can be explained by the fact that, in this country, the governments are usually exceedingly bad, or the state in an inconceivable abstraction."[14]

The Argentine thinker goes on to say that for this reason the citizen of his country sees himself as an individual rather than as a citizen.

Other observations on Latin American reality can extend not to one nation nor to the entire hemisphere but to an area or a group of nations. Puerto Rican writer Luís Rafael Sánchez has waxed eloquent over what he calls "Caribbeanness," describing the pervasive influence of the water that surrounds the islands of the Caribbean that he calls his home. "Caribbean nature has more pleasing sounds that any guitar. The ineluctable sea sends its sound through the islands — the fickle ocean sound that either rocks you to sleep or scares you out of your wits."[15]

The same author claims as well that music is an integral part of all of life in the Caribbean, for it is a basic part of human existence there that accompanies the natural music of the ocean waters.

However the questions are cast, whether in national, regional or hemispheric terms, it is true that the quest for identity is one of the hallmarks of Latin American reality. Far from being simply an abstract question, the domain only of ivory tower theorists, many Latin Americans see this as a vital personal issue — for whatever my nation is, therefore am I. In the Buenos Aires area of Argentina alone, there exists the highest concentration of psychotherapists in the world and it often has been said that the main reason that patients there feel the motivation to seek therapy is their desire to answer the questions posed by their identity problems. "Who am I as an Argentine? Am I basically a person of European cultural heritage or am I more American — a person historically cut off to one degree or another from the European cultural tradition? If so, does that mean that I am automatically a cultural second rater? Or further, am I a member therefore of the so-called Third World? If so, what does that that term really mean and what are its implications for me and for my country?"

Unity and Diversity

Nor does the issue stop there, for the next logical step is the question is there one Latin America or are there many different aspects of the Latin American reality? Or to pose the question another way, is there more unity than diversity among the member states of this segment of the globe and is the term "Latin America," which implies a great unity of characteristics among all the nations, really valid?

The differences between one nation and another are pointed out by Mexican essayist José Luis Martínez. "Mountain chains, deserts, tropical and equatorial jungles, high plateaus, large rivers, pampas and flat lands, as well as national borders, contribute to the division and lack of communication of Latin America."[16]

Then again this loyalty to one's country is often matched by a profound attachment to one's province or state. Indeed the differences between various regions of the Latin world, both in Europe and in Latin America, are often so great as to make inhabitants of each province or section of a country believe that they are actually living in separate countries rather than in unified nations. The strength of such local identities is more than adequately demonstrated by the Basque separatist movement in that region of Spain or in the movement to revive local culture and the traditional language of Brittany in France, as well as the French Corsican independence movement.

Traditionally, however, Latin Americans do sense a basic unity among themselves as they view their collective differences with the United States, which they often believe is the "other America," what Nicaraguan poet Rubén Darío has called "a wealthy country joining the cult of Mammon to the cult of Hercules."[17]

In his influential poem, "To Roosevelt," he claims that the United States possesses economic and military power, but Latin America has maintained its traditional values and its prominence in matters of art and of the spirit, an attitude similar to that expressed by the Uruguayan thinker José Enrique Rodó, in his well-known book *Ariel*.

Yet paradoxes exist here as elsewhere. First and foremost, whenever the spirit of Latin people is mentioned, the well-known solidarity which exists between family members comes to the fore. Here in this part of Western civilization, family values are alive and well and this strong identification of the individual with his or her group extends from the primary social unit to the worker's identification with his place of employment. The Latin American worker, like many of his Asian counterparts, often feels a loyalty to his company and his employer which extends far beyond that of employees in many other societies, and he likes to believe that this loyalty is reciprocated. In fact, in Colombia, a company is expected to care for its employees to the degree that if a worker commits suicide, his employer may be fined by the national government.

This commitment extends to the place where an individual lives as well. In highly industrialized countries there exists an implied belief that an individual's work should demand greater loyalty than that which he or she gives to the value of personal roots in terms of family and place of origin. It is often taken for granted that if an employee is asked to relocate to another part of the country and leave extended family and friends behind he or she will do it without hesitation. After all, work defines life and therefore it should command the ultimate degree of loyalty.

At one time, however, researchers in a small Latin American town asked the citizens there where they would like to live if they were to move to another locale. Not only did they not want to move, they didn't even understand the logic of the question in the first place. To them it was inconceivable that a person would ever want to live anywhere else.

U.S. citizens tend to see their destinies tied up with the government of their nation as they wonder how changing tax policies and interest rates will impact them. In spite of a super-strong sense of patriotism, paradoxically it may not be an exaggeration to state that Latin Americans often believe that they will prosper individually and as a nation in spite of, not because of, policies of their political leaders.

In lands where politics has often zigzagged from the extreme right to the extreme left in recent decades and democracy has followed a difficult road, Latin Americans have learned to harbor limited expectations of their national leaders and this in turn often leads them to depend more on themselves, their families, their friends and their employers than on the nation state.

Past, Present and Future

On visiting the United States, Chinese visitor No Yong-Park reflected that its citizens "are the ones who live in the future tense. Their mind and soul are always bent for the future. They never move backwards."[18]

The impact of industrialization has been so great that its influence is still to be completely understood even after two hundred years since it began in Western Europe.

One aspect of this is society's change from a preoccupation with tradition and past events to a much greater interest in what is happening now and what may occur in the future. After all, what is being produced and sold is being manufactured and marketed today, not one hundred or two hundred years ago.

Latin Americans are able to balance this preoccupation with the present with an appreciation of historical events and trends. It is rare to find, for example, Americans complaining about the influence of England on the development of the United States, theoretically blaming England for pushing this country into a revolution that has separated this society in one way or another from our Anglo-Saxon political overlords and cultural forebears.

There are, however, Latin Americans who harbor an acute sense of history — individuals who still proclaim that Spain stole the natural treasures, the gold and silver from American mines, while it hampered the Latin American search for an end to feudal social injustice and economic stagnation.

Brazilians have staged protests against what they consider to be "cabralismo" or the European influence brought to that country by the Portuguese explorer of the same name. Furthermore Brazilian writer Osvaldo de Andrade has called for a cultural independence in his poetry and his essays. "We want the Carahiba revolution, bigger than the French Revolution. Without us Europe would not even have its meager Declaration of the Rights of Man. The golden age proclaimed by America."[19]

This interest in the past extends to a pride in cultural traditions of former days, including the rich heritage of pre–Columbian societies. More than a decade ago, ancient Indian masks were discovered to be missing from Mexico's Museum of Anthropology and the national outcry was immediate. A state of cultural emergency was declared and airports were sealed off. Perhaps most remarkable was the national sense of outrage that accompanied this theft. This was seen as a direct assault on the national cultural and artistic patrimony, a reaction that might be hard to imagine if Indian masks were to be stolen from a museum in some other country that might possess a different attitude towards its heritage.

This pride extends to the creative achievements of the present day. We have noted that writers frequently are called upon to be the diplomatic representatives of Latin American countries as in the case of Nobel Prize winning author-diplomats such Gabriela Mistral and Pablo Neruda from Chile, and Octavio Paz from Mexico.

Streets, boulevards and parks are often named after important cultural and historical figures. The country of Bolivia is named after the important hero of independence Simon Bolivar, while the nation of Colombia is named after Christopher Columbus.

The enduring influence of native culture as opposed to the European traditions is still a vital issue as Latin Americans question whether they are basically heirs to the indigenous cultures with a smattering of European influence, or is it really the other way around? The former Mexican minister of culture, José Vasconcelos, in his influential work, *The Cosmic Race* (*La raza cósmica*), states that Latin Americans are neither the one nor the other. Rather they are a combination of both traditions which have come together in a totally new way so as to create a completely new "third race" and a hybrid cultural system.

The Caudillo

The Latin American reality in terms of European expansion began under the aegis of a feudal system in which vast numbers of workers held their allegiance to the lord of the estate who naturally possessed great wealth. Such individuals traditionally maintained a power base so strong that it rivaled or even exceeded that of the federal government of individual countries. Such estate owners or *hacendados* have often been referred to in the same way in which Latin Americans have identified any person of great power, as *caudillos*. Even the term "Usted" in Spanish, which means "you" in the formal sense of the word as opposed to the more familiar term "tú," comes from the older expression, "Vuestra Merced," the equivalent of "Your Excellency," the term which humble farmers used to refer to the owners of the feudal estates or *haciendas*.

Such *hacendados* often had a literal life and death power over their workers. The vast authority of the leaders of such estates can be appreciated if we stop to realize that before the Mexican revolution, just one such estate was larger than the current state of Texas.

This feudalism and the rivalry among these local landowners, political bosses and the federal governments of countries in Latin America is longstanding. More than one hundred and fifty years ago the Argentine writer Domingo Sarmiento wrote in his classic essay, "Facundo," which he refers to as a study of civilization and barbarism, that his native country would never become truly civilized until it rid itself of political bosses and pockets of regional power that he saw embodied in the figure of the "caudillo" known as Facundo.

Latin American history is full of the names of absolute dictators, yet in spite of this, there still exists a heritage of local power bases by which new governments have overthrown old ones and new leaders have come to power as a result of *golpe del estado*, better known in English by the French term *coup d'état*. Of course this has occurred simply because central governments did not have the power to overcome such attempts to overthrow a sitting government. As a result, Latin Americans still do not have the blind belief in the power of their federal armed forces and government officials that equals that which exists in the rest of the American hemisphere or in Western Europe.

In our modern era many political observers perhaps forget that numerous governments throughout history lacked the power and budgetary prowess that now lies in the hands of a nation that happens to be a world power. Nor does such power lie in the hands of government leaders in Latin American today. In fact, the very name for revolutionary or guerrilla warfare comes from *guerra*, the Spanish word for "war."

The effect of this reality can best be seen today in the case of the nation of Colombia, which after the *Bogotazo* rebellion in 1948 plunged into a series of armed battles led by guerilla forces, a de facto civil war that still goes on today.

The Mexican revolution of 1910 lasted for some ten years before the central government came to the fore, just as the contra opposition to the Marxist Nicaraguan government of President Daniel Ortega dragged on for years.

Perhaps because of a history of such instability of national institutions, Latin Americans direct their sense of pride, to their artistic and cultural traditions. Such an emotional solidarity also extends to national and local pride in sports, especially soccer.

Mr. Omar Tapia, a world famous soccer announcer for the CNN network, has stated in the case of another Latin nation that shares a fanatical devotion to this sport, that when Italians go to church they go there with a soccer ball in their hands.[20]

Stereotypes on Top of Stereotypes

This pride in the national reality extends to personal pride, as Latin Americans take offense at negative stereotypes regarding their part of the world as insults to them personally as well as to their nations. Some Mexicans complained for years after President Jimmy Carter said that he was going to be careful about drinking the water in that country. Mexicans understood drinking water differs in various countries, but they didn't want those realities thrown in their faces.

Not long ago a U.S. government report on Brazil offended citizens of that country because it stated Brazil had great potential as an economic power if it could only overcome longstanding and pervasive government corruption. Brazil's response was to ask American officials who made such statements. Why did they think that the United States was a perfect nation? Did they think it was free of corruption and why did they believe they were necessarily in a position to pass judgment on other nations?

Latin Americans in today's world are increasingly impatient with patronizing statements and with age-old stereotypes such as those that describe them as living outside the mainstream of the modern world or of Western civilization itself.

However the cultural complex of Latin American attitudes and living patterns are interpreted, one thing is certain — the mass of nationals known as Latin Americans defy a simple explanation of their way of life and of their way of looking at themselves and the world. Latin America is the product of a recipe for a complex, historically-formed stew in which the component parts have mixed together in such a way that it is extremely different to tell where one ingredient starts and another one ends, where one tasteful social enigma may have completely blended into another in a way which often appears to defy our complete understanding.

III

Communication

The principal languages of Latin America, Portuguese and Spanish, are derived from ancient Latin, and they maintain a certain resonance in their tonalities that carries through much of written expression in both languages. Rhetoric, or the mellifluous sound of words, often appears to be an end in itself rather than the directness and conciseness which is often aimed at in English-language written communications.

Business Communication

Written and oral business communication is often highly stylized with a free flow of rhetoric, even in reference to matters which might otherwise appear to be cut-and-dry.

Expressions such as "in response to your kind communication" or "in the greatest appreciation of your kind communication which we are greatly pleased to reply to," often substitute for short, abrupt phrases such as, "Thank you for your letter. We will send the merchandise on such and such a date. Sincerely...."[1]

As a result, letters from the Anglo-Saxon world often appear cold and overly direct to many Latin American business men and women. Telephone calls which are extremely abrupt are likely to make the same impression. One Latin American professional complained that American telephone conversations tended to take his breath away to the point that he didn't believe that he could formulate an answer to statements which were given in such a machine-gun-like manner.

Likewise the mail is not used with the same degree for business matters as it is in many other countries. Although great strides have been made in mail delivery in recent years, traditionally many countries have been inefficient or extremely slow in mail delivery to the point that many businesses have hesitated to rely on it exclusively for their communications. One business package which was sent across the border to Latin America through international overnight delivery at a very high cost was said by one U.S. post office official to have entered an untraceable, no-man's-land once it went over the border.[2]

Of course in this era of e-mail, faxes and other means of communication, these considerations are not nearly as dramatic as they once were. Still, businesses sending packages or bulky material often invest in courier services at a high price in order to make sure that their mail does arrive quickly and safely.

Oral Communication

Latinos enjoy talking. Since they are generally not governed by the clock as much as more pressured societies, they take their time to express their views and to exchange ideas. As we were told once in Lima, Peru, when making ready to finish a conversation just as soon as the information we were seeking was given to us, "Aquí se habla." "Here we talk," meaning that conversation was not limited just to the pragmatic end of getting a piece of desired information; people talk for the sake of enjoying conversation without being dominated by the clock to the same degree as might be the case elsewhere. Indeed conversations can go on for hours and hours with little regard for the passing of time. Business people may go out for a work-oriented lunch that can go on for most of, or perhaps the entire afternoon, without looking at their watches to worry about the need to return quickly to their offices.

The topics of conversation are a hallmark of the educated Latin's broad interests. Again, a less pragmatic approach to communication appears to be the norm. Informal conversations may range from trivial topics to wondering about one's national identity or about historical patterns that have formed Latin America as a whole. Latinos sometimes can be heard blaming Spain for errors in the past. Historical realities and traditions are topics which Latinos take seriously. This author has never heard U.S. citizens discuss the problems cast upon their society by England, for better or worse, yet speculations about the historical patterns of Latin America can be an informal subject of conversation as well as a topic for university classes in history.[3]

The range of subjects themselves can vary, as humor and serious discussions often go hand-in-hand. One Latin American professor was overheard discussing profound philosophic matters, then abruptly switching to discuss the origin of certain characters in children's cartoons. The subjects can indeed range abruptly from the ridiculous to the sublime as Latinos embrace an apparently holistic view of life — it all fits together in some kind of grand design about which they love to speculate endlessly.[3]

In Latin America, speech is not just an exchange of words in order to get a job done to reach some pragmatically important goal; conversation is valued in and of itself. Well known is the tradition of the after dinner conversation or *conversación de sobremesa*, which can go on for hours on end. Latinos do not usually look at their watches to budget their time when they engage in social intercourse — the art of conversation is definitely not dead south of the U.S. border.

In fact, many people in that part of the world see language as an expression of their culture and of their respective nationalities. Culture and language often go hand-in-hand. As the Mexican novelist Carlos Fuentes states in his book *Tiempo mexicano*, the Spanish language in Mexico is still considered to be the language of the foreigner. It is "the language of the other man, the conqueror.... [T]he mass of the common man had to learn the language of their masters and forget their own language."[4]

Language is still a matter of identity and national pride. When Latin Americans from different countries get together it is not unusual for them to have difficulty reaching the main topic of the conversation without arguing over vocabulary. One may hear comments like, "We say 'autobús' in my country for bus," while a speaker from a Caribbean country may object that the most common word for bus in that part of the world is "Guagua." Then a speaker from an Andean country may object that the same word is used in his nation, but there it means "baby." Each speaker may tend to believe that his or her term is the best one and thus the potential for linguistic rivalry and confusion is great indeed.

It is important to keep in mind that facial expressions and body language are often more expressive in Latin American countries than they are for speakers in other parts of the world. Likewise an observer from another society may watch movies and television dramas from Latin America and may realize that the decibel level of normal conversation and of emotional reactions to events in the drama can and do reach great heights of expressiveness.

Another aspect of daily conversations which has not usually been covered by more traditional studies of Latin American culture is the tendency to tailor remarks to what the speaker believes that his listener wants to believe.

This is a trait often found in Asian cultures. Those areas try traditionally to use speech to enhance harmony between the parties taking part in a conversation rather than by engaging in overt differences of opinion or in a direct confrontation. Phrases like, "Perhaps, let's see," "Let's discuss this more," and "Let me think about it," often override the tendency to reject ideas outright. This trait can be considered to be very pleasant but it can have some decidedly negative consequences, such as when a Latin business person tells his or her counterpart from another part of the world that "of course we can supply you with the product you want, by the deadline that you want, at the price that you want."

Listeners from what have been called information-specific societies such as the United States usually believe that the business person who makes such statements means what he or she says literally, because, why would someone get himself involved in a foreign commitment if he has little or no intention of meeting his obligations?

This type of exaggeration is by no means always the case, but at the same time there always exists the possibility that cultural perspectives may lead to statements that may diverge somewhat from the absolute reality of the situation.

Television and Radio

The reader may be tempted to believe that there may be little difference between a newscast in the United States and one in Latin America. Actually the differences are very notable. Latin American announcers often cultivate a show business voice pattern in which there is a dramatic modulation from one tone quality to another with exaggerations of sounds, such as the tendency to over pronounce the trill of the double "r" sound in Spanish more than is heard in normal daily conversation. One may hear an announcer say, "Buy your car at dealer X...." In Spanish it becomes "Compre su carrrrrrrro en...."

In addition, some Latin Americans are struck by what they consider to be the fear mentality of American television commercials which predict direct consequences if a product is not used by consumers. Those who feel this way claim that Latin American advertisements tend more to emphasize the positive results which will arise if a certain product is bought and used by the public.

More importantly, perhaps, the concept of what constitutes the news or what is actually newsworthy is radically different. The average American viewer of international news broadcasts as presented by the major networks is shocked to learn that international news is not really very international since it often gives little understanding of what is going on in most of the world. American news claims that it gives world-wide coverage of important events, but even the most superficial consideration shows the tendencies of networks to limit reporting to what happens in the United States, a handful of Western European nations and several nations in the Middle East at the expense of reporting on Africa, Latin America, India and a large part of Asia as well as Eastern Europe — all of which account for a good 90 percent of the world in terms of land mass or population.

It has been claimed that even our distinguished neighbor Canada is like a veritable no-man's-land. Many adult Americans do not know the name of the capital of that great nation, the name of the prime minister or the names of the major political parties — all simply because we rarely hear news reports about Canada.

Latin American news broadcasts take a much more democratic look at the world. Each and every corner of the globe is potentially important. Of course much greater coverage is usually given to Latin American countries. For this reason perhaps, television and radio news reporters who try to cover events in many parts of the world in a short report or news bulletins are frequently pressed for time and often speak with a rapidity which is noticeable.

As is the case throughout the world, comedy and satirical shows are very popular, with comic characters often presenting themselves in some kind of exaggerated dress or facial makeup. Lavish musical shows are extremely popular, including full orchestras or small musical groups and dancers, often presented with sophisticated lighting effects and stage backgrounds.

Undoubtedly the most popular television dramas of all are the soap operas called *novelas* or *telenovelas*— television novels. These programs occupy a somewhat different place in Latin American society than they do in the United States. First, they are considered to be mainstream dramas, which are shown literally day and night, not just during the daytime. The actors who take part in these dramas are often major Latin American celebrities and working in a *novela* is not considered to be playing second fiddle to their colleagues who work exclusively films. Indeed the *telenovelas* appeal to a mass audience — people of all ages and all social classes. Watching a soap opera in Latin America is not considered to be a frivolous waste of time, but rather time spent in pursuit of serious entertainment.[5]

These shows, which are shown in translation in much of the world outside of Latin America, frequently reach audiences of hundreds of millions of viewers. They often feature lush natural background settings as well as historical presentations based on a wide variety of themes, not simply romantic relationships. One other important difference between Latin American soap operas and those shown in other countries is the limited presentation time of each drama — usually about six to eight months as opposed to soap operas in the U.S. which can go on indefinitely.

In the case of radio, Latin America has a unique phenomenon — a proliferation of micro-transmitters, some of them powered by as little as five watts, that serve far-flung rural areas as well as urban neighborhoods. Such radio stations promote a unique type of solidarity. As communications commentator Jesús Martín Barbero has stated, "These stations transform radio into a meeting and organizes solidarity by a little parallel 'culture industry' that stamps records of regional music and organizes fiestas or championship football contests among people of the region."[6]

News, Magazines and Comics

The reporting in Latin American newspapers truly attempts to give international news and does not ignore other parts of the world. Readers can find a wide variety of editorial styles and viewpoints from just the sheer number of important newspapers in a given major city of a given country. It has been said there have been no less than thirty daily newspapers published in modern times in Buenos Aires, Argentina, with an estimated half of them in German, the other half in Spanish.

Such a variety, linguistically as well as editorially, may appear to be astonishing. But a more or less free press is operative in Latin America today, where all countries boast of democratic governments with the notable exception of Cuba. This is a far cry from the days when Nicaraguan dictator Anastasio Somoza cut out an article critical of his regime from all copies of a certain issue of *Life* magazine before it went to newsstands in his country so that his citizens could not read it.

An aspect of Latin American popular culture which combines television drama with journalism is the photo novel, a short, almost comic book-style dramatic story not based on drawings or cartoons but rather on photographs, thus giving the impression almost that one is seeing a television drama. Obviously these are designed to appeal to a mass audience and are not considered to be serious examples of national literature.

Cartoon figures are universally popular on television, in comics and in newspapers. The name for comic strips varies from one Latin American country to another. They are sometimes called, *muñecas, historietas cómicas* or *caricaturas*, among various other names. Many figures popular throughout the world are imported into Latin American cartoons, such as El Pato

Donald (Donald Duck), El Gato Silvestre (Sylvester the Cat) and El Ratón Mickey (Mickey Mouse) or even El Ratón Jerry and his archenemy El Gato Tom (Tom and Jerry).

Some characters' names are hardly recognizable from their originals, such as Picapiedras (The Flintstones), Carlitos (Charlie Brown), and Piolín (Tweety Bird), while there are home-grown cartoon figures which are very popular, such as the irrepressible bird Condorito.

As in any other part of the world, magazines are widely available. They include those from other countries, which may be translated or may have a local Spanish-language counterpart, as well as local publications. Some of the most famous international magazines such as *Reader's Digest* are distributed widely south of the border, both in Spanish and Portuguese. This world-famous publication appears in its Spanish-language format under the title *Selecciones del Reader's Digest*.

Other news magazines are nationally-based journals which appear to follow a traditionally established format such as *Ercilla* in Chile and *Panorama* in Argentina — publications which are remarkably similar to *Time* magazine in the United States. The same could be said of *Oggi* in Italy and *Der Spiegel* in Germany among others.

Naturally there is a wide variety of local magazines that are specialized and appeal to a particular reader's interest. In addition there traditionally are a great number of literary journals which have a history of publishing important and often experimental writers who give a good indication of the direction that serious literature may be taking in a certain country or in Latin America in general. Above all, such journals have played an important part in serving as artistic focal points for whole generations of writers, sometimes publishing literary and artistic manifestos which proclaim to readers a whole new, if not revolutionary, approach to literature. A classic example is the *Martín Fierro* journal published in Argentina early in the twentieth century, and *Sur* published in the same country. It was formerly an artistic vehicle for such important Latin American writers as the Jorge Luís Borges and Bioy Cásares as well as the Chilean novelist María Luisa Bombal.

Noteworthy also is the magazine *Vuelta* which was published by Nobel prize winning Mexican author, Octavio Paz.[7]

Popular Patterns of Speech

Naturally in any area in which more than twenty countries speak the same language covering distances of many thousands of miles, linguistic variations are considerable. This is as true in Portuguese-speaking Brazil as it is the Spanish-speaking countries. Although some visitors crossing south of the U.S. border may say, "I don't speak Mexican," there is only one Spanish language which is basically the same throughout the Hispanic world in spite of many local differences of vocabulary, speech patterns and intonation. Indeed these differences of vocabulary alone constitute huge numbers of variations of the language, to the point that entire voluminous dictionaries have been published on the Spanish vocabulary of countries like Mexico or Chile. It is likely therefore that no living human being is totally aware of each and every vocabulary word in each and every Spanish-speaking country.

Linguists tell us that the more isolated geographically a particular area is, the more archaic its speech patterns usually are. This is true of rural parts of Latin America where words and expressions that are hundreds of years out-of-date may still be heard in everyday speech, and such local variations of language can cause serious problems. For example, when Fidel Castro gave a speech in Chile, few Chileans understood what he was saying.

Generally the pronunciation and vocabulary differences between the Spanish of Latin America and of Spain are roughly equivalent to the differences of pronunciation and vocabulary between England and the United States, as memorialized in the famous statement by George Bernard Shaw that the United States and England are two countries separated by a common language.[8]

The Spoken Word, Old and New

In addition to Spanish and Portuguese which are the principal languages of Latin America, many Indian languages are spoken as well. These hark back to the era of prehistory so that very little if anything is known about their origins. Paraguay, for example, is considered to be a bilingual country in which Spanish and the indigenous language, Guaraní, are spoken. There may be hundreds of Indian languages with dialects and variations. In Guatemala alone, some twenty-four varieties of the language of the Maya Indians are spoken. In Peru, Quechua, the language of the Inca civilization, is still spoken and is still taught in the schools. In Mexico, Nahuatl, the language of the famous Aztec empire, is still spoken and still shows its impact on many place names in Mexico as well as on common vocabulary words often ending in -ote or -alt such as *guajalote* (turkey), *elote* (corn), and *tecolote* (owl). In addition the English words "chocolate" and "coyote" are derived from Aztec, just as chocolate itself comes from the Mexican Indian tradition.[9]

In rural areas of Latin America, archaic Spanish exists with notable versions of modern Spanish words such as *ainsa* for *así* or "thus," along with words which hark back directly to Latin. Some speakers say *vidi* instead of the modern Spanish term *vi*, which means "I saw." The ancient version was used by Julius Caesar in describing his victory at the Battle of Zela. "I came. I saw. I conquered." (Veni. Vidi. Vici.)[10]

On the other side of the spectrum, you can see the great influence of English in words that are not just so-called Spanglish but are part of modern standard Spanish as it is spoken by educated speakers such as TV personalities and professional actors. These include words like "show" for the traditional word *espectáculo*; "chance" for *oportunidad*, and "control" for *dominio*. Many other examples abound, such as *reporte* for the English word "report," instead of *informe* or *reportaje*, as well as *film(e)* for "film" instead of *película*.

The Spanish-speaking world, however, has traditionally shown great concern over the correctness of written and spoken Spanish, and Spain established an Academy of the Spanish Language hundreds of years ago to regulate vocabulary and grammar. As we have noted, speech in the Spanish-speaking world is more than a vehicle of expression to achieve a practical end of communication It is considered to be an important representation of tradition and culture which is communicated to the rest of the world.

Dialects

What Latin American dialectologists generally observe is that there is often a noticeable difference in the language patterns of speakers that come from coastal areas at sea level and those speakers that come from high altitudes in places like Mexico City, Quito, Ecuador, Guatemala City and others. The former generally speak extremely rapidly, sometimes slurring or omitting some letters, especially the letter "s," altogether. Still there is but one language with all its variations.[11]

Popular Expressions

The Spanish language is full of proverbs and age-old expressions that convey the collective wisdom of the Hispanic world as it has developed over hundreds of years. The great classic of Spanish literature, *Don Quixote* by Miguel de Cervantes, presents the figure of Sancho Panza — whose name means "Sancho Belly" — who represents the common man who lives by his senses, including his liking for food, as opposed to philosophic ideas. Nevertheless, Sancho presents himself as a veritable treasure trove of traditional wisdom expressed in terms of proverbs. Don Quixote himself quotes a proverb when he asks what crime each man has committed upon meeting a group of prisoners being transported to the galleys. He is told that one man was sentenced because he sang, which moves Don Quixote to ask if it is possible that men would be sent to the galleys only for singing. He says this makes no sense because that contradicts the saying, "sing away sorrow, cast away care."[12]

Another criminal answers that this is a different kind of singing because the man in question confessed to being a thief, or "sang" as a proverbial stool pigeon.

Today the presence of many proverbs in the languages spoken in Latin America reflects society's respect for traditional wisdom over the importance of mere facts and numbers. Of course, many such sayings have their equivalents in English, such as the expression, "*cada oveja con su pareja*" (each sheep with his partner), which is similar to the English expression, "birds of a feather flock together."

But the number of such proverbial expressions is literally endless and they are generally heard in daily conversation more than equivalent expressions might be heard in the English-speaking world. There it may be said that the manipulation of technically derived information and data storage is considered to be a creative enterprise, so that, perhaps, takes precedence over age-old observations of folk wisdom. The other is a culture where age and tradition are indeed respected, as reflected in the Spanish saying, "*El Diablo sabe más por viejo que por Diablo*" (The devil knows more because he is old than because he is a devil).

Other expressions include, "*El león cree que todos son de su condición*" (the lion thinks that everyone else is a lion) while "*de limpios y tragones están llenos los panteones*" (cemeteries are full of people that are clean as well as those that are drunks). Also we may note the following:

Én el pecado lleva la penintencia. "The punishment for the sin is in the sin itself."

Tal palo, tal astilla. "Like father like son."

Poderoso caballero es don dinero. "Money is all powerful or money talks."

Hijo de tigre pintito. "The tiger's son is just like he is."

El amor, el humo y el dinero no se puede esconder. "You can't hide love, smoke or money."

Gota a gota, el agua se agota. "Water disappears drop by drop."

En la casa del herrero, cuchillo de palo. "In the blacksmith's house the knives are made out of wood."

The Spanish language also includes colorful expressions which may have their equivalents in English, but which are expressed in a different form in Spanish. These include:

Ir de Guatemala a Guatepeor. "To go from the frying pan into the fire."
Hay gato encerrado. "There's something fishy."
Lo vimos con la mano en la masa. "We caught him red-handed."
Tomar gato por liebre. "To take a pig in a poke."
Tan malo el pinto como el colorado. "One is just as bad as the other."
En todas partes se cuecen habas. "They cook beans everywhere." (This means that life is basically the same all over.)

In addition, there are stock phrases used in social relations which are often an expression of deeply ingrained Hispanic traditions. When a guest leaves a host's home it is not unusual for the host to tell the visitor, "*aquí tienes tu casa*" (this is your house), or literally, "You have your home right here."[13]

Likewise when a friend admires another friend's new acquisitions, be it furniture, a work of art, or jewelry, it is not uncommon for the person who purchased the article to say, "*Es tuyo*" (It's yours). In the context of the culture this is understood as a social formality that is not meant to be taken at face value. The author has heard of at least one American, however, who visited a Latin American friend and expressed great admiration for an impressive ring that his host had just acquired. On mentioning his fondness for the item, his friend told him in Spanish that the ring was his, not meaning that his words were to be taken literally.

The American, who was not aware of the ins and outs of Latin American culture, took the ring, only to be told by other Latin Americans that what he had done was terrible. He protested that he only took his friend at his exact word. However, eventually others prevailed on him to understand the expression figuratively and not literally, and he eventually gave the ring back to its rightful owner.

Other expressions of historical origin include "*hay moros en la costa*" (the coast is not clear) as well as "*no veas moros con tranchete*" (don't see danger where there is none).

From the days of Spain's overseas empire comes the expression indicating that one has made a major achievement, "*Eso es poner pica en Flandes*" (that is like setting your pike in Flanders). In addition, "*averígüelo Vargas*" (God knows) goes back to the heyday of the Spanish empire, when overwhelming amounts of data were collected in the era before computers. The man who supposedly had the best memory for trivial details was a Mr. Vargas, hence the expression when nobody could find a piece of information came to be "let Vargas find out about it."

Gestures and Body Language

It is commonly known that people from Latin, sometimes called Mediterranean, countries, such as Spain, Italy and Portugal, are dramatic in their facial expressions, their gestures and in their body language in general. In commenting on the expressive nature of Italians, author Luigi Barzini has stated that many of the finest actors in the world live in Italy but only a small fraction of them work on the stage. The vast majority of them are to be found out in the street.[14]

The same can be said of countries which are of Hispanic or Portuguese heritage in America, such as the majority of countries south of the U.S. border.

Perhaps the first observation that could be made is that Latin Americans are not as afraid of touching each other as are members of some other cultures, particularly those derived from Northern and Central Europe. It is customary for men to greet friends or relatives by embracing them. Likewise students of comparative cultures have commented that the space between individuals who speak to each other, what is referred to as personal space, is frequently closer than the distance at which speakers face each other in some other cultures.

In addition there are gestures which are not usually seen in the United States nor in other Anglo-Saxon countries, such as the pulling up of one's forearm to meet the upper arm, then touching the bottom of the elbow. When this happens the skin becomes very tight which means that the person being referred to is especially "tight" or stingy, just like the skin at the elbow.

Likewise the finger placed under one's eyes means *ojo*, or be careful, in a reference to the Spanish word for eyes.

Fingers clenched together in front of the mouth indicate that something one is eating is especially delicious, while the thumb pushed forward towards the fingers as the hand is raised up and down in front of the speaker's body brings special attention to the comments being made.

There are certain gestures, movements or examples of body language that foreign visitors would do well to avoid. These include putting one's feet up on a desk, stretching in public, or a man loosening his tie, rolling up his sleeves or being the first one to take off his jacket while in a professional environment. Also, pointing a finger at a person to whom one is speaking is often considered to be discourteous.

Latinos like to greet others with good handshake, neither too weak nor too overwhelmingly strong. Good eye contact is important in a conversation and some observers have commented that visitors to Latin American countries, especially some Americans, tend to slouch down in their chairs as opposed to their hosts, who appear to make a greater effort to maintain good posture.

There is a subjective element in the opinions of those who may form such judgments, however nomenclature is very important. Latin Americans are not nearly as informal as Americans when it comes to speaking to others on a first-name basis. If one meets a Latin American and right away begins to refer to that person by his or her first name without being invited to do so, this can be considered a classic example of presumption or downright rudeness.

These considerations are extremely important since conversation for the sake of conversation is one of the hallmarks of Latin American society, and the degree to which a visitor succeeds in making a good impression in conversational experiences may well be the barometer that indicates the success of that person's social image south of the border.

IV

Aspects of Daily Life

There are aspects of daily life which are fundamental to human society yet they often do not fall within broad categories. When a visitor to another country suffers from what is usually called culture shock, this condition is not caused, in most cases, by one aspect of existence such as food or educational tendencies, rather it is caused by dozens if not hundreds of patterns of life that cause a shock or a surprise that can upset the mental balance of that particular visitor. We will attempt here to consider a number of these factors of daily living that may well have the capacity to take the tourist or business-oriented visitor completely by surprise.

Transportation

Public transportation is an important part of the daily life of millions of Latin Americans. Not only is driving difficult in the heavily congested urban areas of Latin America which have in many cases grown tremendously in recent decades, but the price of an auto in most areas, especially in countries where there is little or no automotive production and cars must be imported, has risen with the rise in population. Mexico City, for example, is the largest city in the world, with a population of 35 million inhabitants if one considers all the suburbs and the central city as part of the total metropolitan area. The smog from the traffic jams has gotten so troublesome that the Mexican government long ago put a limit on the number of days per week that an individual can use a car. This is to say that each driver must stay off the roads one or more days per week to alleviate the traffic congestion. Automobile use is thus regulated by decals which are supposed to be put on each car indicating when they are authorized to be driven. Those who do not obey these laws are subject to heavy fines.

It is for these and other reasons that taxi and bus public transport is widely used. Because of this, more such vehicles are in circulation, so the average person will most likely not have to wait as long for a bus as he might in other societies that do not depend as much on this type of service.

One visitor from the United States in Chile noted that a bus driver will pick up a passenger who is waiting some distance from the bus stop, while in the United States, perhaps because of the tradition of the scientific or pragmatic frame of mind, a driver will usually only stop to pick up a waiting passenger directly in front of the appointed bus stop.

The need for and prevalence of public transport in Latin America is in large part because the possession of a car has long been considered more of a luxury than a necessity.

Perhaps because of this, the structure of Latin American society has traditionally centered more on the activity in the capital city of a given country, with less commercial activity occurring in the provinces. It has always appeared most important to be able to move through the main metropolitan areas, and it has not been as important to travel to secondary urban centers by way of the automobile. Even the whole ambience of travel may appear radically different to visitors. Latin American highways, especially through mountainous areas, are famous for their twists and turns, while at the same time lights are not as frequently found along rural highways as in other parts of the world.

One immigrant from Central America was asked what impressed and surprised her the most on coming to the United States and her answer was that she was shocked to see how many street lights there were to light up avenues and highways at night.

There are subway lines as well as bus and taxi service, combined with what are called *colectivos*. These are cars which function as a kind of combination of traditional busses and taxis. These collective cars run along an established route as do busses, and they charge rates more closely aligned to what one might expect from a bus. They are usually not as expensive as private cabs, yet they are customarily sedans or minivans rather than larger vehicles.

They do not provide private service as do taxis, rather they collect everybody that they can along their route, which is to say that they pick up everybody that can possibly fit in them, as do busses.

Such vehicles can be utilized along a given route in an urban environment or they can be hired for long trips such as an hours-long trek from sea level up to the heights of the Andes mountains in Peru, which ascends up to heights of some 18,000 feet. Of course for the unsuspecting tourist who is not used to the rigors of such travel compressed into a one day trip, the weakness that he or she will feel on reaching the final destination, almost in the clouds themselves, can cause a monumental physical shock to the body along with a potential culture shock.

Travel by horseback is still prevalent in rural areas, as is travel by donkey. Horses did not exist in the American continent until the arrival of the Spanish colonists, while the American cowboy tradition, which is often considered to be one of the most quintessential aspects of American life, is actually, in large part, a continuation of the traditions of the Mexican cowboy. The so-called *charro* worked on ranches in the western part of the United States for hundreds of years before many parts of the United States which had belonged to Spain and then Mexico became possessions of the United States after it invaded Mexico in the Mexican-American war.

It is also true that modern technology exists alongside traditional modes of transportation. Fisherman in Peru, Bolivia, Chile and in other countries still practice their profession as did their ancestors by traveling in *totora*, reed boats which have been used for thousands of years.

Mealtime

The schedule of meals is very different in Latin America. The principal meal comes in the middle of the afternoon. This is often a long meal that can take two hours or more. In the past this was sufficient time for office workers and others to travel home, also giving them time for the traditional siesta, or rest time in the middle of the day. This nap, which is a well-known aspect of the Hispanic world, derives its name from the Latin word *sexta* for the sixth hour of the work day. In recent times, with the tremendous growth of large urban areas and intense traffic, many people simply cannot manage to make it home, nor will they even try, so that it is customary to eat lunch at a restaurant. The important difference for visitors to Latin America to remember is that restaurants may well be empty at noon, however they usually will be bursting at the seams with an overflow of customers at two or three o'clock in the afternoon.

Likewise restaurants are likely to have few customers at five or six o'clock in the late afternoon since Latin America continues the Spanish tradition of having dinner at eight or nine o'clock or even later. Since lunch is considered to be the principal meal of the day, this supper is frequently more like a snack. Of course as anywhere else a snack of *merienda*, or *bocadillo* in Spanish, can be eaten at any time of the day. Some Latin Americans may prefer, however, to continue the custom which is well known in Spain of eating tapas or light snacks strategically placed very often between the hours of the lunch and the late dinner.

One of the myths of the Hispanic American world is that only so-called Spanish food is served to the public. Nothing could be further from the truth. The cuisine of each country is different, and often the food of each part of the each country varies considerably from the specialties in another region of the same nation. More important to remember, however, is that Latin American cities are as truly international as cities anywhere and virtually all types of cuisine from any or all parts of the world are available. As an example, the Chinese restaurants in Peru, called *Chifas*, are some of the most lavishly beautiful oriental restaurants that could be found anywhere.

It is important to be aware that overt gestures of hospitality are a long-standing aspect of the Hispanic tradition. Given their pride in their nations and in their traditions, Latin Americans are also proud of their local cuisine and visitors from abroad would be well-advised to keep it in mind.

Another notable difference in mealtime customs relates to the preparation and purchase of food. Middle- and upper-class Latin Americans frequently have household staff— maids and/or cooks who prepare the meals. Given the prevalence of local as well as open air markets, citizens of these countries are accustomed to buying grocery items on a daily or almost a daily basis, with the result that much of what they eat has not been frozen or packaged. This is by no means true in all cases, and large markets, especially supermarkets, are also common in today's Latin American large urban areas. Those who live outside of these metropolitan centers tend even today to adhere to more traditional modes of food consumption.

It is perhaps because of this and because of the number of fresh plants and herbs which are commonly used in food preparation that Latinos are not overly conscious of the nutritional value of what they eat, and the custom of taking vitamin and mineral supplements is much less common than it is in the United States.

Forms of Address

You will find a tendency towards formality in business and professional dress as well as in the use of titles such as *doctor/a* and *licenciado/a*. The English language once used "thee" and "thou" for "you," however this difference is no longer commonly observed in modern usage. It is well known, however, that the distinctions in forms of address that are used in any language usually correspond to the degree of formality as well as the rigidity of the system of social classes that exist where that language is used. Social classes exist everywhere, even in so-called classless societies, and in Latin America that awareness of a person's social class is much more obvious than it might be in some other sections of the globe. This is reflected in the distinction between the formal and the familiar form of second person address. *Tú* is used in informal social situations when the speaker knows the other person in the conversation on more or less a first-name basis. *Usted* or *Ustedes*, referring to more than one person, is the preferred form of "you" when speaking to a person on a more formal basis. Unlike the common usage of the Spanish language in Spain itself, the plural form for *tú*, which is *vosotros* or *vosotras*, is not commonly used in Latin America, although a dialectal form *vos* is quite common.[1]

The use of last names causes great confusion to non–Latin people since Latin Americans use two last names, the father's family name first and the mother's maiden name second, such as in José Romero Santiago.

Unlike in the Anglo Saxon tradition, in which the last name really is the last name, the name of record in the Spanish-speaking world is the first last name rather than the second one. Thus José Romero Santiago might be called José Romero or José Romero Santiago but not José Santiago. This distinction is important since his name should appear in a phone directory or a school roster as José Romero, not as we have said, as José Santiago.

In the case of a woman, her family name is supplemented by her husband's first last name when she gets married, preceded by the word *de* which means "of" or "from." Thus a woman named María Delgado who marries José Romero would then become María Delgado de Romero.

The title for a man, the equivalent of "Mr.," is "Señor" abbreviated as "Sr." "Mrs." is *señora*, abbreviated as "Sra.," and "Miss" is *señorita* or "Srta." Likewise "Mr." is "Senhor" in Portuguese while "Mrs." is "Sehnora."[2] These are alternative forms of address which usually are used when speaking with older persons and are terms indicating a good degree of respect.

It is important to note that nicknames are very popular in Latin America not only for the average person but even for movie stars and other celebrities. The tendency to use such names is so common that police officials in the United States who deal with the Latin American community are cautioned to make sure that a name which is given to them for a friend of family member who has disappeared is actually that person's real name. Nicknames are so commonly used for long periods of time that it is not uncommon for family members themselves to forget that the names that they give to the police are not real names but are just informal nicknames.

In the business and professional world, terms of address in Spanish in correspondence are the following: "Dear Sir" usually becomes *Muy Señor Mío* and "Dear Madam" is *Muy Señora Mía* or some similar term; and a common way to end a letter, such as with the word "sincerely" in English, becomes in Spanish *atentamente.*[3]

The jargon of a business letter is traditionally so complicated that whole textbooks and complete college courses are given in Business Spanish and non-native speakers are forewarned that attempting to write a business letter in the Spanish language can be much more complicated that it may seem at first glance.

An Awareness of the *-ismos*

MACHISMO

Any attempt to describe the popular culture of Latin American must eventually try to deal with some emotional and mental trends which are referred to by the ending *-ismo* This includes the famous machismo of the Latin male. This particular behavior and attitude pattern lends itself to the superfluous and often gratuitous display of manliness, power, aggressiveness and lack of fear — however one may wish to define it.[4]

The macho man may never show too much emotion. He must never cry and he should be in control of just about any situation. Since he should not show fear, perhaps the most classic example of this Hispanic attitude is the ancient sport of bull fighting. The bull fighter or "matador" must of course conquer the bull, and while he does this he must conquer his own fear of injury, and even death for the slightest movement of the bull's horns in his direction can be fatal.

Of course the fans enjoy the tension between the raw power of the animal and the bullfighter's ability to stare death right in the face, coming closer and closer to the head of the beast as the crowd eggs him on to even more dangerous stances in close proximity to the horns of his opponent.

Many matadors in Spain and in Latin America therefore have been victims of the crowd's desire to see him (or her) get as close to the bull as possible, so that even a split second's thrust of the bull's horns can cause a fatal blow.

Though this is a stylized and highly dramatic expression of power and control of visceral emotions such as the instinct for preservation, Latin American men have been known to display an attitude which can imply to the rest of the world that "I am the king of my castle and I am the master of my fate."

Recently there has been a reaction against the extremes of this kind of attitude, with some groups trying to get men to accept their more tender emotions. Perhaps the most classic expression of this mindset can be found in the Latin American short story, "Espuma y nada más" ("Foam and Nothing More") by the Colombian author Hernán Téllez. This story, which has been anthologized many times in Spanish and in English translation, tells of a barber in a remote town in Colombia. In a country which has suffered through a civil war for decades, this barber, who is a part-time guerrilla fighter trying to kill government forces, is surprised when one day an important general in the federal army comes in for a shave.

As he uses an old fashioned straight razor and applies foam to his customer's face, he reflects that he, as a guerrilla fighter, had tried to kill this general. Now as the general is seated in his barber's chair, killing him would be the easiest thing in the world, and he could easily claim that his death had been an accident. Who could prove otherwise?

At the end of the story, the barber decides not to commit the crime, realizing that ultimately he is a barber and not a killer. The general pays the barber. However just as he is about to walk out the door, he turns around and tells the barber that he wants him to know that people had told him that if he went to that particular barber shop the barber would kill him.

Here, of course, the general's courage allowing him to face death without hesitation and without flinching, may be compared to the bullfighter's ability to face the same danger and in both cases courage alone is not satisfactory in itself, for the macho must let everybody possible know that he is ready to face death without fear in a highly dramatic and visible way.[5]

FATALISMO

The Hispanic personality can be easily characterized as possessing a fatalistic view of life. Destiny is important for all of us for "man proposes but God disposes." This could be described as a basic part of Hispanic thinking. In other, more individualistic cultures such as that of the United States, great emphasis is given to each person's initiative and aggressiveness in obtaining a goal. In other cultures which believe that we are all part of a greater plan which is controlled by a higher, supernatural power, equal importance is given to the grand scheme of life of which we are all but one tiny part. As a result, one almost never sees a character in an American movie or television show kneeling down to ask God for help in a difficult situation. Such scenes are common in Latin American movies and television programs. There people believe that destiny has a part to play in all our lives, and as such none of us is really the complete master of our fate.

Perhaps the quintessence of the American attitude in this regard is the fictional characters portrayed by an actor like John Wayne. When situations get out of hand he just uses his fists and his gun to make them right. He does this all by himself or with the help of few others, and in one movie, when another character asked him if he ever prayed to God, his answer was that he never had the time.

Hispanic fatalism can be seen in many works of Spanish literature such as *El gran teatro del mundo* (*The Great Theater of the World*) by the classic Spanish author Calderón de la Barca. In this drama human life is likened to a play in which all people are actors and God is the director who controls the life and death or the dramatic roles of each person.[6]

It is for this reason that many persons of Latin American heritage can be heard saying that human life is measured and no one will live one second longer than his appointed time — no longer than God wants him to live. Along with this idea, much in consonance with the traditional Christian view of the purpose of life, each individual has a role and a God-given purpose in life, and when a person has accomplished that job, or has fulfilled that goal, his or her life will end.

AMIGUISMO

Just as family values are extremely strong in Latin America, the bond of friendship can appear to be just as strong. Latinos pride themselves on their loyalty to their friends in a type of friendship that can often constitute a life-long commitment.

A sense of belonging and of roots is extremely important. In Argentina, for example, one of the common themes of traditional tango is the importance of one's neighborhood, of what is called there the *arrabal*, not only as a series of buildings, but more especially as personal relationships that go so deep into the human heart that the *arrabal* can never be forgotten nor replaced. Such sentimental associations often extend to an entire city, thus inspiring the Argentine writer Jorge Luís Borges to declare about his native Buenos Aires in his poem of the same name, "Love doesn't unite us but rather surprise / It must be because of that, that I love her so much."[8]

This bond of deep and special friendship extends to what are frequently called *compadre* or *comadre* relationships. These terms refer to friends that are so close that they in effect become like members of one's family in their willingness to offer advice and moral support in times of difficulty. These relationships are longstanding and are very traditional in all Latin countries including the countries of southern Europe.

Such bonds can transcend simple friendship, and can and do become important in the world of work, when personal and family contacts are often considered to be the bases for business and professional relationships in ways which are perhaps more dramatic and more insistent than they might be in other cultures.

The Scale of Life

We have noted that small business has a greater importance in Latin American society than it does in countries which appear to be more and more dominated by chain and franchised businesses. Not only is this obvious to any visitor to Latin America, but the actual size of many stores is often smaller than what a tourist coming from another social tradition may expect. Boutiques and small shops abound. Since drug stores do not usually sell beach balls, greeting cards, toys and the myriad other items that are to be found in large chain pharmacies in other countries, specialized stores will sell pens and pencils and writing paper rather than drug stores. These are often called *papelerías*.

In some countries decorative masks may be purchased in specialized mask stores to mention only a few examples of retail specialization.

Of course American franchises and chain stores have entered Latin America, and it is not rare to find stores like Wal-mart that carry just about any consumer item.

Still Latin Americans suffer from culture shock on entering the United States, exclaiming that they are surprised that everything appears so large and impersonal. Not just the stores, but the multi-lane highways and the malls and shopping centers (not that they don't exist in Latin America. They do but perhaps are not as common).

In addition, the colonial tradition in the layout of towns and cities is still common and as such the ability to move through the streets in many places is still much more oriented for foot traffic than it is for cars and busses. Even so, traffic in major cities is certainly as dense or more dense than one might expect.

To get an example of this difference we may consider the cities of El Paso, Texas, and Ciudad Juárez, Mexico. These two cities face each other on both sides of the Mexican-U.S. border, and they exist in such close proximity to each other that on looking at these urban centers from the air, they in effect comprise one vast city. Yet their construction is very different. On the American side, it is often difficult to walk to shopping, since much of the city is made up of masses of shopping malls and super highways, while Ciudad Juárez is generally built on a smaller scale with many areas of the city more accessible for pedestrians.

We may be tempted to extend this comparison to state that, in general, Latin American cities and towns center more on pedestrians while American cities, especially large ones, may be more oriented to automobile traffic.

Although major urban areas of Latin America have large shopping centers and very large supermarkets and other types of mega-stores, this is more a reflection of the U.S. lifestyle than it is of traditional Latin American approach to retail business. Latin Americans like to relate to store owners on a more personal, one-to-one basis, and they like store owners to know them and cater to their tastes. As in the case of fast food restaurants, however, this is a value which is changing. Still Latin-America has countless small, franchise-free, small-scale retail stores and restaurants. This includes many stands or improvised restaurants that sell food literally in the street.

The prevalence of small business and a generally smaller scale of daily activities can also be seen in the abundance of open-air markets and street vendors, especially those that sell lottery tickets. While magazines and newspapers are often sold in retail establishments in other cultures, in Latin America they are frequently sold in kiosks or small stands that are right on the street. In addition to newspapers and magazines, frequently such establishments also sell a very select group of books.

In Mexico, open-air markets are frequently called *tianguis*, while in Brazil the days of the week carry the Portuguese names which are derived from the number of open-air fairs that occur on a certain day, such as First Fair, or Second Fair, etc. Though there are countless open air markets in Latin America, among the most famous is the market or fair found high in the Central American mountains in Chichicastenango, Guatemala, as well as one found in Huancayo, Peru.

Also indicative of the tendency towards local or small-scale production are the great and world-famous handicrafts traditions, including sophisticated, ornate jewelry production. In just one case, the Mexican city of Taxco has perhaps more jewelry stores per square foot than any city or town in the world. This small, colonial-style city boasts of more than one thousand jewelry stores.

The great hallmark of Latin American handicrafts of all kinds is the incredible variety of styles and mediums in which craftsmen and women work. As opposed to mass produced articles, handicrafts in Latin America reflect the traditional styles of one city or area of a given country as well as important national traditions.

Being vs. Becoming

The Spanish humorist Julio Camba wrote a satirical book on the reflections of an imaginary frog that traveled from country to country. In this work, called *La rana viajera* (*The Traveling Frog*), he commented on the national character of many locations that he visited. On coming to the U.S. in the 1920s, he wrote that he was not surprised to see either the rise of important gangsters like Al Capone or the development of organized crime itself. After all, the United States was the country of mass production of everything, so why not the organized mass production of crime ?

Whatever the reason that mass production and big business have come to be hallmarks of American society, it still is true, as we have just noted, that business and life itself frequently exists in Latin America on what might be called a smaller scale.

Perhaps one of the reasons for this is the distinction between those societies in which individuals are constantly striving to meet some type of goal, whether this be an ideal weight, a financial or professional goal, or whatever objective one may think of.

On the other hand, in more traditional societies, individuals are more concerned with living and surviving in their natural environment, and their main objectives are simply to obtain sufficient food, clothing and shelter. This has been mankind's prevailing frame of mind since the inception of human life on the planet.

To the extent that traditional societies are more prevalent and have a greater cultural influence on the mainstream of Latin America than they do elsewhere, it is only logical to assume that the more traditional and historical view of life does and can hold sway. If we believe this to be true then it is also logical to assume that for vast numbers of people, the success of a modest, small business may be more desirable than the development of a corporate conglomerate.

We would suggest such a possibility. But at the same time, any such observation remains largely in the realm of theory — an area of social psychology that may present a veritable field day of speculation for qualified researchers. But if this is true, then it may also be true that the well-known U.S. interest in "keeping up with the Joneses" may be less attractive to millions of Latin Americans. Could it be traced to less interest in "becoming"? We can leave such observations to the studies of socio-psychologists, but speculation may make us wonder if strong family bonds, which in Latin America make family members more concerned with themselves and less concerned with their neighbors, may make individuals less concerned with whether a neighbor has installed an in ground pool or has put a new roof on his house.

Even in the United States the keeping up with the Jones syndrome may be waning in light of the apparently arbitrary and ever changing fluctuations of the national economy. Or as one American put it, "I used to be worried about keeping up with the Joneses until the recent recession when I learned that the Joneses went bankrupt."

Dress

Certain trends in dress and personal appearance have been slow to catch on and become acceptable in Latin America. This includes men wearing Bermuda shorts, men wearing pony tails or shoulder-length hair, and other styles which have caught on in other places in recent years.

There is a general tendency in the United States for people to prefer comfort over fashion, while Latin America and elsewhere are concerned with being up-to-date in style and making a good appearance when going out in public. This includes just walking along the street to routine, everyday errands.[8]

As far as corpulent individuals are concerned, many Latin Americans remark that the obsession with the loss of weight is not nearly as great in Latin America simply because being overweight seems to be much less of a problem than it is in the United States. At the same time, the ideal of feminine beauty as an extremely thin figure does not appear to have taken hold nearly as much in Latin America as it has in other areas. In the Latin world, what might be called full-figured women believe that they will be more readily accepted by society than might be the case elsewhere.

A great change has occurred in the United States in recent decades in women's fashions. A vast majority of women feel more comfortable appearing in public in jeans, informal shoes like sneakers and very informal shirts such as sweat shirts and other sporty attire.

Wearing dresses and skirts does not appear to be as common as it once was, nor is wearing tight-fitting undergarments apparently as common as it once was. Ditto for wearing hats and gloves in public, as opposed to what still might be found at formal social occasions.

While this is a great generalization, one can easily find out it if is justified by going to the nearest U.S. shopping center and looking around to see how the average shopper is dressed. Undoubtedly the public appearance of men is just as informal. If one looks at picture taken 80 to 100 years ago of a gathering of people in almost any kind of social context, the formality of clothing of both men and women is striking. Men frequently wore jackets and ties even for a day in the country — an outing or a picnic — while in schools and businesses they were *de rigueur,* and the idea of dressing down to be more comfortable simply did not exist. Until not too many years ago women could not wear pants in a formal business or professional office setting.

Latin America has seen a great move toward informality in dress in modern times, but not as much as in other societies. Women generally wear much more makeup than their American counterparts, and lotions and perfumes, even in professional and corporate environments, are often used in more potent quantities.

Especially in rural areas, many individuals still conserve dress styles that represent their indigenous origins, such as the wool knit caps with long ear flaps commonly worn even in urban areas in Andean countries such as Ecuador and Peru. Also derby hats, shawls and long skirts often are worn by women in such places as Colombia, Ecuador, Peru and Bolivia, to give just a few examples.

Indigenous influences are still in the forefront of the popular cultures of Latin America much more so than in the United States.

One may wonder if it might not be possible to make the generalization that the mass produced qualities brought on by the industrial revolution of several hundred years ago have never taken hold as they have in some other societies.

Latin America may be ahead of its time in anticipating what some observers call the "human scale movement," which advocates a post-industrially based social unit which is more individually and more community-oriented, without the dominance of so many national and multinational companies in large urban areas.

Opinions may vary on such issues of course, but for the very least, an awareness of these aspects of Latin American daily life may at least give us extensive food for thought.

V

Government

The very notion that government can be viewed differently in Latin America than in other areas of the world may appear at first to be a difficult one. After all how could we make assumptions about nations which have such different histories and political realities? To do so would seem to call on an observer to delve into detailed histories of each and every government, which would be in itself a monumental task.

Such a study, interesting as it might be, is not really our goal here. Rather we are concerned with the popular attitudes which allow such political realities to exist.

The very first hallmark of Latin American political history is the fragility of many of the regimes since Latin America's independence from Spain early in the nineteenth century Rather than focusing on each twist of the government each country, we may be able to make an initial generalization that in Latin America there is respect for the spirit of the law while in countries with an Anglo-Saxon heritage, or perhaps a Central European rather than a Mediterranean cultural heritage, there may exist a greater respect for the letter of the law. This distinction is far from being abstract or theoretical. On the contrary, it has vast implications for the lives of countless millions of people. Such a difference in viewpoint has been brought down to an apparently trivial level in the hypothetical case of a Latino driver arriving at a red light in the middle of the night in a deserted street. For some reason this driver is in a great hurry.

A driver from the United States finds himself in the same situation, thus presenting the following question. Will either of these drivers stop at the red light or will both stop? In this hypothetical situation some theorize that the

U.S. driver will likely stop while the Latino or Latin American driver may not. Why might this be the case?

If our theory is correct we might say that the U.S. citizen tends to obey the letter of the law. The law clearly says that a driver must stop at a red light. It doesn't say that he or she should stop only during the daytime, or only when there are cars in sight, or only when the driver feels like stopping. It says that the driver should *always* stop at a red stoplight.

The Latin American driver will tend not to stop because he obeys the spirit of the law. He views the basic motivation for the law, which is clearly to prevent accidents. He sees no cars and at that late hour he assumes that there are no cars in his vicinity, so he reasons that there is no chance of having an accident. He is in a hurry and therefore he is doing nothing illegal since he is merely being faithful to the spirit of the law if he does not stop at the red light. He is sure that he will not cause nor be the victim of an accident, thus complying with the basic spirit of the law.[1]

Such a difference in philosophy goes a long way towards explaining many aspects of Latin American history. Governments and governmental institutions frequently have lacked the stability of those in other countries. In the United States, for example, the Constitution was written shortly after the end of the American Revolution. The precepts formulated in this historic document are slavishly followed as they are interpreted by the U.S. Supreme Court in its decisions. In a country which has a great respect for the absolute letter of the law, no matter how controversial a Supreme Court decision may be, the United States has never witnessed a popular revolt against such decisions, though they sometimes go against the common sense of many citizens. We may take for instance the recent ruling that prayers may not be said at a football game at a public school, when the Congress of the United States begins its legislative session with a prayer — all this in a country whose motto is "In God We Trust."

The law is the law, even though at times it may violate basic common sense and even a belief in the sacredness of human life, in the eyes of many millions of U.S. citizens.

Historically, on the other hand, many Latin American countries have changed constitutions to meet what they believe to be changing historical realities. Citizens of countries whose legal traditions vary from those of old English law have often experienced a vastly different reality. Although it may be hard actually to keep track, one Latin American country is reputed to have made more than one hundred different constitutions since its liberation from Spain almost two hundred years ago. Likewise Venezuela under the administration of President Hugo Chávez has recently struggled with the decision to possibly impose an entirely new constitution.

In Colombia a civil war has raged for more than thirty years with an uncertainty as to what forces or political groups will ultimately rule, possibly bringing along an entirely new constitution. Indeed as one citizen of Bolivia expressed it, "Emergency is a normal state of affairs for us.... Ours is a history of crisis. We've learned to enjoy it. It makes us feel important."[2] Latin Americans are less likely to accept judicial decisions based on arcane or obscure legal findings in some distant past that go against a basic sense of right and wrong.

The mere reference to what a constitution says or is supposed to say, or to what some legal decision said in a case one hundred years or more ago will not automatically satisfy the populace's thirst for order and justice. In a country that depends on the strict letter of the law, the situation can be very different. Latin Americans often voice the opinion that such nations generally do not question whether the law makes sense or whether it should be upheld in the first place — the law is the law. Possibly as a result of this the United States is undoubtedly the most legalistic country in the world, boasting more than one million lawyers among its citizens. Latin Americans find the lawsuit mentality of Americans to be strange indeed, for they are not nearly as liable to begin legal action in courts nor do they endure the mind-boggling accumulation of government regulations that hold sway over virtually all aspects of life in more legalistic nations.[3]

The love which Latin Americans have for the flag of their country may suffice as an example. Given the exalted degree of patriotism in these nations, the flag of each country is an especially sacred symbol of national integrity and national traditions. Some years back a U.S. celebrity was reported to have made a vulgar gesture towards an American flag in public. Americans can and do argue the fine legal points of whether such insults should be legal, and the Supreme Court can decide whether Americans can burn an American flag in public as an expression of their free speech. In Latin America it is not a matter of legal wrangling. A common sense of patriotism tells millions of citizens that such behavior is wrong and it should not be tolerated. Numerous Latin Americans exclaimed after the aforementioned example of public disrespect for the American flag that if such an event had taken place in Latin America there would be no need for a court decision for local authorities to take action. The matter would never go that far. People would have instantly arisen in outrage. They would have rushed out of the stands of a ballpark to attack this celebrity. Many Latin Americans claimed that it would have been very doubtful if the celebrity left the ballpark alive.

In Argentina after the end of the administration of President Carlos Menem, the citizens rejected one president after another in the space of just a few weeks. At one point in Menem's administration, he separated from his family by moving out of the Argentine equivalent of the White House. Then the wealthy Argentine family which loaned that house to the nation as the president's residence demanded that the house be returned to them since it was intended to be the residence of the president, and if he wasn't going to live there the government shouldn't have it.

It's difficult to imagine the president of the United States losing his residence in the White House. Perhaps the main reason is simply because the power distance between the public and the president of the United States is greater than it may be in other nations. This is to say that Americans have traditionally viewed their national leaders, especially the presidents, as almost superhuman figures. This is why the revelations of the Watergate scandal during the Nixon administration were so devastating. Before that time there was a greater tendency for the American public to believe that its president could do no wrong.

This difference in attitudes between the northern and southern parts of this hemisphere was well illustrated by a comment by the then-president of Nicaragua, Anastasio Somoza. He stated during a visit to the United States during Watergate that he wondered why Americans were so scandalized by the whole matter when, after all, in Latin America they had a Watergate every single day.

Government by the People?

It may not be going to far too say that the basic Latin American view of national government has often been radically different than the view held by people in the U.S. and by many citizens of Western European countries. Latin Americans often say that people living elsewhere are naïve. For Latinos, no government is immune to corruption, although they state that it is simply much more flagrant in their own backyard, for, as they say in Spanish, *En todas partes se cuecen habas,* or life is the same all over the world. As a result, Latin Americans may be seen to be more tolerant of corruption and they may take a more resigned or fatalistic view. It would be unwise, however, to push this generalization too far, and it certainly is true that criminal charges are brought against offending public officials.

Nevertheless, it may be interesting to note that in one Texas court a driver from a Latin American country was found guilty of attempting to bribe a police officer in order to not receive a ticket. The driver's defense was that he was from Latin America, where this was considered a normal way of dealing with such issues, whether this actually was the case or simply a disingenuous excuse. For better or worse, a Texas jury in a state known for its strict adherence to the value of law and order accepted this excuse and found the defendant not guilty.[4]

Walk on the Wild Side

In light of this traditional adherence to the spirit rather than the letter of the law, drivers in Latin America have a reputation for taking driving regulations with a grain of salt. As we have noted, an American driver cannot always depend on Latin drivers to stop at a stop sign or a red light. Indeed in some countries governmental regulations relating to how one would get a driver's license in the first place are relatively informal to say the least in comparison with other nations that emphasize strict adherence to the letter of the law and the fine print in each and every statute. Readers can form their own opinions as to whether this is positive or negative or whether such an observation corresponds to any experiences they may have had south of the border, however, in the meantime they may be well served if they think twice about driving in areas where attitudes to driving regulations may bend according to local cultural norms.

Such a relaxed attitude towards regulations may be part of the reason why, according to recent estimates, there may be millions of uninsured Latino drivers currently in the United States. At the same time, U.S. drivers who wish to venture south of the border with their cars would do well to check first with their insurance companies, since these firms do not always insure American drivers once they go over the border into Mexico.

Yet such differences in regard to legalities would hardly help us to account for some of the more flagrant crimes of some Latin American presidents in the past and in modern times, for they go against both the spirit and the letter of the law.

In the year 2006, former President Echevarria of Mexico was found guilty of genocide in 1968, while past Peruvian President Fujimori is still wanted by Interpol for real or imagined crimes, depending on one's point of view, and the military junta which ruled Argentina in the 1970s was, by all accounts, responsible for the deaths of thousands of innocent citizens.

In addition, Latin American countries in modern times have frequently experienced violent swings from one form of government to another, such as the Marxist regime of Salvador Allende in Chile, which was overthrown only be replaced by a violent right-wing government led by General Pinochet.

In the case of the Chávez government in Venezuela, we now have a regime that is trying to strengthen its ties to Cuba while it attempts to spread its own leftist orientation to other parts of the South American continent in what has been described as a struggle for the soul of Latin America.[5]

Because of their often turbulent history, many people in this area of the world may be more used to political changes than citizens of the United States. This observation, however, has to remain just theory since we are not aware of any polls or studies that would bear this contention out. It may in fact be the case that because of this very turbulence, Latin Americans actually fear political change more than inhabitants of other regions, since they know from experience that the political pendulum often swings from one extreme to another.

The tendency to adhere to the letter of the law may actually make U.S. citizens fear such changes in government much less, accustomed as they are to a stable governmental system and a stable currency without the wide swings in inflation and devaluation which have marred the Latin American experience into very recent times. Basic changes such as the ones mentioned above are unthinkable to most Americans. They also believe that their political decisions will go unchallenged by the rest of the world. During the George H.W. Bush administration, the U.S invaded Panama and took the president of that country prisoner. What would the reaction of the United States be if Panama were a world power and if it had invaded the United States and took former President Bush prisoner?

Come to the Promised Land?

Another basic difference in the way the average man or woman looks at government has to do with the limitations of general expectations. The United States has a great concern over fiscal and other policies of the federal government and their impact on the economy. What will the inflation rate be next year? How much unemployment will there be?

Latin Americans on the other hand do not usually look to government to solve their problems and to create conditions that are conducive to their wellbeing. On the contrary they often believe that they can and will succeed not because of, but rather in spite of the politics of their central government, not to mention the policies of state and local governments.

This limitation of governmental trust extends to national postal systems, since Latin Americans have traditionally been less likely to trust that the mail that they send or receive will arrive in a timely fashion if at all. Undoubtedly, with the advent of new technology, such attitudes are changing, however, in the past a stoical attitude towards postal service as well as many other governmental services was accepted as a fact of life.

Likewise Latin Americans are not nearly as liable to look to their governments to solve social problems, such as upholding family values or religious values. Nor does government power extend as much to the realm of employment and careers. Latin American governments do not usually employ millions of people, so that the central government is not a possible employer for a considerable percentage of the population. This is true both for desk jobs as well as for military employment. Costa Rica is most notable in this regard, since it actually has no army. Costa Rica has been called "the Switzerland of Latin America." It abolished its military forces with its president expressing his belief that this world needs guns but it also needs music and poetry.[6]

Voters in many countries have traditionally had limited faith in supposedly democratic elections. In a government like Anastasio Somoza's Nicaragua, those citizens that ventured to the polls knew that their dictator would always win every election since it would dangerous for anyone to vote for another candidate. In Cuba, Fidel Castro has always held a lifetime position, excluding any chance that he could be voted out of office. In Mexico from the end of the Mexican Revolution of 1910 until recently, all presidents were elected as representatives of the PRI — the Institutional Revolutionary Party — that supposedly always upheld the ideas of the revolution.

Though Mexico had presidential elections every six years, no one thought that a candidate of any opposition party such as the Party for National Action would ever win an election. But eighty years after the revolution, President Vicente Fox, the candidate from the Party for National Action, actually did become president. Later in the elections of 2006, representatives of three major parties were viewed as viable candidates for the presidency.[7]

Perhaps because of this and because of the fatalism which is part of the Latin temperament, Latin Americans can sometimes be heard to express their own cynical feeling about politics. People say, *Los países tienen los gobiernos que se merecen* (countries have the governments that they deserve), implying that citizens in corrupt or violent regimes are too ignorant to vote correctly, too lackadaisical to care. Perhaps they are also implying that the political infrastructure is too weak and too corrupt to change.

Given a Hispanic regard for history and tradition, Latin Americans blame current governments for their political and economic problems, but also look to the past. They sometimes will argue that Latin America is not as economically progressive as some other regions simply because Spain and Portugal imposed feudal systems of agriculture and land division which stifled democratic progress for centuries — right up to the current time.

Perhaps because of this cynicism (some may wish to call it simply realism) or fatalism, Latin Americans voters are not used to the proliferation of political polls found in the United States, where gathering data, political or otherwise, has come to be a national obsession. Although many Americans may differ with this view of the importance of polling data, this disregard for statistics and data collection may be considered typical of the Latin American mind. Political analysts do not usually make a living predicting future political events, and political pundits are not found in over abundance.

It is true, however that Latin Americans may be less likely to be influenced by the power of the media that centers its attention, in the United States, mainly on only two major political parties, thus creating an implicit establishment mentality which implies that only the candidates of the two most important political sectors are really worth any serious consideration. Thus third party candidates find it next to impossible to rise to the highest political office in the land.

In Latin America, voters are much more likely to seriously consider the candidacy of a wide number of candidates and political parties. This is negative or positive depending on one's point of view, since although it can permit a great variety of opinions and policies, it can also be seen as opening the door to governmental extremism.

Sylvester Paradox

The great Spanish author Pío Baroja once wrote a novel called *Paradox rey* (*Paradox the King*), presenting a main character with the name *Sylvester Paradox*. This title was well chosen since the Hispanic world may be seen as nothing if not a series of great paradoxes. Many relate to political realities — the great sense of patriotism which has existed for centuries in Spain and throughout the Spanish-speaking world is balanced by a strong, perhaps an even stronger attachment to the traditions of one's province or local area. The strong adherence to cultural and social values relating to either the national or the local identity is also often counterbalanced by the strong individualism of the Hispanic character, by which a person may come to believe that political realities are secondary to the desires and impulses of his own persona.[8]

One foreign observer, Richard Ford, has gone as far as to say that Spaniards lack, "a sense of civic responsibility, and [have an] apparent inability to make any effort for the good of the community at large," while a member of the National Spanish Symphony was quoted as saying that every musician in that orchestra has his own conception of a certain note.[9]

The Spanish thinker Julián Marías notes another paradox that he believes is basic to the Spanish character, which may well have been inherited by the Latin American psyche, when he claims that in many countries when a person has a problem with bus transportation he will criticize the bus company. In Spain when a person has a problem with a bus it is more likely that, "the Spaniard hardly thinks about the bus, nor of course about the organization that runs it." His comments go further. According to Marías, the Spaniard immediately says, "Nothing works in this country."[10] The abstract enthusiasm for Spain is common among Spaniards — it is the best place in the world — united with a general hostility for everything in Spain. Nothing which is Spanish appears to be acceptable.

It is undoubtedly true that this enthusiasm in the abstract, which is then united to specific criticism, even to a basic negativity towards national politics, is at the root of much of the cynicism at the bottom of national life. In Mexico this problematic stance towards one's nation even has a name, *malinchismo*, which refers to a Mexican's preference for foreign locales, products or cultures over the Mexican equivalents. The term is a reference to La Malinche, or Doña Marina, the native woman who helped the Spanish adventurer Cortés conquer the Aztec civilization, which led to the Spanish conquest of Mexico.

Pan America

Attempts have been made to reconcile all these paradoxes and conflicting identities into a great pan-American union. This was the dream of the great liberator Simón Bolívar, who wrote of the possibility of uniting Latin America in democracies free of Spanish rule. In recent years, the past president of Peru, Alán García, has spoken highly of Bolivar's ideals, but his administration has not been able to unite all of Latin America in any ideology nor any political philosophy.

Most recently, president Hugo Chávez of Venezuela has begun what has been called a struggle for the soul of Latin America, trying to unite many countries in a left, socialist-veering political orientation that has led him into an apparent friendship with the Marxist president of Cuba, Fidel Castro. Chávez has sharply criticized policies of the United States. He has paid the foreign debt of Argentina and he has aligned himself with the current president of Bolivia, Evo Morales.

Flush with oil money in the midst of a rising international oil market, Venezuela has promoted populist policies not only on its own turf; it has encouraged indigenous people to seek educational opportunities outside of its borders. In May of 2006, for example, Venezuela sent money to enable 5,000 Bolivians, many coming from disadvantaged families, to enroll in university education programs at government expense.[11] Most recently Hugo Chávez played a large part in a worldwide conference of non-aligned nations held in Cuba. This grouping included a number of other Latin American countries besides Venezuela and Cuba itself.[12]

The Color Line

This comes at a time when a renewed interest in the values of native cultures is reaching new heights. Although some historians have long claimed that racism had little to do with the development of political realities in Latin America, there has long existed a so-called Black Legend by which historians of other countries claimed that Spain was especially cruel in its conquest and development of the lands now known as Latin America. Still other historians claim that a White Legend has also persisted for centuries. This is the myth that racism had little or nothing to do with development of Latin America since the days of the European conquest. The truth is just the opposite. Blacks, Indians and various mixtures of both races were for hundreds of years considered to be social outcasts not really capable of taking a full role in the government of their countries. As a result, aspects of popular Indian cultures were looked down on including indigenous languages, works of art, oral literature and traditional music. The dominant political classes traditionally believed that Latin America's cultural aspiration would grow only to the degree that they imitated the artistic and cultural traditions of Western Europe.[13]

Cultural values started to change as political realities changed. The Mexican painter Diego Rivera and his contemporaries such as José Clemente Orozco went to pains to put the Indians and their heritage front and center in their works. Later on in the twentieth century, native elements formed an important part of the literary exploits of some of the authors of the so-called Latin American literary boom of the 1970s and 80s.

President Morales of Bolivia, who worked early in his life herding llamas, is said to be considering establishing an indigenous university within his country, while the study of Quechua, the language of the Inca civilization, has received a new impetus in recent years in Bolivia and Peru, to mention only a few instances in which age-old indigenous cultures are gaining a new importance.

Still Latin Americans do often not believe that their government, as we noted before, has all the answers to their personal problems. Given the much smaller infrastructure of Latin American governments, millions of college graduates do not aspire to a life of comfortable government service, enjoying high salaries and good benefits, as do many graduates in countries with a larger governmental structures. Nor do Latin Americans aspire to finding a professional niche in large corporations to the degree that countless people in other countries do. Big business is nowhere as big, which has made professionals in many countries south of the border seek out opportunities in other lands.

Countless Cubans escaped from the Communist revolution of Fidel Castro with the clothes on their backs. Thousands of Nicaraguans fled their native land during the Sandinista-Contra civil war, as did many Salvadorians during the civil war that recently rocked that country. Many Chileans left their country after the fall of the Allende regime while many Argentines sought relief from turbulence and the monumental inflation of the 1970s by seeking opportunities in other countries. These are only a few instances in which government seemed to fail to meet the needs of its citizens. At the same time, the most pressing example of this trend is the grave problem with illegal immigration at the Mexican-U.S. border.

Globalization and Government

Although there may not be a hemispheric sense of political reality in the vast region known as Latin America, the growing trend towards globalization has sparked a different set of popular expectations of government. What happens in one supposedly isolated country can have world-wide consequences. When the Marxist government of Daniel Ortega was voted out of power in Nicaragua, popular elections in a country that had been marked by dictatorial corruption in the past were overseen by foreign observers who agreed that indeed a non–Marxist government, the government of Violeta Chamorro, had actually won.

As we have already noted, for some eighty years presidents of Mexico came from only one party, the PRI. In 2006, citizens of the country were amazed that their elections were fair enough for a candidate of the opposing PAN party, Vicente Fox, to actually win the election and become Mexico's president.

In the hotly contested presidential elections of 2006, foreign observers who watched the voting booths agreed that the PAN candidate had been elected despite massive protests by almost one hundred thousand people congregating in the Zócalo Plaza in Mexico City, claiming that the socialist candidate had won and the votes had not been correctly counted.

Politics and culture go hand in hand and paradoxes abound. As a purported globalized outlook is taking hold in Latin America, some Latin

Americans, perhaps as a result, continue to cling to their national and localized identities more than ever. As the Hispanic soul is analyzed in the seminal work by the Spanish thinker Ortega Y Gasset, *España invertebrada*, Spaniards for many centuries have tended to think of separate provinces as separate nations. This tendency which was the hallmark of the medieval world, continues to persist and perhaps has become more pronounced in our own day, as clearly seen in the Basque separatist movement.

Perhaps Latin Americans, just as people in many other parts of the world, feel that their local and indigenous cultures are being threatened as never before by mass culture, mass production and multinational companies. Perhaps these realities have led some Latin Americans to actually increase their appreciation for the traditions that they believe may be slipping away from them. Government has a part in this in stimulating the study of ancient languages, in supporting the spreading of native handicrafts, music and dance and in allowing people of native backgrounds greater access to the mainstream of their society.

This development is noteworthy in light of traditional prejudices. For example, in Bolivia, one man of Indian background who wanted to study to be a lawyer was told not to waste his time. He was informed recently that if he opened a law office, anyone seeing that his name was indigenous would not patronize his professional services, and he would surely have to close.[14]

Surely then in order to understand political realities in the land that is the subject of our study it is important not only to learn historical facts and theories as they might be presented in a textbook on political science. It is necessary also to understand a radically different way of looking at historical and current phenomena relating to these same realities.

It is also important to understand that citizens of this other part of the world are not simply middle class Americans who speak different languages, and who will come to see the logic of other attitudes as soon as they become better educated and more sophisticated. Business and political leaders of Latin America are extremely sophisticated and very well versed in what is going on in the world. They often speak two or three languages and often they have a much clearer idea of what is and what has happened in this hemisphere and what is happening in the world, not necessarily because they are more intelligent, but rather because the Latin American press often contains a wide perspective on world events.

We may also realize that their view of themselves, of their country and of the world often springs from a different set of attitudes which, as we have seen, may indeed go back many centuries in time. Or, as it has been said so well and so often, history repeats itself. It frequently appears that "the more things change, the more they stay the same."

VI

The Business of Business

Traditional views of world business centered on the idea that business was business — this was a sphere of practical realities that had little or nothing to do with national cultural patterns. This view has matured greatly in recent decades to the point that it is very common for schools of business in numerous colleges and universities to include at least one course in the cultural background for international business. The realization has grown that business is conducted by human beings and human beings are always a product of their culture. Far from being the realm of those who spend their lives with abstract theories that have little to do with the real world, the realization has finally come home to managers and professors of business alike that countless important business dealings hinge on supposedly small details of human conduct and communication. This blind spot has existed in traditional studies of national cultures as well. Rarely have textbooks or other book-length studies dealt with the role that business activities have in national life, nor the way in which the cultural patterns of a particular country or a certain part of the world have a deep and dramatic effect on the way business is conducted.

In the case of a study of popular culture, which in itself is a rather new way of approaching social patterns, little thought has been given to the daily activities of millions of people that either own their own businesses or work in commercial offices. At the same time, the term "business" could and should be a broad one, for government offices, although they do not ostensibly operate on a commercial profit basis, conduct business all the time, as do other sectors of society that are not always lumped together under the title business activity. We are therefore dealing here with a basic and extremely important part of life and therefore of popular culture.

What then is the Latin American attitude towards business? Americans become impatient when citizens of other countries take exception to what they consider to be the excessive materialism that is a hallmark of American life.

It would be foolish to argue that this is not a basic motivation for the Western world in general if not for most of the world, but Latin Americans often state their deep-seated desire for materialistic welfare, and say we all share it. After all, who does not want to get rich?

However Latin Americans, and Latins in general, including residents of southern European countries such as Spain, Italy and Portugal, say that they know how to combine prosperity or at least the search for it with an ability to enjoy life as well. Or, to put it another way, they repeat the old cliché that in the Latin countries one works to live, while in the United States one lives to work.

In order to prove this they may be quick to point out that when two Americans meet, invariably the first question is, "What do you do for a living?" This implies that the hallmark of life is work itself.

Observers of Latin American life often agree that Latin Americans share the tendency of Mediterranean peoples to value business and profit making as a part of life that is to be balanced by family and personal values — more than may be the case in more highly industrialized cultures. Of course such generalizations are very broad and comments on the lives of hundreds of millions of people must be approached with great care.

The traditional break during the day, what is called the siesta in Spanish, a rest period that can go on for hours, contributes to this stereotype to the point that many foreign observers are quick to point to the *mañana* attitude towards business in general. Such a view of the Hispanic way of life goes back hundreds of years. In fact there is a well known satirical story in Spanish literature written by the author José de Lara, *Come Back Tomorrow (Vuelva Ud. mañana)*. In this story a visitor from France decides to finally become a Spanish citizen and live in Spain for the rest of his life in order to complete some minor business transactions that he originally thought would take him only several days.

Lest this type of generalization lead us far astray, it might be wise to remember that the Latin American work day frequently goes until the evening, with office chores demanding the attention of employees for at least two or three hours after the end of the day in the traditional 9-to-5 schedule. In addition, the increasing pressures of international business, in light of the current globalization of commerce, have forced Latin American business methods to resemble more closely those in other parts of the world.

Still time has a different value south of the border. A well-known aspect of Latin American society is the relative sense of time. Absolute punctuality is not considered as important in business and personal life as it is in some other societies. Indeed Edward Hall, a pioneer of intercultural research, has stated in his book *Hidden Differences* that lateness up to five or ten minutes is normally allowed in business and professional appointments in the United States and the Anglo-Saxon world in general, however in Latin America as well as in many other parts of the world, a wait of twenty to thirty minutes is often considered to be acceptable.[1]

One caveat — the recent globalization of business and a growing internationalization of business mores in recent years, especially since the implementation of the North American Free Trade Agreement (NAFTA), has made such tardiness no longer as acceptable as it once was and at least one country, Ecuador, has made a national effort to combat tardiness.[2]

Nevertheless, one aspect of this different sense of time relative to the implementation of Latin American business and commercial practices in other cultures is the strong emphasis on personal harmony between the parties that wish to enter into a business agreement. In the United States, for example, sales people tend to believe that they are selling their product alone, and that the personal relationship they might strike up with their business counterparts who may become their clients is not the main issue at all. In Latin America business people have a traditional desire to take the time to get to know those people with whom they wish to do business.

In effect Latin American business operatives like to establish a harmonious personal relationship with those who seek a commercial deal with them. Indeed they may go beyond merely feeling what might be considered in colloquial terms "good vibes" to get to know potential associates to the point that they actually have a basis to judge whether others are responsible and sincere people who can be trusted.[3]

In this sense business deals can take time and a person who simply appears on the doorstep of a potential client and states the nature of his or her business, expecting to conclude a deal on the spot if the price and the merchandise fit the bill, may be in for a surprise. Protracted or at least a time-consuming contact with Latin American counterparts, extensive conversation and perhaps social invitations may be required.

It is important to keep in mind that conversations do not necessarily always deal with business, at least not right away. The Latin American who is considering entering into a deal, especially with a person who represents a different culture, may wish to talk about a wide variety of topics before getting down to business. Indeed one of the hallmarks of Latin American conversation is the tendency for a wide variety of subjects to weave in and out in ways that may surprise visitors from other parts of the world.

Since this approach to a possible lucrative venture may strike foreign visitors as odd, it would be wise to bone up on local history and the artistic contributions of the country which is the home of the Latin American counterpart. Keep in mind that conversation in which a visitor speaks only of his own experience in his own country will certainly appear, sooner or later, to be shallow and one-sided.

Moreover it is important to keep in mind that the Latin American concept of education or *cultura* goes beyond the mere attainment of educational titles and degrees. The Latin American mind sees education as the total formation of a person. How do they dress? How correctly do they speak? What are their table manners and to what degree are they aware of the world in general? Do they know not only what has happened in their own country but what has happened in the business counterpart's section of the world? Does the visitor know something about history, art and literature or does his intellectual horizon start and end with the world of business?

Nor is it an exaggeration to state that the higher the level of business that one conducts in Latin America the more important these fine points and details of personal amenities become. And this means business in the fullest sense of the word, for business can be conducted on the governmental and professional level as well as in the world of commerce and large corporations.

Image and Reality

Considering the great pride that Latin Americans have in their countries and cities of origin, it is not surprising that they also have great pride in themselves, to the point that any word or gestures that may imply a lack of recognition of a person's dignity or importance can have an extremely negative effect on the possibility of concluding a business deal.

This author once asked a high official of a Latin American government what his response would be if he asked for a new pen during a governmental negotiation with representatives from another country, and another person carelessly tossed a pen in his direction.[4]

The discussion would immediately be terminated was his answer. Could a deal worth hundreds of millions of dollars be immediately sidetracked because of a pen? The answer was again that the way in which a pen was casually tossed in a person's direction was definitely more important than the millions of dollars that were under discussion.

Likewise the extreme formality of names and titles often comes as a surprise to visitors from other countries that may be accustomed to different modes of address. Latin Americans, for example, are continually surprised that

Americans would call a president of the United States, "Bill" Clinton as opposed to "William" Clinton. How can you be so informal as to use an abbreviated name for the most important political official in the world, they ask?

By the same token it is expected that in a business or professional environment people will be addressed on a last-name basis unless a specific invitation is given to speak to the other person on the first-name basis.

Likewise for those who engage in conversation in Spanish, a choice must always be made as to whether to use the formal *usted* or the informal *Tú* form of the word "you."

Here again the desire to export the informality of other countries may come to the fore in the tendency to use the latter form of address immediately. It is most likely that the more formal *Usted* would correspond more closely with a person being addressed on a last name basis.

A heightened sense of personal pride also extends to the frequent use of titles in daily conversation, above and beyond the well-known title of "Dr." Latin Americans will frequently address members of other professions as "Engineer" (*Ingeniero/a*) so-and-so or "Architect" (*Arquitecto/a*) so-and-so.

It is essential to keep in mind that the term *Licenciado* or *Licenciada*, a form of address used to precede the last name of a person with a university degree, is always to be used when applicable.

Clothes Make the Man?

It may come as a surprise to many whose contact with Latin America has been limited to well-known vacation areas where tropical and beach style clothing is most usual that business dress in the southern part of the American hemisphere is actually more formal than that found in a number of other countries. Men tend to wear dark jackets and suits, and traditionally women were expected to wear a dress or skirt, although that dress code has changed greatly in recent years.

At the same time, certain informalities in dress, such as men rolling up their sleeves, not wearing a tie or even loosening the knot and opening the top button of their dress shirt, is usually considered an expression of a lack of professionalism. Ditto for men taking off their jackets in the office or during a business meeting.[5]

Should You Really Take "Yes" for an Answer?

Some societies place more importance on creative harmony among conversationalists than on bringing forth possible differences of opinion.[6]

Although this well-ingrained social tendency unfortunately does not extend to the avoidance of wars and acts of violence, still it can have a bearing on a person's desire to get a direct answer to a business deal or proposition.

As noted before, Latin America is often considered to be somewhat of a non–information specific society. Many possible ways to avoid giving a direct "no" answer to a business question may actually appear appealing. These may include such expressions as "I will think about it," "It is a possibility" or "We will have to see," along with other similar expressions. They may be sincere statements of the situation, but it is also possible that these and other similar phrases of a tentative or non-conclusive reality may be gentle ways of turning down a business deal without directly saying "no."

Why is there a similar tendency in Asia, which is superficially at least so different, we may ask? It may be helpful to realize that there is more than a small dose of oriental heritage within the Hispanic world. This need not be as surprising or even as controversial as it may appear at first glance. After all, history tells us that Moslems of Middle Eastern cultural heritage invaded Latin America's mother countries of Spain and Portugal and took up residence there for hundreds of years, thus making a vast cultural impact. In the Spanish language alone there are some eight to ten thousand words which come directly from the Arabic language, such as the commonly used phrase *Ojalá* which literally means, "Oh I pray to Allah."

It may be because of this heritage that this oriental tendency to try to create harmony to the point of telling listeners what the speaker thinks they want to hear rather than what is the literally true, exists to a certain degree in Latin America.

This is not to say that speakers tell untruths on purpose, for it is likely that this tendency to satisfy the listener is so ingrained that it becomes a subliminal or subconscious way of thinking. In any case, for whatever reason, it is very possible that a foreign business visitor to the Latin American world may get a "yes" answer to a business question when such an answer is not always warranted. Therefore it might be wise to check on the status of a matter many times, asking various levels of management of the same company if the assurance already given will turn into reality, rather than a imagined goal.

Over-optimism may run through various levels of the organization, so it may be advisable to get the agreement in writing and then check and double-check again.

Many U.S. residents believe that Latin America is wide open area where anyone can do business any way they want, with little or no government control. Perhaps this is a holdover from the cowboy movies about the old West in which outlaws frequently headed for Mexico, implying that they would always be safe there because Mexico was a lawless land where anything goes. Old stereotypes die hard and this false assumption has foiled more than one business attempt south of the border.

A little-known aspect of the Hispanic mind is the love of red tape, bureaucracy and governmental regulations. Part of this tendency is the Latin belief in the dignity of the individual. An extension of this characteristic is the bureaucrat's or functionary's belief in his or her self-importance, which has historically been expressed in tangible form by the Hispanic love of rubber stamps and important-looking seals, as well as duplicate and triplicate copies of official and semi-official documents.

The popular culture of business extends to personal banking, such as a deposit or withdrawal from an account. In Latin America an apparently simple transaction may be more complicated than it looks, since it may involve waiting in more than one line and filling out more documents than might be expected. More than one Latin American has found that he had to take part of a day or a full day off from work just to complete a simple financial transaction.

On a very common, everyday level even the most trivial purchase in a retail store may be the occasion for a mild dose of culture shock for those who are visiting the region for the first time. Rather than picking out an item and paying the casher, it is customary for a person to approach one cashier or clerk with the item. The customer pays this person, who writes out a receipt and marks it as "paid." Then the customer is directed to present this receipt to another clerk, thus having to go through two procedures to make a simple purchase.

The tradition of mounds of official-looking documents and red tape in the Hispanic world goes back centuries, to the era of the Spanish *conquistadores*. In the days before Xerox machines or computers there were so many thousands of pounds of documents and assorted papers in governmental files it is said that few if any officials of the Spanish empire could really keep track of them.

Caveat Manager — Manager Beware

All of the aspects of popular culture in general, as well as those that specifically relate to business, come into play when personal relations are at issue.

To understand this we must remember that pride in oneself and in one's place of origin is paramount to the Latin American mind. Therefore workers who protest that they will not work on a certain local holiday or days of special celebration may cause a foreign manager to scratch his or her head, wondering what possible importance such a local holiday could have in the greater scheme of things.[7]

Traditionally, worker turnover is the biggest problem for foreign firms with production facilities in Latin America. Many employees in large organizations in Latin America work on a temporary or almost seasonal basis — long enough to be able to send money back to their families in outlying districts or just long enough to make the money necessary to attain some immediate goal. Keeping workers on the job has been a formidable task for some companies. Of course the best way to create worker satisfaction is to pay good wages. That much is obvious, but not as obvious, perhaps, is the importance of holidays, especially local or regional holidays, to the employees. Mexican author Octavio Paz has even gone so far as to state in his book *The Labyrinth of Solitude* that to the Mexican mind, life is characterized by celebrations.

Likewise it is important to remember that to a group culture rather than an individualist oriented society such as the United States, family and family obligations are often of the utmost importance. Workers who come to their supervisors saying they cannot work on a given day because of a problem or illness relating to a cousin or uncle or aunt may raise the eyebrows of supervisors. Supervisors may carry their own set of values to the point that they may not be able to believe that relatives in the extended family can be considered by Latin Americans to be close family members. It is important to remember that in many cases, however, these relations are indeed close and Latin American workers may well in all sincerity believe that an illness or other problem relating to members of the extended family is exactly the same as illness or emergencies relating to a member of the immediate family.

In Latin America, citizens have a sharp sense of the differences between the social classes. It is for this reason that students of comparative culture and comparative business refer to varying levels of "power distance" in businesses throughout the world. This may be defined as the degree of formality that exists between employees and their supervisors.

Though this power distance may differ from one country to another within Latin America, most students of the popular culture of business in Latin America believe that the relationships among staff and managers are much more formal than in other parts of the world.

When asked if they would enjoy a more informal relationships with their bosses, such as the right to address them on the first name basis, Latin American workers say, "No. We don't want that type of familiarity, since it is only skin deep. It really isn't sincere at all." They believe that it expresses a false sense of friendship between the boss and the employee that will not stand the test of time; or to put it another way, this cordiality is often misleading since a supervisor who express a very friendly relationship with a worker will turn on that person at a moment's notice and fire him on even the slightest pretext.

At the same time Latin American working personnel traditionally have not been as ready to second-guess managers as might be expected. In fact, when asked if they wanted to give suggestions to management on how to improve production, some Latin Americans have said they didn't even want anyone to ask their opinion. They often express the sentiment that they are workers and the managers are management. That is the way it has always been and that is the way it should remain. Managers are paid to make administrative decisions. They are not.

It is precisely because of these complicated sets of values that our education in these matters lags behind this reality. Consider the case of one executive in a major Fortune 500 company who complained to the author that his employees in a Latin country did not seem concerned with time. They almost always handed in their reports four or five hours late, to say the least.

"What am I going to do?" asked the U.S. executive. "This is driving me out of my mind."

"Very simple," was the answer. "Just tell them to get the material to you at least five hours earlier than you really want it, and if it comes late they will hand it in right on time. Don't fight it because you're not going to overcome habits ingrained by a lifetime in a few days or even in a few months."

Soon after, the businessman called to say that he was really grateful for the advice, expressing wonder that he hadn't thought of that. "It works great," he said. "This has made everything a thousand times better." He went on to explain that his international corporation had not given him any training to prepare him for working in another country with another culture.

Mass Society, Mass Production

Business visitors from abroad may also carry their own perspectives on the nature of business enterprise, which may mean a universal desire to do bigger and better business. We might take a minute to consider this assumption more carefully, since traditional textbooks on the culture and civilization of Latin America do not explain the attitudes of the popular mind that constitute daily life in general, nor the daily life of business.

If we accept this as a possibility then we may consider that a business person from another culture may believe that a Latin American business that produces its product on a limited scale would be delighted to receive an order to purchase ten thousand items per month. This is big business indeed and being in business is all about conducting commercial enterprises on as large a scale as possible. After all, a basic difference between Latin American and U.S. business is the latter is largely populated by chain and franchised businesses while small businesses appear to be losing ground all the time, especially in terms of retail sales.

Though one might assume that all small-scale Latin American businesses want to become big chain businesses, this is not automatically true at all. The owner of a small Latin American business might be making enough money to live, and that might be enough for him or her. Perhaps the so-called American dream has not penetrated that far south of the border. This business owner may think that to expand would demand a greater risk and assuming a greater number of responsibilities than he or she is willing to take on.

As a result a foreign company may, in accordance with tendency of Latin Americans to say what is most acceptable or what they believe another person wants to hear, promise to deliver a certain amount of goods at a certain time and yet a foreign company may find it wise to look at this commitment through the prism of a different set of cultural values as we have described them.

But how could this possibly be the case? After all business is mechanical, practical, and cut-and-dry. Well yes, but we have already noted that business is human enterprise conducted by human beings, as well as computers and other modern technology. We must keep in mind that custom has a way of reigning supreme in human affairs and what is customary in one part of the world may appear to be irrational and outrageous in another. It is not always self-evident, for it is human nature to believe that what we do and think makes perfect sense and it should make sense to everybody. We frequently forget that human beings that are just as rational and logical as we are have developed ways of living and interacting with other people which may be radically opposed to our values and our perspective on life.

As we consider these differences in the popular and the commercially trained mind, let us realize that this is true just as much in the world of business as it is in any other aspect of human existence.

VII

The Business of Business in Daily Life

The question as to how these general concepts of cultural sensitivity relate to business practices in Latin America brings us to a more detailed consideration of the workplace in today's world. Could a business deal, whether large or small, actually be derailed because of one or more intercultural mistakes? This is hardly an academic question, since large amounts of money may be at stake as well as the future of one of more business enterprises. And "business" may be interpreted in many ways. It is not simply commercial transactions, as important as they may be, but also professional and even government business, which frequently hinge on the same principles of human relations and intercultural sensitivity that we have studied in our examination of commerce in Latin America.

Let us take two concrete examples of an American businessman who tried to complete a transaction south of the U.S. border only to encounter series of pitfalls which could have easily been avoided had he paid attention to the details of business culture.

Mr. Sage Freeman, let us call him, called on a Latin American business. He was directed to a manager whom he addressed by his first name, calling him "Carlos," instead of calling him by his last name, which was Delibes. He also forgot to use the term of address "*Licenciado*," the absence of which is often considered to be a direct insult when such a form of address is relevant.

He was presented with the business card of his Latin American counterpart. On searching in his own wallet, he could not find his own card. On top of this lack of professionalism, he immediately took the card of his counterpart and put it in his own pocket without looking at it, which made his opposite number feel that Freeman was not really impressed by the Latin's name and position in the company.[1]

After they sat down to discuss business, our American friend carelessly tossed a copy of a piece of correspondence which he had already sent to a high official in the Latin American company. There was, of course, nothing wrong in presenting such a letter, but by carelessly tossing the letter in the other person's direction he committed an affront. He did not take the time to carefully place the piece of paper in front of the other businessman, giving proper acknowledgement to his business counterpart and his side in their conversation.

Such an act, which would be considered completely acceptable in the normal conduct of business in many other countries, was taken as a grave personal insult — enough to ruin any business deal in that part of the world.

To make matters worse, Mr. Freeman came to the meeting without wearing a tie and a jacket, which is often considered to be a breach of proper business etiquette south of the border except when deals are to be consummated in regions which actually do have a tropical climate, which was not the case here.

Contrary to his name, he was unwise in stretching his arms behind his head during one part of the conversation and clasping his hands, another bit of body language which does not make a favorable impact.

After a very brief conversation about introductory matters, Mr. Sage Freeman began to get right into business matters by bringing up the subject and purpose of his visit. Although in U.S. culture "time is money," and few people like to waste their time let alone the time of others and therefore want to get right down to business, in Latin America this comes across as bad form — an unwelcome representation of the overly aggressive and pragmatic mindset.

Whether the visiting foreigner or his company want to agree or not is not as important as the consideration that his Latin American counterpart and the rest of *his* company feel this way, and this can and often does have a negative impact on business success.

After that, Mr., or rather Licenciado, Delibes suggested that the two men continue their discussion at lunch. Knowing that lunch is usually the principal meal of the day in the Latin world, often taking more than two hours, the American glanced at his watch and estimated that his busy schedule would not allow him to dedicate that much time to lunch.

This was certainly an understandable reaction, or at least it was meant to be, yet his counterpart felt in the depth of his heart that his U.S. colleague was living up to the stereotype of North Americans. These are people who do not want to take time with others. They are ruled by the clock and in this case Licenciado Delibes apparently was not important enough for Mr. Freeman to spend more than a few minutes talking to him. Even though this was not the case, Delibes couldn't help the negative twinge in his nervous system that told him that this was because he was a Latin American. Perhaps he was considered to be a second-class citizen for whom Freeman had carefully budgeted his time. He was worth only a few minutes and no more than that.

Though this might not have been the intention of the casual glance at a watch, this was the result. Hardly a good way to initiate a business relationship that could have lasted for years and years if Freeman had actually been wiser and more careful.

A Latin American in the Corporate World: Survival on the Job

Problems of an intercultural nature are not limited to Americans trying to do business south of the border. The differences are an important part of daily business life everywhere. Take, for example, the case of one very bright Latin American who brought himself and his cultural mindset into the corporate world inside the United States.

How did he fare? Were there other conflicts between the popular culture of business in Latin America and the United States which caused concern or problems that might have had the potential to actually ruin his career?

Well, let us consider the experiences of Mr. Juan Santiago Contreras, who achieved a very fine middle management position in a large American corporation known simply for our purposes as company X.

He had worked in the Mexican office of a large multinational U.S. company. Even in his own country he had experienced cultural-based problems in the office, since the American manager insisted that all of his staff speak only in English because he did not speak in Spanish even though he was working in a Spanish-speaking country. It goes without saying that this did not go over too well with a large part of the staff, many of whom had only a passing knowledge of English which they had learned in school but which they had not practiced for many years. They found it difficult and stressful to communicate, and they inevitably thought to themselves, why should I have to go through all of this aggravation right here in my own country?

The American official was never trained in the fine points of working in Latin America, and therefore he was never told about the importance of what might be called social details of interpersonal communication. To be specific, he often forgot to greet all members of his staff with a "good morning" salutation just as he often forgot to say "thank you" and "good-bye." Not an important point in a culture where the bottom line is all important — the issue is to get the job done not to make friends — but in a culture where the social graces and interpersonal harmony are of a much greater importance, these supposedly trivial items of communication can and often do take on a special significance.

The manager insisted that lunchtime was from noon to 1 P.M. which seemed extremely strange to Juan Santiago Contreras and his colleagues since the Mexican lunch is usually eaten in mid-afternoon and it can go on for several hours, even for office workers with a tight schedule.

The American manager found it unusual that female workers would use so much perfume in the office, and that men would sometimes overdo it with cologne. Personal appearance and dress can be seen from a different perspective than is usual in the United States.

The boss would sometimes appear at work without wearing a tie and sometimes without a jacket. Such dress smacked of non-professionalism to Juan Contreras and some of his colleagues.

Eventually this American manager lost his job due largely to these and other cultural mistakes which led to discouragement and very low morale among his local staff. In the meantime, however, Mr. Juan Santiago Contreras thought himself to be fortunate to have been offered a better-paying position in the main office of his company in the United States.

Juan was ecstatic. However his excitement was short-lived. On going to work in the United States he soon found himself in the middle of another group of dilemmas that he could never have anticipated.

A Latin in Manhattan (or Elsewhere in the U.S.)

Juan found his colleagues somewhat cold and unfriendly. Whereas work in Latin America was often a team effort, and he was used to a great deal of camaraderie at the office, he soon concluded that the business culture of the United States was "everyone for himself or herself." Whereas in Latin America many people looked at work as a great opportunity to socialize and enjoy themselves, the work ethic in the United States struck Juan Santiago Contreras as much more oriented to the bottom line, not to the individuals who worked for the company. For this reason he began to sense that his colleagues expressed less concern or even loyalty to their bosses and to the company in general, preferring to worry about the future of their organization in terms of their welfare alone.

At times he wondered if he was overreacting to his new environment. After all there was no need to make snap judgments. A person had to give himself time to get accustomed, but as time went on his opinions only became more hardened than they were in the first place.

But that was only the beginning. After two weeks on the job he was asked to fill out a performance questionnaire which contained, among other considerations, questions about his supervisor. He knew that this form would be forwarded to the company's main office. The top management of his company was sure that their employees like Juan would be very pleased at this newly instituted democratic approach to management, as opposed to traditionally rigid management. However Latin American workers like Juan were not usually asked their opinion on the competence of high-level management.

For Juan, language itself was a problem. Not just the differences between Spanish and English, for Juan could perform very well in both languages, but the brevity of the language of business telephone calls and business letters. The style was different because the mindset was different.

Not only that, but the pragmatism of his American colleagues was so extreme that even taking the time to say complete words was often considered to be unnecessary. Therefore when his supervisor said at a meeting, "OK, the VIP told the CEO that the SOP [standard operating procedure] had to be revised ASAP, just FYI [for your information]," Juan was taken aback. It began to dawn on him that he would rarely if ever have the opportunity to have long conversations with the people that he was supposed to report to because they didn't believe, within the parameters of the culture that they were a product of, that they had the time to engage in discussions of theoretical matters. The expression of ideas, even as they related to the business of making money, had to be expressed in concise terms with the main idea of a conversation coming to the fore in less than one minute. Few colleagues had time for small talk about the weather or how their favorite baseball or basketball team was doing that season.

Furthermore he was in culture shock to see how much the Americans peppered their statements with references to graphs and statistics. No one would believe anything he might want to say in relation to commerce without his being able to back up his statement with facts and figures. He soon came to the conclusion that what he considered to be an obsession with polls, numbers and figures amounted to a national cultural trait that struck him as odd and unnecessary. He had a hard time adjusting to it.

In addition, his superiors would often criticize the performance of his colleagues with little or no concern about how this would affect the employee's morale, let alone the morale of the staff in general when word of what was often blunt, if not actually devastating, criticism got around. He heard somebody refer to this as "the General Patton style of management." In addition he found it hard to adjust to the extreme importance given to absolute punctuality. After all, anyone's watch could be a few minutes late. Who was to say that the boss's watch ran exactly in synch with Big Ben in London? The boss was always sure that his time was correct and his employee's time was not, though this was never proved to absolutely be the case.

His company featured a "dress down day"—one day a week in which employees were invited to come to work in sports clothes. This was fine for most of his American colleagues, but Juan could never feel completely comfortable wearing what he considered to be less than professional apparel.

Furthermore his secretary called him by his first name (which to his dismay, some New Yorkers adapted to the local vernacular, making it sound more like "foist" name) rather than by the title that he was used to in Mexico, which was "*Licenciado.*" For Santiago Contreras, that was a shocking step down in dignity and professionalism.

But the biggest shock of all, the hardest change that he had to become used to was the basic difference in the value of work and business in his new world in contrast to the Mexican environment. Though change was afoot in Latin America as in many parts of the world, and globalized attitudes were developing rapidly, still the traditional attitude towards work was that it was more of a means to an end, with the end or goal being the enjoyment of a good life, while in his new surroundings he couldn't help getting the feeling that the attitudes he encountered on an almost daily basis were radically different.

This came home to him when his wife endured more of a climate crisis than a severe culture clash. This was like the classic Latin American fiction writer José Eustacio Rivera, who endured the life-threatening dangers of the jungle as the basis for his novel *La vorágine* only to come to New York City to die of pneumonia.

Juan's wife contracted this same sickness during her first winter in the Big Apple. When Juan, deeply concerned, communicated this news to his boss and his co-workers he was surprised to find that they expected him to keep up his normal pace of work with the same degree of attention to detail as before, as if his wife's health were a small detail in his life. He came to feel that it really was true that the business of America is business, while in Latin America he was used to others realizing that grave personal matters were all important as *the* defining characteristics and values in life, not business.

This was a cultural clash that upset him as it took him off emotional balance. He lost an equanimity of spirit that he never really regained while he worked in a country that he came to admire, a country which, however, he never believed that he could accept as his home.

Add to this his shock at finding that American workers had little or no security on the job. He noticed that it was actually part of the American culture to feel that one could and should be able to deal with any challenge, even losing one's job, and survive with little support from the outside world.[2] He found that his company's lack of regard for the security and welfare of his co workers matched their lack of concern for a group-based approach to living in which an individual is encouraged to develop a real concern for the welfare of his company and a real dedication to a place of business. He found that the lack of concern was mutual, and American companies would fire large number of employees to relocate their production base to another country, if only to save a few pennies an hour in the cost of labor.

Sometimes he berated himself for having developed this cynicism regarding his work experience, but coming as an alternate reality so to speak, he could see clearly that business, like so many aspects of life, is a product of culture, since business is conducted by human beings and all human beings are to one degree or another a product of their culture.

Juan thought to himself that the traditional wisdom that he had been taught as a child was true as it was expressed in sayings like, "El que se acuesta con perros, se levanta con pulgas" (he who sleeps with dogs, gets up with fleas), as time went by and he found that he himself was changing as he became part of the vast melting pot of a new land and a new way of doing business.

But that was not all. In the new teamwork environment which has taken hold in international business in recent years and which many business experts believe is going to be the wave of the future, specialists are brought in from all parts of the globe to work on a particular project for a limited amount of time. Juan has recently been asked to be part of such a team of experts, and he has many questions about how his own cultural perspective on business will fit in with specialists from all over the world.[3] For example, how will time be handled? Will their work be governed by the strict American concept of punctuality or will there be a certain flexibility, not only in their daily work schedule, but as far as deadlines? In what language will the work sessions be conducted? In what language will the final report be written? The styles of business writing vary from country to country. They can be somewhat verbose and ornate in the Spanish-speaking world whereas in other countries pragmatism dictates a simpler, more direct writing style. What is the proper dress code for the meetings of this international committee? When will meals be eaten? The differences in work schedules can be great. In Latin America offices are frequently open until well after the normal supper hour in the United States. The list of questions was almost endless for Juan and for others coming from his cultural perspective.[3] In this time of globalism, the reality of the culture of daily business, is an acute one that encompasses the need for one cultural perspective to work well with another. It is truly an international issue with profound implications for the day-to-day world of business both here and in Latin America.

VIII

Home and Education

Any student of Latin American life can go to a local library and obtain a book on the colonial architecture of Latin America. The styles that are found in elegant picture books are striking indeed, especially since the very elaborate baroque form of architecture took hold in Latin America during the early days of the colonial period, while it had little or no influence in North America with the exception of the French cultural influence in Canada.

This baroque style included twisted or fluted columns, ornamentation to an almost unbelievable degree, imposing domes, complicated carving and elaborate gilding, especially in churches. Churches were designed to make the faithful feel they were in such an august atmosphere that they could look up to the ceiling to be overwhelmed by the power and beauty of architectural detail — to almost believe that they were in heaven already.

Colonial style plays an important part in Latin American life since its presence can be seen in almost any part of Latin America from colonial-style buildings and entire traditional-styled neighborhoods in large urban areas to the very same style of architectural heritage in small towns and rural areas.[1]

Such historic forms of town planning as well as the design of homes and public buildings are often characterized by narrow streets, since these were built before the advent of automobiles. Such streets are often made of cobblestones, and roads often twist and turn. They do not usually conform to the geometric patterns of modern superhighways.

The buildings that face these narrow streets often have balconies adorned with elaborate wooden carvings. In Latin America as well as in Spain, some streets are actually so narrow that those who live in the second story can step from one balcony on one side of the street to another balcony right across the street without actually crossing the street below.

Builders and homeowners in that former age must have loved color, because many of the structures that have been preserved still maintain bright and pastel colors such as yellow or ochre, ultramarine blue and various shades of red or maroon. The shingles that adorn rooftops even today also give evidence of this love for color. These tiles, often laid on top of each other in a half-moon or arched formation, come in various shades such as orange, yellow and red among others.

Doors of many colonial buildings, especially public buildings and churches, are mammoth affairs that are often built to double or triple the height of a normal adult. These entrances were meant to accommodate pedestrians as well as horsemen. The door knockers were large and heavy enough to require a major effort to hoist them.

The early settlers used the same architectural plans for the layout of towns as had been used in Europe for centuries. Houses often follow a rectangular structural pattern. A fountain and an array of plants was set in the middle of an open patio with the rooms of the house, usually constructed on several floors, surrounding the open patio. Many houses or haciendas conform to this arrangement even today.[2]

It would be a great mistake to believe, however, that all of Latin America's architectural styles, whether in the Spanish- or Portuguese-speaking areas, conform to historical patterns. Contrary to popular opinion, ultramodernistic office buildings and family homes can be found in just about all parts of this vast area of the globe. The furniture found in such edifices is frequently as spare and modernistic as the buildings themselves.

In homes of a more traditional mode, architectural styles differ from those in North America without an overt English influence, especially the Victorian and neo-Victorian style. Inside, especially in the dwellings of upper middle- and upper-class Latin Americans, furniture styles often show the influence of a French rather than a neo-Anglo style. This includes reproductions in the curved style of what has been called Second Empire furniture which originated in nineteenth century France.

Of course furniture showing the influence of the Spanish tradition is also in evidence, bearing the hallmark of heavy, if not overly comfortable, styles of workmanship. These patterns have been continued in heavy wooden articles of furniture that make up a modern version of colonial, Hispanic furniture styles.

The floors of homes may be wood as is common in many countries. (Setting aside ridiculous stereotypes as seen in a question once posed to the author by a supposedly intelligent adult, who asked whether people south of the border had floors in their houses or whether they simply sat and stood on the dirt.) Floors made of many other materials including marble or onyx may be also found with some degree of frequency.

Wooden homes are not nearly as common as they are in the United States and few homes have an attic or a cellar. Houses of middle class and upper class Latin Americans have separate rooms for servants, while metal grillwork or *rejas*, which sometimes are very ornate, are common outside of the homes. Wealthy Latin American are prone to hide the entrance of their large homes behind high retaining walls, some of which contain barriers to unwanted visitors such as shards of broken glass.

In the United Sates, front and back lawns can be very large. In Latin America, front yards are generally smaller than back yards. Nor do Latin Americans have what has been called the American obsession with the perfect front lawn, devoid of weeds or crab grass.

The distance separating one house from a neighbor's house represents a different sense of privacy. As Raymond Gorden has observed in relation to the structure and placement of homes in Bogotá, Colombia, "Privacy in the United States is obtained by increasing the open space between a person and his neighbor, while in Bogotá it is achieved by double abutting walls with no doors or windows."[3]

The living room of the house is the showcase of the whole dwelling. It demonstrates the best and most formal articles of furniture, antiques, or highly prized works of art. U.S. residents who have visited Latin America and have been overwhelmed by the beauty and variety of handicrafts, including jewelry, art, textiles, and statues, may imagine that Latin Americans love to fill their homes with these colorful items. Actually, middle- and upper-class Latinos frequently eschew such decoration, preferring more formal European-inspired designs.

Given the formality of the living room setting, the informal use of this space as a den or TV room would be highly unusual, except in very small homes where families are pressed for living space.[4]

Family

The house is the dwelling and the gathering place for the entire family. This usually includes not only the immediate family but also the extended family. At any given time in the home of a Hispanic family it is not unusual to find both the immediate family and members of the extended family. Living is truly a group enterprise. Since friendships can also be very strong, a person will have *compadres*, or friends who are so close that they are literally considered to be part of a family, and *comadres* as well, women who fill the same function.

Elder members of a family are revered for their experience and wisdom, and their advice is taken seriously. This respect is evident in terms of address. Concern for family members beyond the immediate family is great both in terms of health, money, and general welfare. For example many Mexican immigrants who come to work in the United States do so to be able to send money back home to their families in Mexico. They do not simply forget them as they come to seek their fortune, and as such, this transmission of money constitutes an important part of the Mexican economy each year, involving billions of dollars that are turned into pesos.

A sense of belonging and the adherence to one's roots remains very strong. This is traditionally aided by the relative size of the capital and other large urban centers in Latin America, where the most important business and government centers tend to concentrate. Therefore job seekers don't have to move all over the country to innumerable branch offices as they do in the United States.

Family traditions and the family name are very important in business and professional life, especially for members of very prominent families, and especially in those countries which have a large concentration of wealth and power in the hands of relatively few families. Just as in Massachusetts it was said that the Cabot family only spoke to the Lodge family, and the Lodges only spoke to God, social stratification is strong and the tendency of prominent families to restrict marriage and business relations to themselves is still strong.

It is a common belief that all Latin America has only two social classes, without the presence of any middle class. This is definitely not the case and the idea that everyone who is not wealthy lives in abject poverty without access to education or culture is a common stereotype of Latin America that should be discarded or at least be examined once again in the light of reality. Business and professional relations are frequently commenced after an inquiry of "who do you know that I know?" and "who sent you?" or "who recommended that you contact me?" Although such considerations may be important in any part of the world, they are especially important in the Hispanic and Luso-Brazilian world. Important families often are familiar with their familial coat of arms and with the historical traditions that their families have played in national life. The strong Latin American interest in tradition and history as well as Hispanic pride play a large part in such attitudes.

Latin families have a strong patriarchal tradition, a logical outgrowth of the *machismo* attitude which makes a man believe that he is the king of his castle and the lord of his manor no matter how humble it may be, and therefore his authority within the family unit should go unquestioned. It is for this reason that the father's authority often reaches to control almost all of the family's business and financial matters, in light of the very traditional idea that such matters are the province of men alone.

In upper middle- and upper-class homes where it is very common to have one or more persons who provide domestic help, the wife and mother tends to function more as a manager of household affairs than as a house-wife who personally takes care of domestic chores. Such fortunate individuals look with a good degree of wonderment at their middle-class counterparts in the United States who often have to juggle a part-time or full-time job with domestic chores and other family responsibilities.

Family responsibilities are considered to be a sacred, and a holiday such as Mother's Day is an important day indeed. Similarly the relationship between a godmother and a godfather and a child is taken very seriously, since it constitutes more than a nominal relationship.

Children are accustomed to socialize with adults from a young age and they continue to do so throughout their lives. This includes the teenage years when young people are looking for their own identity and their own independence. The work and dedication which are expended in the upbringing of children within the family is not considered an afterthought — after one's work experience outside of the home. Traditionally, young women from upper-class families were expected to be educated and prepared for their roles and wives and mothers, and it was not considered acceptable for them to work outside of the home except in charitable organizations. Indeed in wealthy families in nineteenth century Mexico, wives and mothers rarely if ever left their homes.[5]

Such isolation from centers of commerce may be better understood if one keeps in mind the feudal heritage of much of Latin American and the vastness of large family estates. It was not uncommon in the past for powerful families to own more land and to have more authority in certain parts of a nation than the federal government itself.

Perhaps it is not surprising to find the strong sense of social class that exists even today in Latin America and to find as well the strong sense of parental or patriarchal authority which has always existed in the Latin world in general.

Along with the question of family tradition comes concern with the racial heritage of a given family. From the earliest days of the Spanish and Portuguese colonization of the New World, the conquerors had a strong sense of the inferiority of native people and, African slaves. Aristocratic Spanish families prided themselves for centuries on being of pure Spanish origin.

This prejudice against the local cultures was so strong that before the independence of the Latin American colonies from Spain, even individuals of direct Spanish descent who were not actually born in Spain were forbidden from holding the highest political offices. These *criollos* resented such restrictions to the point that their knowledge of the progressive ideas of European writers like Rousseau and Montesquieu led them to propose a series of revolutions, which led the majority of Latin America to gain its independence from Spain in the early nineteenth century.[6]

This cultural bias against the native cultures, as we have noted, continued well into the twentieth century and it continues today, so that when the Mexican artist Diego Rivera put Indians front and center in his paintings and murals, they shocked the sensibilities of many middle-class Mexicans.[7]

But remember that the indigenous and the African cultural element remains strong in many areas of the societies under study here. It is important to mention that indigenous groups everywhere tend to be family, clan, and tribal based, and that is true in Latin America. Indeed one may make the assumption that it is the natural form of human society since man is, as everyone knows, a social being.

This sense of reverence not only for elders who are living today, but for ancestors is deep and immensely traditional. It transcends life itself, since indigenous peoples believe that they maintain contact with departed loved ones and ancestors in ways which are direct and powerful. This is evidenced, for example, in the Mexican celebration of the Day of the Dead.

Education

Contrary to popular opinion, higher education in the Western Hemisphere did not begin in what is now the United States or Canada. The first universities on this continent were already in existence before the very first North American university opened its doors. By the middle of the sixteenth century, educational institutions like the University of San Marcos in Lima, Peru, and the National University of Mexico in Mexico City were already turning out graduates.

As a matter of fact, the Peruvian author Juan del Valle y Caviedes as early as the late 1500s wrote a satire about a graduation ceremony of the medical school of the University of San Marcos in which a student was told, half in doggerel Latin and half in Spanish, that the medical school was conferring on him the right to kill just about any patient that he wanted to. Apparently such was the state of medical practice in colonial Peru.[8]

Again contrary to popular opinion, which believes that advanced education is all but nonexistent south of the U.S. border, Latin America has a long tradition of public and private universities dating back to earliest colonial days. In colonial times the curriculum closely followed the medieval view of what education should include, however towards the end of the eighteenth century, the church began to lose ground to secular viewpoints. New ideas and concepts of the French Enlightenment began to be introduced in the intellectual atmosphere of Latin America.[9]

Today, private universities provide education for an elite class of students while public universities offer similar opportunities on a more democratic basis. But this tradition is far from universal, since in some countries public education is extremely selective, while capable students with less money look for low-cost institutions of learning such as night schools.[10]

In recent years some countries, especially Venezuela and Bolivia, have taken the lead in providing special educational opportunities to students of disadvantaged indigenous backgrounds. Likewise the push to provide opportunities in higher education for handicapped students is growing.[11]

At the same time, institutions common in other places such as educational accreditation boards and peer professional evaluations are slowly beginning to appear in Latin America.[12]

The cultural prestige of the countries of Western Europe, especially France, has been strongly felt in much of Latin America, and for this reason wealthy families have long felt the need to send their children to Europe for their higher education. This was certainly true in the case of Simon Bolívar, the great hero of Latin American independence.

Latin American universities have been in the forefront of political developments in countries where political parties were strong. For example, in the classic Mexican play *El gesticulador* by Rodolfo Usigli, the protagonist, César Rubio, chides his son for ostensibly being a student at a Mexican university while not really being a student at all. He criticizes him for using the role of student as a kind of cover for all types of political activism, while he really did little or no actually studying.[13]

Teachers and professors and learning itself are held in extremely high regard. Latin Americans are proud of their professors and of their universities and education is regarded as a quasi-sacred commodity. This reverence for education and culture reaffirms our stated acknowledgement of the high degree of patriotism and national pride in these nations. The literary and artistic traditions, for example, are much revered and are emphasized in each educational system, and prominent writers frequently hold high diplomatic posts since the countries that they represent believe that they could not find better representatives of their nations than those who help to develop national artistic traditions.

The Latin American concept of education goes beyond mere book learning. For affluent families, the acquisition of a truly international perspective on the world, travel and the ability to speak more than one language are highly prized.

A writer and pioneer of Latin American studies, Thomas Merton, has said of the educated classes in Latin America, "They [North Americans] have never awakened to the fact that Latin America is by and large culturally superior to the United States, not only on the level of the wealthy minority ... but also among the desperately indigenous cultures, some of which are rooted in a past that has never been surpassed on this continent."[14]

As a result, true education for Latin Americans includes proper dress; the ability to speak well and to engage in intelligent conversation on a wide variety of topics including history, literature, art and music; and understanding of correct table manners and general politeness. Frequently, educated Latinos can be heard expressing the view that visiting professional Americans are well trained in their fields but lack true cultural breeding, which they believe can handicap them in the business and political arena, especially at the highest levels of international relations. In a class-oriented society like Latin America, a person who shows such desired qualities and who has higher educational credentials as well is clearly regarded as one who stands out. Such individuals are accorded a special respect such as may have been given to a "gentleman" or "lady" in the old European concept of such terms.

Such ideas are especially significant since traditionally, higher educational opportunities for women have been limited. Mexican author Sor Juana Inés de la Cruz, called the first important poet in the Western Hemisphere by Nobel Prize-winning author Octavio Paz, found it necessary to dress as a man to attend the National University of Mexico in the sixteenth century. In those colonial times such advanced education was not considered proper for women, whose role in society was limited to getting married and raising a family or entering a religious order, which is exactly what Sor Juana did in order to have the time to study and access to a library of books, which were a rare and highly expensive commodity in those days.[15]

Generally the European traditions of education have held sway in Latin America, where, for example, professors present their lectures while giving little or no time to comment or discussions of the topics by students. Traditim says that professors are there to teach and students are there to learn, and the two roles should not be confused. This attitude has been slowly changing, while in the United States with the newly developing interest in interdisciplinary studies, many have come to realize that no human being can have complete knowledge of a wide number of academic fields and the opinions of others, including students, may be of the greatest help. In addition, with a new emphasis on interactive education, less emphasis is currently being given to a variety of pedagogical approaches to learning.

Traditional approaches to academic requirements have long held sway in Latin America, where students are obliged to complete a thesis even for undergraduate degrees, while in other regions the submission of a thesis is more common for graduate degrees.

As in the old European tradition, students are required not only to complete and hand in a thesis to their advisor or mentor, called the *sinodal* in Spanish, but they must adhere to the old tradition of presenting themselves in front of a committee of professors in order to defend their thesis, a process which is much more common as a requirement for graduate degrees in other countries.

The School Experience

Many students in primary and secondary schools in Latin America attend private schools. Many, although by no means all of these schools, are oriented to certain cultures, traditions, and national origins, such as an American school, a German school or a French school. The discipline of Latin American schools is strict, and given the great respect that these societies accord to teachers as representatives of learning and culture, a less democratic attitude to the educational process reigns supreme. This is to say that parents may be less likely than in some other societies to take what might be called a consumerist attitude towards education, believing that if they pay taxes that gives them the right to demand a certain grade for their children or to try to tell professionals in the educational system how to teach — something they would never consider doing in the case of other professionals such as doctors or lawyers.

This great respect for educators and for those who represent the educational process, namely teachers and professors, also extends to speech patterns. Teachers are routinely addressed as "Sir" or "Madam" and professors are likewise addressed by their titles so that a Latin American student speaking to a professor is likely not only to say "Good morning," but rather, "Good morning professor," or the equivalent of, "Good morning, sir," thus giving an almost military-like formality to daily forms of personal address. This may be a holdover from the great prestige that professors have had in Spain over the past centuries, when a professor's word or his decisions were rarely challenged, let alone his grades.

One Spanish professor, Julián Marías, visited the United States and was amazed at the lack of respect for professors. As part of the American democratic spirit, any student could lodge a complaint against a professor for almost any reason, with a good chance that the student's opinion would be more highly valued than that of the professor.[16]

Indeed within the Hispanic tradition, the holder of an academic chair, or the chief professor in any academic discipline was considered to hold a position of national importance similar to that of a nationally important political figure in our day and time. So deeply felt are these attitudes within the European tradition that when the renowned Italian literary scholar Mario Praz, author of such brilliant works as *The Romantic Agony*, passed away, the whole nation of Italy mourned his death. Likewise one literary conference in Spain in recent years was front page news in dozens of Spanish newspapers while the national government ordered the mayors of the cities and towns visited by the attending scholars to host a formal reception.

The regard for education transcends mere pragmatism, which is to say that schooling is not just viewed as something that will lead to a satisfying career, although such concerns are of course very strong.

In general Latin American students and teachers are impressed with the physical infrastructure of public and private schools in the United States, which boast laptop computers for students, Olympic-size swimming pools, extensive after-school group activities and TV monitors and computers in each classroom. Still, basics are strongly emphasized in Latin America and such subjects as, world history as well as national history, literature and geography are stressed to the point that few students would be able to graduate without a strong foundation in each area of knowledge.

Students proudly wear school uniforms. They take the identity and traditions of their particular school very seriously as they take the traditions of their country and *patria chica* equally seriously. Despite the widespread idea that only traditional Hispanic and Luso-Brazilian cultures make up the bulk of the school curriculum, there are whole areas of the subcontinent where one may hear other languages and have to think twice to believe it is really Latin America. This is true, for example, in German-speaking communities such as might be found in Guatemala, Argentina, Brazil or Paraguay. Remember that a past president of Paraguay named Stroessner was a direct descendent of a German family, while a past president of Peru, Alberto Fujimori, was of Japanese descent.

A new sense of nationalism in many parts of Latin America in recent years has given rise to a renewed emphasis on the value of traditional, indigenous cultures, not only in terms of cultural richness but also in terms of ancient languages. In Peru, for example instruction is given in some schools in the Indian language of Quechua. In Guatemala classes are taught in the language of the Mayan civilization, which encompasses dozens of recognized dialects. In Brazil, the government of the state of Río de Janeiro has ordered two of its universities to set aside at least 5 percent of their admissions for disabled students and students representing indigenous minorities.[16]

Education is the product of any given culture and it is a basic aspect of each and every culture. Because of this, Latin American countries place less emphasis on amassing data on the performance of students in a given school system, in a given city, or on a state or national level. Polls and statistics do not appeal to the Latin psyche to the degree that they do in other societies, including the United States. Latin Americans also do not join a multitude of professional organizations. In this sense the United States, which is considered by experts in the field of comparative culture to be a highly individualistic culture, may be seen more as a group enterprise. As a result it is not as common for educators south of the U.S. border to belong to multiple professional organizations or to attend a myriad of professional conferences.

While standardized testing has become extremely prevalent in other educational systems, starting even with youngsters in grade school, Latin Americans eschew such testing and the pressures that come with such tests, both for the students and for teachers and administrators. Latin Americans believe that their schools and the courses that are taught in their schools are rigorous enough. If students achieve a passing grade in a given course they have shown sufficiently well that they have learned the basic material and therefore don't need an outside organization to validate their pedagogical efforts.

Likewise the emphasis on technology and the need for schools and universities to keep up with each development is felt to be less pressing in many educational systems, especially in rural areas that usually lack the funds for expensive products. Even so, Latin America is becoming highly developed in terms of modern communications and some educational systems are on the cutting edge of the newest technologies, including the latest developments in computers and robotics. Such centers of teaching and research garner international renown.

Above and beyond high-tech instruments of learning, however, the people believe that education is based more on a true desire to learn, with a firm grounding in fundamentals and a respect for the opportunity to learn, than on expensive materials which could enrich the basic learning experience but which do not necessarily constitute a substitute for the desire and disciplines which are basic to real learning.

Although schools offer opportunities for sports, the tradition of athletic rivalries between competing schools and colleges has not had a great place in the educational life of Latin America. Nevertheless, student pride in any given school or college is high, and Latin American schools have alumni organizations even in foreign countries outside of the nation in which the school is located.

In addition, the U.S. concept of graduation ceremonies as well as fraternities and sororities have traditionally been absent from Latin American university life. Spanish does not even have a word for "college," only a word for "university." The similar word "*colegio*" can refer to any school, not just a college.

Nevertheless an alumnus's identification with one particular place of higher learning could theoretically be stronger in Latin America simply because he will study at one particular university rather than getting a college degree from one school and a graduate degree from another. Certainly numerous Latin Americans possess graduate degrees from a Latin American or foreign university, however the entrance to some professions such as architecture, engineering and law are usually based on one university program which lasts longer than the typical four years to achieve a bachelor's degree in the U.S.

As is the case elsewhere, however, the prestige of schools and universities varies greatly and some countries or universities many have a stronger reputation in certain fields than in others. Chile for example, possesses an international reputation for excellence in university training in the field of economics. It also true that certain schools and universities have the reputation of catering to an elite student body from privileged families, and in such institutions the students who enroll may be more aware of their special position in society than the average U.S. student, who is the product of a generally less class-oriented social structure.

Because not all Latin Americans have access to education, even in the most elementary grades, education is in general is viewed as a great privilege rather than as birthright. Because of this, and because the society is less litigious in the first place, teachers and administrators have less fear of frivolous lawsuits over things like violations of a dress code or a careless word or two that might be directed at a student. The result is that discipline is not as much of a problem as it can be elsewhere. Here the teacher and the professor are the authority figures, and authority is authority.

IX

Religion

In their book that bears the simple title *Spain*, Dominique Aubier and Manuel Tuñón de Lara comment that it "is a country quite capable of leaving the would-be visitor standing at the doorstep. How many people, when they think that they are making discoveries, or understanding and admiring, are in fact still traveling on the other side of the frontier!"[1]

Undoubtedly the Spanish character does have its own mysteries. Spain can be seen as a hermetic land of paradoxes which defy, as the authors have stated above, easily classifications and facile explanations. Perhaps in no sense of the word is this as true as in the case of religion, where a fervent belief in the Catholic faith has for centuries existed side-by-side with a strong tradition of anticlericalism.[2] Yet the Catholic religion is so much a deeply felt hallmark of the spirit of Spain that the state and the church have historically gone hand-in-hand. When, for example, Father Hidalgo declared that Mexico was going to be independent from Spain, not only was he considered to be a political rebel, a criminal according the Spanish law, he was also excommunicated from the Catholic church.

Indeed there is a story which is told in Spain about a protestant missionary who came to Spain to try to make converts to his own church. On stopping to have his shoes shined in Madrid he reflected that he should take advantage of every opportunity to make converts. He began to tell the shoeshine boy of the virtues of his own faith. On listening to this, the boy interrupted the clergyman and said to him, "I'm sorry but I think you are wasting your time. After all, if I can't believe in the Catholic Church which is the only one true church, how could I believe in your church?"

The great Spanish writer Miguel de Unamuno, in his novel *San Manuel*

97

bueno, describes a Spanish priest who agonizes over his inability to be a believer. All the while, he refuses to let his flock know of his own lack of faith, for he feels that the common people, known in Spanish as the *pueblo*, need faith, since it forms the very core of their being as well as their personal and national identity.[3]

Much of this Spanish approach to religion should be carried over into a study of religious beliefs and practices in Latin America. Religion itself was a motivating force behind much of colonial Latin American society. Spanish priests, for example, not only believed that native religions were unacceptable, they actually thought them to be the product of the devil himself. Therefore the clergy did their best to burn all books referring to indigenous belief systems, and they often made it a point to build a Catholic church on any spot in which they found a pyramid.

The first explorers doubted the humanity of the peoples of the new world. They believed that all humans were, as the Bible stated, children of Adam and Eve, so how could these beings separated by thousands of miles from the original Eden be descendents of the very first parents? Serious theological discussions took place in Spain during the sixteenth century by prominent theologians to the question of whether Native Americans were human enough to receive the sacraments of the Catholic church.

Missionaries were of course extremely active in Latin America at that time and many Indians were converted to Christianity, however the Christianity of Latin America has and continues to differ from that found in Spain, since the cultural blend which makes up that section of the globe is often radically different. The Latin American mélange is the combination of European (basically Spanish and Portuguese) cultures as well as African and Native American cultures. Far from a remaining clearly distinct, these ideologies have blended almost from the start of European influence in the New World.

This fusion of beliefs, traditions and customs has formed a kind of syncretism which manifests itself in unique ways. Perhaps a basic difference between these traditions can be seen in the role religion in daily life. We may wish to consider that the dictator Mussolini in Italy, like other demagogues, feared the opposition of intellectuals that could see through the falseness of his propaganda perhaps better than could the average citizen. As a result he sent the Italian writer Carlo Levi into internal exile, forcing him to move into the extreme southern part of Italy.

The author's culture shock at experiencing a different lifestyle than he was accustomed to in central or northern Italy is well expressed in his thought-provoking book *Christ Stopped at Eboli*, whose very title indicates the author's apparent belief that when he ventured into another part of his own country he was in effect entering a society that seemed so strange that it hardly seemed to still form part of the Western world.

At one point in the narrative, Levi comments that he was curious about the religious beliefs and practices of the people with whom he was living. He found that they often appeared to lack traditional beliefs about the supernatural powers of God, his saints and his angels. To his surprise, however, this did not mean that they lacked spirituality. On the contrary, he learned they appeared not to believe that only some things were sacred. They believed that everything was sacred.

This highlights a basic quality of traditional, native religion in Latin America and the religions of indigenous societies throughout the world. Their worldview sees the sacred in each and every aspect of life, especially in nature.

It is for this reason that we will find in another part of this study that traditional healing practices such as are conducted today by Latin American *curanderos* and shamans combine religious beliefs and practices with medicine. They do not mark a bold demarcation between the two as is done in Western medicine.

Furthermore, the distinctions between popular culture and religious beliefs are blurred in components of life such as art, music, and healing.

Such blurring of lines was common in the Western World since during the Middle Ages, when knowledge of the world was often interpreted in terms of religious dogma rather than empirical investigation. Our modern, scientifically based conception of the natural world differs greatly. The contrast between a viewpoint based on religion and another based on science is well described by the American anthropologist Wade Davis, who researched native religious beliefs in Haiti to write his interesting work *The Serpent and the Rainbow*. He found, for example, that upon asking a Haitian about the formation of a very common tree, he was given a complicated cosmology of deities that was beyond his own imagination. He goes on to observe that "every society, including our own, is moved by a fundamental quest for unity; a struggle to create order out of apparent disorder.... The voudo society ... spins a web ... that generates an illusion of total comprehension ... and what's more the belief system works; it gives meaning to the universe."[4]

It should be evident that the indigenous, or as in this case, the strongly African influence on religious beliefs of this young Haitian reflects not only purely religious viewpoints as they are understood today in the Western world, but extends to an encompassing view of the natural world itself.

As a result some may wonder if the good intentions of missionaries who attempt to convert indigenous people do not reflect a Western understanding of the place which religion has in the popular culture of daily life. They may wonder if they represent a view that religion and religious practices are a separate part of life that may not have a great deal to do with the more mundane characteristics of our understanding of the natural world and the supernatural realm. Or to put it another way, is destroying their indigenous belief systems tantamount to destroying their culture itself, for religion in such societies is much more than simply a way to spend time on Sunday morning.

However, all is not lost, since the indigenous religious beliefs of Latin Americans have mixed closely with Christian traditions from the very beginning of colonization, just as this combination of theologies continues today. Frequently Catholic priests have found it necessary to let their flock worship local gods before or during their worship of Christ and his saints and angels.

African slaves, as we have already noted, were forbidden to worship their ancestral gods under pain of punishment. As a result, they often feigned worship of Christian religious figures while in their minds and hearts they believed they were actually worshipping the deities which originated in their own African traditions. As a result, to this day there is great confusion about the real names and identities represented by figures of traditional Christian worship among those who still practice voodoo and other religious such as Santería, since these images may at times be called by the names of African saints or gods and at other times they may be identified as Christian based figures of worship.

Not long ago when the eruption of a volcano was threatened in an area not far from Mexico City, a citizen who lived near the volcano, who may have been raised in the Christian tradition at least to a certain extent, was asked if he feared for his life, living so near to where the molten lava might fall. His answer was that he was not really worried because there was a local god that lived inside of the volcano. He believed that the volcano only erupted when the god was upset and as a result he and other people in that area of Mexico were in the habit of offering gifts to this god to placate him.

In Guatemala it is not unknown for Maya Indians who still worship their traditional gods to also worship in a Catholic church and to make prayers and other offering to their gods on the steps or in the vicinity of a Catholic church. This is because the desire to see the sacred in daily life still goes on and if native peoples do not find that Christianity supplies this need sufficiently, they are prepared to supplement it with a worldview which tells them that all of creation is sacred.

More important still is the inability of adherents of traditional religious to see any inconsistency between one set of religious beliefs and another. Clearly then for many Latin Americans, religion is not a part of life, it *is* life. In societies that have maintained the ability to see the sacred in each and every aspect of their existence, their art is religious, their dramas and ceremonies celebrate the great achievements of the gods, government and laws are theocratic, and they do not abandon deep traditions of non–Christian origin, for they are as much part of the habits and thought patterns of daily life as is their personal theology.

In a sense, however, this is not really different from the religious orientation of traditional Spain itself, a country where the great Spanish saint, Theresa of Avila, once made the statement that God was to be found among the pots and pans. This is the same Spain that has immortalized the great literary figure Don Quixote, who has been called essentially Spanish and essentially human at the very same time, since he personifies the urge to search for the highest ideals of human life. In this way do members of Latin American indigenous cultures combine basic aspects of their daily existence with transcendent thoughts and aspirations, seeing God or the gods in nature. In the same way, the hero of Alejo Carpentier's novel *The Lost Steps* comes to abandon the alienation of his existence in the modern urban world when he returns to his roots in the jungle of Latin America and wonders why men cannot see the leaf of each and every tree as a poem in and of itself.[5]

It is in this sense that Latin America has traditionally lived more in harmony with the natural world than it has tried to tame it and to destroy it. Surely the natural world has appeared to be an enemy, and the theme of man against nature is a basic and recurrent one in the literature of the southern continent. We can see it is a constant theme in the morbid tales of the author Horacio Quiroga as well as in the classic of Colombian literature *The Vortex* (*La vorágine*), the story of a man who ventures into the jungle to undergo harrowing experiences that nearly cost him his life. This same theme appears in the Peruvian play *Collacocha* by Enrique Solari Swayne, and in the Chilean work *The Land of Fire Goes Out* (*La tierra de fuego se apaga*) by Francisco Coloane, as well as in countless other works of art. Yet the Latin American pioneer did not rush to conquer nature and join the coast of one country to another, or to pave over the land and to create a megalopolis such on the East Coast of the United States.

The need for land conservation has not appeared to be as pressing as in the United States, though this attitude continues to change in a very dramatic way with the rise of ecotourism, spawning concern over the maintenance of rain forests and the balance of nature in general.

Not too many years ago the Mexican government urged every family to plant a tree and within a short time some twenty million trees were planted in that nation. To this day the concern over air pollution in Mexico City has caused the government to limit the number of days per week that a single vehicle can circulate in traffic.

It is because of this sense of harmony that spirituality, if not religion itself, often is concomitant with harmony in the natural world. The Latin American sense of spirituality springs from indigenous and European roots to the point that religiosity often accompanies religion itself. This outward manifestation of religious traditions and beliefs as seen in the abundance of religious images, statues, and acts such as lighting candles and wearing religious objects such as medals and crucifixes, illustrates "religiosity" as a hallmark of Latin American popular culture.

One example would be the Mexican custom of lighting a *veladora* or candle which is left burning in the home as a continuous act of dedication and worship to God and the Blessed Virgin, who is especially revered as the Virgin of Guadalupe, the patron saint of Mexico.

The overwhelming belief system of the vast majority of people in Latin American forms the backbone of the country's social values in terms of education and public life in general. This contrasts directly with a country like the United States, where a completely legalistic tradition has taken over in recent years to the point that some citizens object to the teaching of religion in public schools (unless they be "exotic" religions), questioning whether one set of beliefs should be emphasized over another. They may object to a Christmas nativity display, claming that not everybody is Christian therefore this may constitute a violation of rights of those who are not. Whereas in Latin America, commonly accepted values trump the legal hair-splitting, for as we have noted elsewhere, in Latin America the spirit of the law takes precedence over the letter of the law.

However it is because religious traditions are at the heart of Latin American society that citizens of other cultures may make the mistake of confusing Latin religiosity with true religion in the most noble sense of the word. A law enforcement officer in the United States may have to deal with a criminal suspect whose house is full of religious images and who may wear religious articles, indicating at first glance that he is truly a seriously religious person who tries to adhere to the high moral principles of organized religious. However, this may or may not be the case, for such displays of religiosity may be a kind of ingrained sense of religion which has accompanied that person all of his life without his necessarily practicing the highest ideals of that religious tradition.

In education, especially university-level education, the curriculum was greatly influenced by the basic Thomistic intellectual tradition, based on the writing of St. Thomas Aquinas, whose teachings are considered to be of great importance in the Catholic tradition. Nevertheless, medieval religion presented a worldview which purported to explain the physical mysteries of the cosmos in a pre–Copernican era in which the earth was still considered to be the center of the universe with the sun revolving around the earth rather than the other way around.

The religious authority of the Spanish inquisition was inextricably bound up with the state and the inquisition carried over its power into Latin America as well as those parts of the present-day United States that were under Spanish control. As a result, as Irving A. Leonard explains in his informative work *The Books of the Brave*, novels were forbidden in Latin America as supposedly immoral works of art. Not just some novels, but all novels, so that literary historians tell us that the very first novel published in the Spanish language in Latin America was in 1816 with the publication of the Mexican work *The Mangy Parrot* (*El periquillo sarniento*) some three hundred years after the first European settlement in Latin America.[6]

In many areas the struggle between conservative forces, mainly rich landowners who supported the Catholic Church in wanting to preserve the status quo, vied with more liberal social concerns. In the case of Mexico, President Benito Juárez, often considered to be the founder of modern Mexico, began to limit the financial and temporal power of the church which previously had maintained vast tracts of land often belong to wealthy religious orders.

This political move only increased tensions in that country, which led to a breaking point with the revolution of 1910 in which an estimated two million Mexican citizens lost their lives. As a result of this conflict increasing restrictions were placed on the Catholic church, which led to closing some religious communities and a complete separation of church and state.

Though Mexico, like most of Latin America, is a devoutly Catholic country, one regulation forbade clergy from appearing in public in clerical garb. As a result, a recent Pope violated Mexican law when he visited that nation dressed in the traditional garments of the leader of the Catholic Church.

Such restrictions were not completely accepted by large numbers of people and a revolt against what were considered the anti-clerical measures adopted by the Mexican government led to the *Cristero* revolt of the 1920s.[7]

Controversy continued and when Alvaro Obregón, the first president of Mexico after the Mexican revolution was assassinated, a Catholic priest, Father Miguel Pro, was accused of committing the crime. Though he is considered to be a kind of Mexican Lee Harvey Oswald, the Catholic church still maintains him on a list of individuals that may be considered for possible canonization since many people believe that he was not guilty of the murder of Obregón, but was framed by the perpetrators.

To this day, church weddings have no legal standing in Mexico because of the separation of church and state. Those who wish to be married in a church may do so, but for their marriage to gain legal status they must also be married in a civil ceremony.

The Liberation of Theology?

As unlikely as is the marriage of African-based religions such as Santería, Voodoo and Macumba with Catholicism and the joining of indigenous native religions, perhaps even more remarkable has been the combination at least in the minds of some individuals of Marxism with Christianity.

As strange as these bedfellows may appear to be, in recent times the reaction against the traditional allegiance between conservative forces led by wealthy feudalistic land barons and the Catholic church has lead some observers to believe that it may actually be more Christian to seek justice by rejecting this ago-old alliance. The new view is to espouse a Marxist advocacy for a radical redistribution of wealth which has long been in the hands of the aristocracy rather than in the hands of the people.

Of course Marx's original doctrine maintained that when a communist state came to power, religion would no longer be necessary and it would wither away. Unfortunately in most communist states this has been interpreted as it was in Stalin's Russia as a call to actually stamp out all religions except what some called the "religion" of the state, and thereby engage in persecutions of churches and the clergy.

Some liberal-minded theologians in Latin America have claimed to believe that the social equality proposed by Marx could be achieved in Latin America without violations of human rights, by way of what has been called Liberation theology.

The extent to which this glaring inconsistency of ideologies is reconciled by religious thinkers who lean sharply to the left is clearly seen in the case of the world-famous Nicaraguan poet and essayist Ernesto Cardenal. A Catholic priest, trained in the Gethsemane monastery in Kentucky, Cardenal is perhaps the best known poet living in Latin America today. His artistic works had special popularity in Russian and Eastern Bloc nations during the Cold War, since he very clearly supported the ideas and the ideals of the Marxist revolution in Cuba and he held an important position in the Marxist government of Nicaragua during the first administration of President Daniel Ortega. This was an administration that was so controversial in the United States that the battle between the Contras, or those opposed to the

Marxist government, and the Sandinistas or Marxists, led to the Iran-Contra scandal.

This author is familiar with the writer's ideological leanings since he visited the poet in his remote artistic-spiritual community on the island of Solentiname in the interior of Nicaragua.[8] Upon reaching the island after a five-hour boat trip through dense jungles inaccessible by road, it was apparent that this Latin American clergyman and author was living out his mentor's, Thomas Merton's, ideal of creating a hermitage for himself in the wilderness. Merton ventured to Alaska to carry out his dream, until he was told that the Alaskan frontier had very large bears that sometimes tried to eat human beings for lunch.[9]

Cardenal spoke in glowing terms about the glories of Cuban society, describing it as a kind of paradise. Only two pictures hung on the walls of his home. One was an almost life-sized photo of the great religious thinker Thomas Merton, accompanied by an equally large photo of the well-known poet and Marxist revolutionary, Che Guevara.

It became immediately apparent that the poet saw no inconsistency between the radically different ideologies of both men. In the building which served as Cardenal's library only one book held a prominent place right on the top of his desk. This was a biography of Augusto Sandino, the Nicaraguan who led the local opposition to invading American troops in the early years of the twentieth century. Since the Marxists of Nicaragua would go on to take the name of this local hero as the inspiration for their own *Sandinista* government, the title of this book in the possession of Ernest Cardenal would seem in retrospect to be prophetic indeed.

The disparity of his views and the policies of the Catholic Church became clear when some years later the Pope visited Latin America. Cardenal was kneeling before him as the Pope emerged from his airplane. On seeing Cardenal, the Pope raised his finger up and down in a gesture that clearly indicated his great disapproval of the man and for what he stood for. The pontiff's words were not audible to television viewers, but from the expression on his face and from his body language it was clear that he must have been expressing a stinging criticism of Cardenal and his Marxist ideology.

At the beginning of the twentieth century one of the major television networks presented news footage of what they considered to be memorable events of the twentieth century, including this piece of television reportage. They showed the pope leaning over to clearly and dramatically admonish the world famous priest-poet.

This conflict between what society should be and what it could be, and which is the best road to arrive at greater social justice is far from over in modern Latin America. In Nicaragua, Marxist Sandinista President Daniel

Ortega has been re-elected once again, and the president of Venezuela, Hugo Chávez, a firm supporter of Marxist ideals, is seeking to extend his political point of view throughout the rest of Latin America as he establishes ties with so called non-aligned nations in other parts of the globe.

Secularization

It was claimed during the Cold War that materialism was preached in the Eastern Bloc nations but that it was practiced in the West, where the power of conspicuous consumption was actually much greater.

In the popular mind in Latin America, the whole idea of a consumer society is identified to a large extent with the United States and the influence of U.S. society in terms of consumer goods, movies, music and television as well as styles of dress and even personal behavior. When the world-famous Argentine novelist Manuel Puig was asked why he entitled his novel *The Betrayal of Rita Hayworth* (*La traición de Rita Hayworth*) in honor of the memory of a great American movie star rather than a Latin American, his response was clear. Rita Hayworth was the popular idol that captured his attention as a young man, as she captured the attention of millions of other Latin Americans, much more than any Latin film celebrity.[10]

The influence of the United States has been and continues to be strong in the popular tastes of the Latin American public. American television programs and films are extremely popular in translation, even though Latin America has its own film and television industry. Equally persuasive is the extension of what has been called the consumer society into Latin Aberica. The acquisition of more and more consumer items appears to have a growing importance. In an era in which it is estimated that the average child will see perhaps ten thousand advertisements for consumer products even before he starts school, some observers believe the growing emphasis on materialistic consumption amounts to what might almost be called a secular religion. This is to say that the public is bombarded year after year with images of individuals or families which appear to have achieved complete happiness simply because they purchased a particular brand of toothpaste or because they purchased a particular brand of automobile.

The social critic Arturo A. Fox states in his book *Spain Back and Forth* (*España: ida y vuelta*) that the influx of millions of tourists into modern Spain, many of them coming from countries with more liberal social values, cannot but have a profound impact on the contemporary Spanish mind. Likewise in Latin America it would be impractical to discount the enormous influence that social mores as they are presented in American television and movies have on the liberalization of social and personal values as well as the extension of consumerist value systems.[11]

The appeal of such a consumer-based nirvana which promises paradise in this world rather than in the next one can be considered to come into direct opposition to traditional religious beliefs.

But then again these are heady ideas which are really the province of philosophers and experts on the development of social and historical trends. In terms of our more limited study of cultural trends what we may be able to state is that as industrialized nations have become increasingly secular during the twentieth century, they have engendered a desire on the part of many to seek even more desperately for meaning in life, a basic set of spiritual values that transcend the twists and turns of the society around them and the vagaries of human history. It is perhaps for this reason that extreme secularism, in historical terms, in a country like the United States has actually spurred, on one level, a desperate search for spiritual values in the formation of extremist and often dangerous religious cults, which according to some estimates actually number more than five hundred.

With the great adherence of Latin American popular culture to family and traditional values and with its greater respect for religious beliefs which are woven into the very fabric of a basically Catholic culture, Latin Americans do not search quite as much for radical solutions in religious extremist groups.

However, religion in its varied form and multiple guises continues to be at the very center of Latin American life, a driving force which encompasses and continues many traditional forms and which represents a wide array of beliefs in supernatural powers, all the way from the worship of a supreme being in organized religions to the rumored use of the dark forces of evil in magical religions.

These have been made most famous by the highly picturesque ceremonies of Haitian voodoo. The purported power of local gods is well represented in the Haitian novel *The Beast of the Haitian Hills*, which presents the story of a sophisticated professional man who scoffs at voodoo gods only to ultimately be destroyed by them.[12]

Do such forces exist and do some people try to manipulate dark powers for their own benefit to harm others? Perhaps one observer expressed it best when he stated that one can't say with complete certainty that such magical spells do work, but on the other hand one can't say with complete certainty that they do not.

What we can say for certain, however, is that Latin Americans, as do almost all people now and throughout history, believe and feel the need to search for spiritual transcendence as well as to sense and understand the workings of transcendent powers in their daily life.

X

Festivals and Celebrations

In his well-known study of the Mexican national character, *The Labyrinth of Solitude* (*El laberinto de la soledad*), Mexican author Octavio Paz states that for Mexico, life is a continual festival.[1] The Canadian literary scholar Erminio Neglia has stated that in Latin America, life is often seen to be so dramatic an affair that it can resemble the same level of excitement, be it positive or negative, as a celebration.[2]

Certainly it is true that popular celebrations and festivals form an important part of life for millions of Latin Americans. Not only is the frequency of these celebrations impressive; the originality, diversity and elaborate nature of the settings and the costumes worn make them a highly colorful and distinctive aspect of Latin American life.

Given the frequency and variety of these festive occasions and events it would be impossible for any one work to attempt to describe or even catalogue each and every one. Some of these special events such as Christmas and Easter are celebrated worldwide, yet they have their own distinctive character in various countries that make up the southern continent.

Christmas carols, known as *villancicos* in Spanish, are sung as the birth of Christ is celebrated. Just as figures of Santa Claus are frequently seen in stores and public places, in Latin America people dress in the Middle Eastern attire of the three wise men to remind everyone of the season which is approaching.

Traditional Spanish dramas, sometimes called *pastorelas*, depicting the events of the first Christmas are staged, especially in churches. Alongside the custom of exchanging gifts on Christmas Day, gifts are also given on the Day of the Epiphany or Day of the Wise Men —*Dia de los Reyes Magos*. A spe-

108

cial bread may be sold in bakeries in honor of this holiday, and Mexicans lead up to the Christmas holiday with *posadas*, or visits to houses of friends and relatives, with guests stopping by supposedly to ask for lodgings, as did the parents of Christ. When guests are accepted in a host's house, a celebration is held in honor of the Christ child.

The Christmas season is preceded in Mexico by a solemn day in honor of the Virgin of Guadalupe, the patron saint of Mexico, who is believed by the faithful to have appeared to St. Juan Diego in the sixteenth century, and to have given him a miraculous cloak with a flowered design which is still on display in the Cathedral of the Virgin of Guadalupe in Mexico City.

In Colombia the Christmas season is likewise preceded by the *alumbrados* celebrations on December 7–8. At these events, papier-mâché figures with a candle in the middle are placed in the streets of Colombian towns and villages on trees and lampposts in public places to illuminate the entire community. On the night of December 8, also known as the Night of the Virgin Mary, many neighborhoods construct a public altar in her honor. The faithful pray around such altars and various communities vie with each other to see which can boast of the finest Christmas decorations. Thus Christmas celebrations as well as the preparations for such events can begin weeks before Christmas day.[3]

New Year's celebrations tend to reflect the inspiration of the peninsular Spanish way of welcoming the new year. This can include eating a bunch of grapes, sweeping dirt and dust out of the front entrance of the house to symbolize getting rid of what was not wanted from the previous year, and carrying pieces of luggage as one walks in and out of the entrance of a house to indicate that one will frequently be making trips to many interesting places during the new year. The arrival of the new year can be a colorful event as sounds and lights of numerous fireworks fill the sky.

Along the coast of Brazil an estimated one million celebrants ring in the new year at the famous Copacabana Beach amidst music, fireworks and religious ceremonies. Men and women wearing white carry lit candles in their hands as they venture down from the surrounding hills, wandering through the streets on their way to the beach, where they enter the water in a wave of humanity that represents the washing away of the negativity of a previous year. Water is the symbol of life and cleanliness. Celebrants welcome its embraces as they look forward to new life and energy in the coming year.[4]

The sacred celebrations of the Easter season also have a special place in the minds and hearts of Latin peoples. Much of Latin America continues traditional Spanish customs. Easter is also sometimes known as the *Pascua florida* or "the Easter holiday of flowers," which was the origin of the Spanish name for the state of Florida. Historians tell us Florida was discovered by the Spanish explorer Ponce de León on Easter Sunday.

In Spain, Holy Week includes such well known observations as that in Seville. On the evening of Palm Sunday, groups of men begin passing through the streets as they carry very heavy floats with religious articles and statues of saints. Stopping every once in while to take a rest, they consider carrying this burden hour after hour to be part of their personal act of penance to God.

The Easter season in Latin America is also characterized by unique commemorations. In Antigua, Guatemala, entire carpets composed of multicolored flowers are woven together in a painstaking and lengthy process which has gone on for centuries. This tradition, which is the pride and joy of this historic city once the capital of Guatemala, is known world wide and attracts numerous visitors every year.[5]

In Oaxaca, Mexico, *La Danza de los Viejos* or the Dance of the Old People is performed after Easter. In this ceremony masked celebrants represent deceased loved ones who are believed to return from the dead.[6]

Other notable ways of observing this special season abound in various part of the Hispanic world. In Popayan, Colombia, people are in the habit of donning costumes to act out the biblical events of Holy Week.

In Mompox, Colombia, the Thursday before Palm Sunday is marked by the appearance of *Nazarenos*, or penitents in turquoise colored robes who throw stones at a church door in order to be ritually allowed to enter. After they get inside their robes are blessed by a priest.

In Venezuela, on Good Friday a procession from the Church of San Francisco in the capital city of Caracas accompanies a representation of the dead body of Christ that passes through the streets.[7]

There are also other ways in which Latin Americans show their distinctive ways of celebrating Easter. For example, in the Spanish-speaking village of Sarteneja in Belize, Easter is crowned by regatta races among the local sailboats.[8]

Mexicans traditionally burn papier-mâché figures of the traitor Judas at this time of the year. This is easily accomplished since these puppet-like figures are filled with firecrackers which explode and destroy the puppets in what is known as *La quema de Judas*.[9] Picturesque also is the custom of the Tarahumara Indians of northern Mexico who perform a Holy Week Dance of the Pharisees.[10]

Related to the Easter season also are what are undoubtedly the most famous and the most outlandish festivals of the entire Latin America calendar. These are the carnival celebrations marking the beginning of the Lenten season of forty days of fasting and penance in the Christian calendar. Known as the Mardi Gras, coming from the French expression "Fat Tuesday" as it was celebrated in French-speaking Louisiana centuries ago, this is the last time to eat, drink, and be merry before the strict observance of Lent starting on Ash Wednesday.

Although the Carnival celebration in Río de Janeiro, Brazil, is without doubt the most elaborate, creative and colorful of these festive events in terms of the number of participants and the intensity of the general air of festivity, similar carnivals are also held yearly in many Latin American locales, especially in coastal areas of Mexico, Panama, Colombia and Venezuela.[11]

Independence Day

Each country remembers its independence from its colonizing mother country with a commemoration of national independence. These traditions go back to the nineteenth century. One U.S. traveler of that time who claimed to have actually walked across the vast Argentine pampas tells of his experience as he attended a local celebration of Argentina's independence from Spain:

> While I was in Mendoza, the celebration and festivities of the 25th of May, the independence day of the republic took place, and was celebrated with unusual enthusiasm. For several days previous the people were engaged in preparing for the festivities, though not half of the lower classes knew for what reason the celebration was made, so ignorant were they of the country's history. The government, for one hundred dollars, secured the services of the North American performers and under their direction a ring of adobes were constructed in the centre of the plaza, and close beside it a rostrum for the governor, his suite, and the musicians. The news of the grand function that was to take place spread far into the country, and three days prior to the 25th the gauchos came galloping into town from all parts of the province. At sunrise, on the great day, I visited the plaza in which the populace was pouring, the whole forming a most picturesque scene.
>
>   Gauchos, gaily attired, were mounted upon horses decked out with silver ornaments, and tails braided with ribbons, and galloping about in little parties.... At such galas one sees a degree of life and animation not to be met with at other times.... Two cannons, the only pieces of artillery in the province, were drawn by foot-soldiers ... dressed in white pantaloons and jackets.... Upon each side was painted a figure, one for Liberty, one for Justice and another, a portrait of General Urquiza and our own Washington.[12]

Of course each nation has its own way of celebrating its independence day. For example, September 18, Chile's independence day, is commemorated not by one day's celebration but by a whole week of festivities including parades, music and dances, accompanied by the participation of the Chilean cowboys or *huasos*. These activities frequently take place in *armadas*, which are temporary structures designed especially for independence day activities. Along with music and dancing, typical Chilean food such as empanadas and anticuchos are enjoyed.[13]

In addition to independence days, other holidays may commemorate days of special national importance. For example, Mexico's *Cinco de Mayo* or "Fifth of May." This special day celebrates Mexico's victory over invading France in the important battle that took place in the nineteenth century in the city of Puebla. Often mistaken in other countries as Mexico's day of independence, this special occasion remembers Mexico's victory over a foreign power that eventually led to Mexico's overthrow of a puppet emperor who ruled in the name of France's Napoleon III.

Another example of a local holiday commemorating an historic event is Belize's Griffin Settlement Day on November 15, distinguished by a three-day festival from November 17 to 19, when the Garifuna people celebrate their first landing on the shores of Belize.

Another water-related custom in El Salvador involves placing a life-sized statue of St. Michael the archangel in a boat. Accompanied by other boats, a priest blesses the waters, invoking the aid of the angel in protecting citizens from violent storms at the same time that prayers are offered for an abundant fishing season.[14]

Some Festivals of Indigenous Origin

It is well known that indigenous societies throughout the world formulate ceremonies and rituals as a basic element of life. As such, traditional celebrations carry through to the modern world in countless parts of Latin America in festivities that continue to fascinate visitors with their unique and colorful displays of music, dance, and costumes. One example is the *diablada* or devil dance of Bolivia, celebrated in the city of Oruro with a twenty-block-long display of masks and costumes. In addition, the festival features music performed with such local instruments as the *charanga*, a stringed instrument, and varieties of flutes such as the *quena* and the bagpipe or *gaita* as well as maracas.[15]

In Venezuela, the Day of the Devils of Yare is a distinctive event of African origin which is marked by colorful masks, traditional dances and lively music. This festival, which goes on for four days, is a major tourist attraction for the small town of Yare.[16]

Famous as well is the Pachamama fiesta in Uruguay, in which the country's rich African heritage is remembered and promoted in a series of ceremonies. Celebrants don colorful and dramatic-looking masks complemented by *llamadas* or processions accompanied by African-American styled music and dances. It is said that such festivals have their origin in the customs of slaves brought to Uruguay from the African Bantu culture.[17]

In Latin America the mixture of indigenous and African religions with Christianity has caused a sometimes confusing mixture of religious traditions and perspectives. As a result, Christian-based ceremonies may take place right next to celebrations which date back to pre–Hispanic days, or the origins of such events may be mixed up to the extent that it is almost impossible to tell where one begins and the other ends. Innumerable cities and towns celebrate the special day of their patron saint, such as San Juan, Puerto Rico, which is named after St. John the Baptist, whose holy day falls on June 24.[18]

The feast of St. John the Baptist or St. John's Day actually is found in many parts of Latin America and throughout the world since this festival in June comes close to the time of ancient celebrations of the summer solstice, which has been the inspiration for popular rituals since long before recorded history. David Guss, professor of anthropology at Tufts University, has said that the "Día de San Juan is one of the most widespread festivals anywhere, probably beginning in pagan times with giant bonfires."[20]

The nineteenth-century runaway Cuban slave Esteban Montejo describes a colorful, old time celebration of St. John's Day in Cuba in the following terms: "The fiestas of San Juan were the most celebrated ones in the region. Two or three days before the 24th the village children would start getting ready for it, decorating the houses and the church with palm-leaves.... Although it was a religious festival and there were altars even in the doorways of the houses, I never got around to praying.... It was the custom at fiestas to dance the caringa.... They danced the zapateo as well, the traditional Cuban dance, and the tunandera.... It was performed in people's homes or in the countryside."[21]

In the mountains of Peru thousands of individuals of Indian descent make a pilgrimage which they believe is required of them at least once in a lifetime in order to contribute to the celebration of Quoyllur Riti. This is a dramatic example of religious devotion which combines adoration of the Virgin Mary and a Catholic mass with the arrival of as many as fifty thousand men, women and children to the upper reaches of the Andes, where they also salute the native god *apacheta*, the deity of roads, and where they kiss the earth, showing their unity with all the creation made by their native gods. Also famous in Ecuador and Peru is the celebration of Inti Raymi from June 24 to June 29.[22]

Such a cultural and religious mixture is also typical of the celebration of the Day of the Dead in Mexico. This holy day is celebrated in a variety of ways. In the town of Olinala in the state of Guerrero, locals dress themselves and wear masks representing *tecuanes*; men often dress like women and wear masks with feminine features.

In Zinacapán in Puebla, Mexico, the traditional dance of the *negritos* is presented in front of the main Catholic church on the feast of St. Michael. Other festivals hark back to rituals that were performed before the Spanish conquest. In Acatlán, men dressed as jaguars fight each other in public just as in pre–Hispanic days when men dressed in jaguar masks fought each other in a mortal battle. It was believed that their blood would please the god of the sun, who would reward such adoration with a fertile crop for that particular year.[23]

In Peru the town of Paucartambo celebrates July 15 as the day of the Virgin Mary, with elaborate floats replete with flowers and statues of the Virgin Mary under a parasol of macaw feathers. Onlookers from the balconies of old-style colonial buildings can look down at the floats in the procession and watch costumed dancers holding ropes and cords that formed a part of ancient dances in pre–Hispanic times.[24]

In Belize, dancers doing the John Canoe dance perform in groups of six to ten. They wear colorful masks, and are dressed in white with straw hats adorned with peacock, parrot or turkey feathers. With their faces covered by African-style masks they make an impressive appearance in this Christmas-time celebration.[24]

Day of the Dead

The Mexican celebration of the Day of the Dead, which coincides with the Christian holy day of All Souls on November 1, is a classic example of the way in which pre–Hispanic celebrations have mixed with Catholic traditions to create a colorful and memorable combination of customs and sensibilities.

In Mexico and in Guatemala, people of Mayan descent fly giant kites of many designs as a way of communicating with their ancestors.[25] Many Mexicans commemorate the day by creating altars in their homes. These structures contain food and other items which remind living relatives and friends of the tastes and preferences of loved ones who have passed away and are lit by candles and other objects that might be fitting to epitomize the day of the dead. It has been said that Mexicans, because of their link to their pre–Hispanic past, do not fear death as do other cultures. Rather they play with death and make it a part of their daily life. This statement is borne out by the presence of skeletons representing figures of death in much of Mexican folk art as well as in the painting of famous Mexican artists like Diego Rivera. His Doña Catrina is a life-sized skeleton figure wearing a woman's hat. Figures and reminders of death are best seen, however, in the engravings of the Mexican artist Guadalupe Posada.

Just as in the celebration of Halloween, in which scary figures like ghosts, vampires, and witches abound, depictions of otherworldly figures and human skulls are common on the Mexican Day of the Dead. However, the spirit of the celebration is very different since these reminders of death and the supernatural are not intended to scare people. Rather, they are intended to link the living with the souls of the departed in a more positive way.

For this reason the Day of Dead is celebrated in Mexican bakeries, which sell cookies in the form of a human skull. Purchasers give these cookies to friends, relatives and co-workers, not as a macabre reminder of death but rather as an expression of friendship. These delicacies are often accompanied by bits of doggerel verse called *Calaveras*, or skull poems. Rather than taking offense at what we might find a morbid gift, the usual reaction of recipients is appreciation, since Mexicans believe that the more skull cookies you receive, the more friends you have and the more popular you must be.

Especially in rural areas where the cultural links with pre–Hispanic civilizations and customs may be strongest, it is not uncommon for friends and families to celebrate lengthy, sometimes all night vigils in a local ceremony, complete with homemade altars, candles and other appropriate decorations.

The Quinceañera Party

An important custom in Latin America is the *Quinceañera* party which celebrates the passing of a young girl into adulthood, from a girl to a young lady. Similar in spirit to a "sweet sixteen" party, this rite of passage takes place when a young lady arrives at her fifteenth birthday. In many families this celebration is taken so seriously that preparations start months in advance with numerous rehearsals of the ceremony. The girl's father gives her away symbolically to society in general, and specifically to the *chambelán* or young man who is chosen as her special escort at the ceremony. So special is this party that many families of limited economic resources may actually start to save for the event years in advance.

In addition to the young lady who is the center of attention, other young ladies who are chosen by her accompany her at this symbolic transition from childhood to the world of adults, and they in turn are accompanied by their own escorts who traditionally appear in formal dress.

This ritual is not only celebrated by families in Latin America but by countless families of Hispanic origin living in the United States as well as in other countries. Among wealthy families, such festivities may be carried out in formal dress in other countries, notably in Europe. The prestige of the cultural traditions of European countries is believed to add to the impressive nature of the event.

Countless local celebrations commemorating patron saints of towns and villages, events of historical importance and religious traditions best known to local residents fill the calendars of Latin American nations. So important are the names and holy day commemorations of the lives of the Catholic saints that it is common for some families to arbitrarily give a newborn child the name of the saint on whose day that baby was born, even if the names were more popular hundreds or thousands of years ago and therefore sound unusual today. This explaining such names as "Policarpo," "Sixtino" or "Hermenegildo." In counties where the names of pre–Hispanic gods still resound with vital importance, children may be found with names that hark back to ancient times.

Indeed the collective memory of many cultures shows that the native traditions still are vital and important not only in the pages of history books but in the streets and plazas of large cities and small towns. They show their importance in innumerable celebrations that are marked by incredible colors, high drama, creative and distinctive costumes and an awareness of the importance of the dignity and worth of local social traditions as well as national and international ones.

The very existence of so many open air markets with their incredible variety of colorful textiles and handicrafts is perhaps a kind of ancient festival of small-scale commerce that exists today. Even in Mexico City, the world's largest urban area, certain streets are closed to traffic on certain days of every week so that tents can be erected a local fair or *tianguis*.

The Celebration of Life

Perhaps the most significant result of a study of celebrations and festivals in the Spanish- and Portuguese-speaking worlds that compose Latin America may be the implications that such activities have for a broad perspective on life as it is lived and conceived south of the U.S. border.

As we have already noted, the Mexican author Octavio Paz has said that celebrations that enrich the social spirit of the Mexican people are but a display of their basic feeling that life itself is a celebration. Festive days are not an exception from the norm, which is the world of work. Rather they characterize basic elements of society. Or to put it another way may, the rich traditions of music and dance, extremely colorful clothing and artifacts and the vast pantheons of supernatural figures represent an outward manifestation of the color, sound and movement which indigenous cultures believe constitute all of nature and creation itself.

This is but another way of saying that festivals which combine ancient gods and cosmic powers with Christian images are a manifestation of the vibrant reality of tradition, a respect for the past and the value of ancestors to a degree rarely found in the more industrialized world. This sense of history and the vitality of past events has been captured very well by the Peruvian author Alfonsina Barronueva, speaking of rituals and ceremonies of the Andes mountains. "Another world of marvels and mystery created by miracles, faith and superstition, in which traditions mix with the customs of the local towns, their hunger and their tenderness, their fear of death, their thirst for justice and their anxiety and their revenge [is seen] in churches that embraced for centuries their anger and their crying, their joys and triumphs.[26]

This World and the Next

The respect for the souls of dear departed friends and family members is more than superficial. It reflects a belief that departed loved ones are with us in a very real way, not just as an idea or as a memory, but rather as a living presence. It is for this reason that the Mexican celebration of the Day of the Dead is not meant to emphasize the scary or spooky aspects of the supernatural as in the day we call Halloween, although figures of human skulls and skeletons do often adorn altars constructed to mark this special time. On the contrary, Mexicans often say that this celebration is designed to celebrate life not death. It is meant to show that those who have left us to travel, we hope, to a much better world are still alive, and therefore their lives and their presence are celebrated in a real way, in the preparation of their favorite foods and presentation of other personal items on the homemade altars. It is for this reason that the death of a loved one in small towns in Mexico is marked by an actual celebration which can go on for not one hour nor one day, but for three straight days.

Man and the Cosmos

The awareness that mankind forms part of the total cosmic balance of powers is well portrayed in ceremonies complete with masks and other items depicting the forces of good and evil, whether these be seen in pagan or in Christian terms or perhaps in a combination of both. Other festivals and rites that commemorate man's unity with nature, whether these be related to the changing of seasons, the summer equinox or any other manifestation of the power of the natural world, form a part of what might be called a holistic or naturalistic view of man's place in the great scheme of life, seen as a basically unchanging natural reality.

The search for the cultural roots of civilization obscured by the modern world is perhaps more acute today than it has been in the recent past. For this reason the emergence of what has been called the New Age is, in the minds of some people, nothing new at all, rather it is the renewed importance of attitudes and practices which are actually thousands of years old, marking in effect a kind of Old Age. The Latin America of the present era maintains its link with the past in a vital way.

As anthropologist G.M. Foster has noted of one indigenous Latin American community, "Rituals are connected with a basic view of the measure and equilibrium of the basic life process. A striving to maintain equilibrium thus emerges as the dominant pattern in Tzanzuntzán culture.... Government activities, religious rituals, agricultural practices, the local pottery industry, family, community, schooling, all are adapted to the basic cognitive orientations and behavior forms." In effect, these people see life as a continuum, a holistic experience where there is little if any separation between man and nature. Healing and ritual often go hand in hand in traditional societies for, according to Foster, in the name of equilibrium, "the steps man takes to restore the equilibrium in a 'sick' society and a sick body are similar."[27]

We may consider then that often celebrations and rituals are much more than mere celebrations for their own sake. Man's desire to constantly renew his vital link with the past and with the heroic actions of great legendary heroes as well as animalistic and supernatural powers betrays not only a vital link with tradition, but is a manifestation of an ancient awareness that life is and should be a balance of energy, belief and action, all of which can work together for the common good.

XI

Popular Music

Music plays a very important part in popular Latin American culture. Not only has it accompanied religious ceremonies and celebrations since time immemorial, but it forms an important part of daily life. The author remembers walking through a street in a city in Mexico to the accompaniment of the vocal renditions of the popular Mexican singer Ana Gabriel. Not only did the songs resound from recordings being played on one side of the street, but the very same singer was to be heard coming from renditions being played on the opposite side of the same street. All the while normal business was going on to the point that these formed a kind of concert-like atmosphere that permeated street life.

So important are popular musical performers in this part of the world that their songs and the music played by groups that continue well known national musical traditions as well as current popular styles are often considered to be institutions that carry forth the character of each nation to all parts of a home country and then to all parts of the world. Such a tradition is certainly to be found in the case of the well known musical heritage of Argentina which is contained and expressed by what is known as the tango.

Tango

Well known as an elegant dance replete with sudden changes of direction and subtle if not seductive body movements, the tango is both a style of dancing and a musical expression. Having originated among the lower classes in Buenos Aires at the turn of the twentieth century, the tango originally had little appeal for society as a whole, yet its charm soon expanded its popularity to include both humble establishments in the colorful Boca section of the Argentine capital as well as the mansions of the highest classes of society.

After it conquered the tastes of the Argentine nation, the tango was exported to the whole world thanks to performances of highly acclaimed tango masters such as vocalists like Libertad LeMarque, Agustín Magaldi, and most especially the genius of the tango, Carlos Gardel. This latter artist is often considered to have been one of the most famous and most popular matinee idols of the twentieth century because of his dedicated if not sometimes hysterical fans, not only in Argentina but in all of Latin America as well as in many other countries.

Being a star in tango-based films as well as a recording artist, this vocalist had the unique ability to move the hearts of his numerous fans as perhaps no other singer has in the Hispanic world in modern times. Upon his death in an airplane accident, a funeral procession was held in the Argentine capital that went on for more than seven hours, with ticker tape so thick and heavy that it was almost impossible to see from one side of the street to another.

The tango is still alive and well in today's world and some dancers and fans of this highly sentimental music, complete with the melancholy grinding of a small version of the accordion known as the *bandoneón*, express the belief that the tango and the sentiments expressed in its lyrics can almost become a way of life. Still the greatest popularity of this famous style of dancing today, outside of Argentina itself, is perhaps in the northern European country of Finland, where numerous tango bars dot the countryside. There the tango is said to help citizens open up and communicate with each other.[1]

Tango music and dance can be found in many countries, however the tango still expresses the passionate soul of Argentina with its lyrics charged with nostalgia for family, the neighborhood or the *arrabal*, lost friends and especially lost or impossible love. The words of these songs frequently express desperate emotions. Indeed the passionate nature of such melodies can run so high that it has been claimed that when news of the tragic death of Carlos Gardel spread through Latin America there actually were female fans who committed suicide.

Above all, the high sentimentality of the tango is a constant reminder that Latin Americans are more likely than many others to wear their hearts on their sleeves. Latinos of all nationalities feel deeply, and show their emotions in a highly visible way, not only in their music, which boasts of deep lyricism and sentimentality, but in body language and facial gestures which accompany the words, and contribute to the conversations that make up daily life.

To go even further, a listener who is entranced by the majestic, not to say tragic, beauty of tango lyrics may be tempted to believe that this music which has captured the hearts and minds of countless millions of listeners outside as well as inside of Argentina represents the sophistication and gentle beauty as well as the sensitivity of the best aspects of the culture of that Latin American country.

Recent Trends

Certainly trends in popular music transcend national boundaries, and such manifestations of cultural popular taste as hip hop and rap music are well known in many countries, however these styles have made relatively little impact on Latin America as a whole. The same could be said of American blues and jazz musical styles. These U.S.-born forms of music have been very well received in some parts of the world. Jazz especially has been taken to heart in certain countries which have become known to dedicated jazz fans as "hip" nations (to use the jazz vernacular term). Such a designation would certainly include Japan as well as the Scandinavian countries, especially Denmark and Sweden, places which have been the home of many expatriate American jazz musicians such as trumpeter Chet Baker, tenor sax artists like Stan Getz and Dexter Gordon and pianists Duke Jordan, Hampton Hawes and many others. Although it certainly is true that jazz and Afro-Cuban styles have met before in works by American jazz musicians like Stan Kenton and Dizzy Gillespie as well as Cal Tjader, whose brand of West Coast jazz betrays the strong influence of Latin American music.[1]

Among the most recent trends in popular music, rock music has perhaps made its impact felt the most south of the border. New rock groups seem to appear almost daily with a bewildering variety of names and styles, yet Latin American rock, at least to some U.S. listeners, comes across in a softer, less abrasive form than the so-called acid rock that has encroached on U.S. air waves in recent years.

Caribbean Music

When speaking of the popular music of the Caribbean, many aficionados of Latin American music may immediately think of places like Cuba, Puerto Rico and the Dominican Republic, and certainly these countries do form part of the Caribbean cultural zone. Very often, however, casual observers overlook the Caribbean coastline of countries like Mexico and many of the nations of Central America as well as Venezuela and Colombia. In these places coastal musical styles are similar to the strongly African-based rhythms that are most typical of what has become known as "salsa" in all its forms, such as the music that accompanies Caribbean dances such as the mambo and cha-cha.

Nevertheless in the minds of most people, Caribbean music is usually synonymous with the music of Cuba and Puerto Rico. The most popular melodies and rhythms heard in those countries today are really continuations of the musical heritage which began in Africa and which existed in those areas before the arrival of Spanish settlers. What is true of melody and rhythm is also true of many of the popular instruments themselves. For example the *guiro* or *Guacharo*, a hollowed-out gourd, began to be used by the Taino Indians before the arrival of European colonists. Even the guitar, an instrument that has for so long been associated with the melodic traditions of the Hispanic world, was adapted by local people into their own version of this instrument. As a result, the *Requinto*, the *bordona* and the *cuatro* are all Caribbean variations on the six-string Spanish guitar, each one with its own inimitable sound quality. Used today in many Latin American countries, the *cuatro* is a ten-stringed guitar with the strings assembled in five different groupings.

Also well known among typical instruments used in Caribbean popular music are the maracas, which bear the same name in English, an instrument that makes a rattling sound as it is shaken. Also commonly found are different-sized drums or *tambores*, which are manufactured today but which were originally built of hollow tree trunks with animal hides tightly stretched across their surface.

In Puerto Rico the dances known as the *bomba* and the *plena* are African-based patterns of movement that are set to music. The *bomba*, which is reputed to have begun in the Puerto Rican town of Loiza, gained popularity in the mainland of the United States in the 1950s thanks to the work of Rafael Cortija and other musicians of Caribbean origin. It is performed with its own special instrument, a small drum called the *subidor* which marks its beat to the tune of maracas. It is beaten with sticks that produce a highly dramatic effect. All of this is accompanied by a chorus responding to the vocalized words of a singer. This dance is also known in variations commonly referred to as the *euba*, the *cocobale* and the *sica*.[3]

Also popular is a musical style called the *danza* or *contradanza*, a musical form and a dance which had its origin in Spain. In Cuba it formed the basis for what has been called the *habanera*. In Venezuela this traditional Spanish style mixed with native African rhythms to be called the *danzón*.[3]

Salsa

The world famous salsa, which means "sauce" in Spanish, is really a name used to describe a combination of musical styles that accompany typical Caribbean-based dances such as the mambo and cha-cha among others. Said to have been originated after World War II in New York by musicians such as the legendary Tito Puente, who brought a big band approach to Latin music, this tradition derives from an Afro-Cuban base known especially for its pounding rhythms.

Undoubtedly the most famous singer who bases much of his style on an Afro-Cuban rhythmic approach is Ricky Martin, the winner of the 1999 Grammy Award for Best Latin Pop Performance. Nevertheless the names of popular salsa singers and musical groups is extensive indeed, including among many others such names as Willie Colón, Héctor Lavoe, the popular contemporary group Puerto Rican Power, Victor Manuelle, Jerry Rivera, Ismael Miranda, Gilberto Santa Rosa and many others.[4]

One other pop star who has gained great popularity is Antonio Muñoz, whose real name is Marco Antonio Muñiz. His first album, *Cuando la noche se acaba*, which came out in 1991, contained at least one song which climbed to the top of the Billboard charts.

This singer claims that he began to sing in the salsa style after hearing a rendition by the great Mexican vocalist Juan Gabriel. After that his first salsa album, *Otra nota*, became one of the best-selling salsa records ever to hit the commercial market. Then in 1995 his recording *Todo a su tiempo* sold 800,000 copies, which earned him a Grammy Award.[5]

The popular music found on the Caribbean coast of other Latin American countries is remarkably similar to that found in the Caribbean nations we have already mentioned. This would definitely include the melodies of the coastal area of countries such as Venezuela and Colombia, although in the case of Venezuela its closeness to islands such as Trinidad and Tobago accounts for the popularity of Calypso-style music as well.

The *joropo* is representative of popular Venezuelan music. This style which originated in the *llano*, or flatlands, of that country accompanies the Venezuelan merengue.

Venezuelan musical instruments include the harp, the violin and the *bandola*, a guitar which is similar to the *cuatro*. Its strings are formed differently in various parts of Venezuela, however it always has four sets of strings.

Venezuelan maracas are somewhat smaller than the better known maracas of other parts of the Caribbean, and they therefore produce a sound which is generally less percussive. Notable among the traditional instruments of Venezuela also are the *claves*, which are oversized drums sometimes referred to as the *mina* the *burro* or the *cumaco*. The *mina* is so large that the musician must ride it as if it were a horse. These drums are then beaten by wooden sticks or *palos*.[6]

Other Caribbean-styled melodies and dances include *guaguanco*, a type of rumba developed originally in Havana, Cuba as well as the *guarachua*, another Cuban song and dance style along with the *bachata*, which is a highly popular style of music and dance in the Dominican Republic.[7]

Uruguay also shares an important African-based cultural tradition. Most notable among its approaches to musical expression are *candombe* and *murga*. The *candomble* is a very typical Uruguayan music based on the special *tambori* drum. Such music typifies the Uruguayan carnival season, which is marked drum-based percussive sound as well as by singers accompanied by other instruments.

The *murga* is the fusion of music with acted-out dialogues at *tablado* performances, which feature musical comments on politics and other aspects of national life.

The Andean Region

The traditional popular music of the Andean countries such as Colombia, Ecuador, Peru and Chile is marked by the use of age-old instruments such as the flute, the harp and assorted stringed instruments. Typical Colombian dance melodies include the *vallenato*, the *bambuco* and the *cumbia*. Also found are variations, the modern *cumbia* and the *cumbiamba*.

The *cumbia* is especially popular as a dance performed during the celebration of the patron saint of any particular city or town. In the lively coastal towns of Colombia *cumbia* celebrations are known to go on all night, accompanied by typical instruments such as the accordion, the Quechuan flute and the maracas along with African-inspired percussion instruments, the *chonta* marimba and the *fototo*, which is an instrument made from a seashell.[8]

The variation of instruments used in typical Andean music is impressive indeed. Flutes made of pieces of hollow wood come in various sizes and shapes which include the *quena* and numerous other forms of flutes such as the *zampoña* the *surisicuria* the *antara* and the *rondador*.

Percussion and stringed instruments are often used in traditional Andean music. These include the *quancara*, a large drum made of goat skins; several versions of drums including the *bombo* and the *caja* made from a hollowed tree trunk; the *chullus*, a ribbon with goat hooves tied to it; the *charango*, a stringed instrument which is unique to the Andean region and the harp, which gives an almost spiritual tonality.

This music has undoubtedly resounded through the valleys and mountains for eons right down to the present. Traditional dress often goes with the dances that accompany melodic styles.

In nineteenth-century Peru, the dramatist Felipe Pardo y Aliaga presented a theatrical classic in which a girl who was supposed to be married into a high society family was rejected by them because she was known to have performed the traditional Peruvian dance known as the *zamacueca*.

Well known also in this area of Latin America are the Peruvian and Chilean waltzes, the latter through classic performances by groups such as Los Huaqueros, Los Trovadores, and Las Criollistas,[9] as well as the melodies of the *huayno* the *yaraví* and *sanjuanito*, the *huayno* being danced by men and women holding hands as they move in a circle.

The *yaraví* is a melancholy love song which has its roots in the ancient Quechuan tradition of Peru. Popular also is the *marinera*, a melody accompanied by its own special dance which is performed throughout that country but which is especially typical of coastal areas. The Peruvian waltz is a highly melodic and often sentimental musical style that has been performed and recorded by countless musical groups, as has the Chilean waltz, which shares the uncommon beauty, pathos and artistic charm of this tradition.

Chile has seen the resurgence of traditional musical genres going back to indigenous Quechuan melodies. This so-called *nueva canción* or new song soon became political protest music in Argentina and in Chile thanks to the efforts of artists like the Chilean poet and singer Violeta Parra, and the Argentine singer Atahualpa Yupanqui Parra. Gilbert Favre, a member of the Bolivian musical group Los Jairas further added to the popularization of this musical orientation.[10]

Paraguay

The indigenous element remains strong in Paraguay, which is a bilingual country where the Spanish language and the Guaraní language are spoken by most citizens. Well known are the Paraguayan polka and the *guaranía*, a musical form characterized by highly sentimental lyrics presented in a slow tempo. The European guitar and harp are heard in the polka and the bottle dance, in which performers spin a bottle on their heads. The composer Agustín Barrios is perhaps best known exponent of popular Paraguayan melodies.

Perhaps better known than the music of this nation itself is the impressive-looking Paraguayan harp — a large, somewhat simplified version of the European harp, with the local instrument having 38 strings.[11]

Mexico

The traditional music of Mexico is usually known almost exclusively by what is called Mariachi music, however, as in all of Latin American music and art, traditional styles vary from one part of the country to another. Mariachi music comes from an old melodic vintage dating back to the eighteenth century. Ironically, however, the name does not originate in the Spanish language but rather in French. At the time of the French occupation of Mexico in the nineteenth century during the administration of President Benito Juárez, people who wanted to hire musicians for weddings used to refer to them in terms of the French word for marriage, hence the term "mariachi."

This sentimental music, which includes violins and a chorus of trumpets along with an oversized guitar known as a *guitarrón*, is very picturesque since the musicians and singers that perform it dress in formal cowboy or charro-style clothing complete with large round hats, waist-length jackets and tight pants. In the case of wealthy performers these trousers often are adorned with silver ornaments in suits that are especially prepared.

In Mexico today, highly popular exponents of this type of music include Vicente Fernández, often called "the king" of the mariachis, and Paquita la del Barrio. Countless mariachi groups abound in Mexico and in other countries that have large groups of people of Mexican ancestry, especially in cities like San Antonio, Texas, and Los Angeles, California. In Mexico City, many mariachi bands can be found in the Garibaldi Plaza area. These groups are routinely hired in advance or even on the spot to serenade a wife or girlfriend, or to celebrate important occasions such as a wedding or a birthday.

In northern Mexico, a distinctive regional musical flavor has developed which can include instruments such as the clarinet or saxophone and trumpets with rhythmic accompaniment, often in the form of the heavy umppa tones of a large tuba. Perhaps what is most distinctive about these musical groups of what is called música norteña or "music from the north" is the drum beat, which is so percussive that it often closely resembles the rapid beats of the Polish polka. Such northern Mexican renditions have traveled ever further north and form part of what has been called Tex-Mex music. A number of northern Mexican, ranch-style ensembles have achieved international fame such as the well known combo, Los Tigres del Norte (The Tigers from the North).

In southern Mexico, especially in coastal areas, melodies and rhythms tend to caress a listener's ears with a softer, broad or tonal charm often expressed by the piano, the guitar and especially the marimba.

Brazil

Brazilian popular music has its origin in the indigenous traditions of many native groups and includes whistles, drums and other homemade instruments used for countless years by the people of the Brazilian rain forest. The first record of a popular musical tradition in Brazil dates back to 1578 when missionary Jean de Lery wrote a history of his trip to that country in which he described the musical inclinations of the Tupi people.[12]

At the same time Eastern Amazonia has been the home of a type of music known as *carimbo*, centered mainly in the area near the city of Belém. This form of musical expression became commercialized several decades ago when it mixed with the traditions of reggae, salsa and the meringue. It was the Bolivian ensemble Los Kjarkas who were credited with beginning what actually became an international dance sensation, the *lambada*.

The first Brazilian popular singer to establish an international reputation was the Hollywood film star Carmen Miranda. Since then, the popular styles listed below have attracted many fans.

CHORO

Based on the Portuguese *fado* songs, this kind of melody, originally from Río de Janeiro, was originally improvised by bands made up of guitars, mandolins, clarinets and flutes among other instruments. Though this style of music had its beginning in nineteenth-century Brazil, it has become popular again through the work of groups such as Os Ingenuos.

TROPICALIA

This musical genre has had a controversial past in Brazil because of the songs presented by musicians such as Gilberto Gil and others who were exiled during the military regime of recent decades because of the highly political content of their melodies.[13]

MÚSICA NORDESTINA

This is the name given to music from Northeastern Brazil. Marked by slow rhythms that are not as highly accented as music of a more obvious

African-styled beat, the flavor of this music has evolved into a popular dance music called the *baião*.

Other popular Brazilian musical forms include the *frevo* and the *forró* played by drums, a triangle and an accordion. Even more contemporaneous styles include the funk carioca, the hardcore and heavy metal rock.

Among musical forms with a more African-based orientation is the world-famous samba. This in turn can be found in its variations known as the *samba de breque*, the *samba-cancão* and the *samba pagodé*.

Perhaps the most distinctive popular musical tradition is that of the *capoeira* which is actually a sport involving gymnastic pyrotechnics accompanied by its own form of music. The songs themselves can be made up as the activities go on and they are frequently accompanied by instruments such as the *berinbau* and the *pandeiro*.

African-based music also includes the *maracatú* played in Recife and the *olinda* performed during the Carnival festivities, and the *afoxe*, a religious-oriented music which is part of the *candomble* tradition.[14]

Some Popular Performers of Note

The list of singers and musical groups that form the panoply of celebrated names within the world of Latin American popular music is truly endless, and new names are appearing almost daily. A list of just a few singers and groups that have achieved international renown in more recent times would include Roberto Carlos (Brazil), José Luis Rodríguez (better known as El Puma, the puma, from Venezuela), Ana Gabriel (Mexico) as well as Yuri and Gloria Trevi (Mexico). More traditional names from Mexico would include Javier Solís, the trio Los Panchos and songwriters such as José Alfredo Jiménez and the highly sentimental Agustín Lara, who was both a composer and a singer.

Such a list would also have to include the ever-popular Jorge Negrete, whose singing in classic Mexican movies still evokes both nostalgia and deep sentimentality from a vast number of fans.

From Puerto Rico have come the singers like Diosa Cordero and Olga Tañón among many others, as well as the already mentioned Marc Antonio and Ricky Martin.

During the wave of popularity that the *bossa nova* enjoyed in the United States a number of decades ago, Brazilian singers like Antonio Carlos Jobim, Astrid Gilberto and her husband João Gilberto achieved international renown with their Brazilian-style songs as well as their adaptation of the Brazilian bossa nova traditions to American jazz in recordings they made with jazz musicians such as Charlie Byrd and Stan Getz.

Other notable singers are listed below.

CELIA CRUZ

Cuban born Celia Cruz has been called the "First Lady of Latin Music," and as such she is generally considered to be one of the most popular Latin music performers of the twentieth century. She made her first recording in Venezuela. Later she became famous in Cuba and throughout Latin America as the lead singer in the musical group called the Sonora.

After the Cuban revolution she moved to the United States and she and her orchestra began her U.S. career at the Hollywood Palladium. She recorded with band leader Tito Puente and performed at New York's Carnegie Hall. Her 1974 recording with Johnny Pacheco, *Celia y Johnny*, won a gold record and her international career was on its way.

During the 1970s and '80s she made frequent tours of Europe and Latin America and in 1990 she won a Grammy Award for the Best Tropical Latin Performance for her recording with Ray Baretto, *Ritmo en el corazón*. After her death in 2003 she won a posthumous award at the Premios Lo Nuestro for the best salsa record of 2004. In 2005 the Smithsonian Institution in Washington, D.C., held an exhibition dedicated to the life and works of this renowned artist.[15]

LUÍS MIGUEL

Luis Miguel has been called the most popular singer in all of Latin America. Born Luis Miguel Gallego Basteri in 1970, he has won nine Grammy Awards — five Grammys and four Latin Grammys. He has won three World Music Awards, and he is now the best-selling Latin American popular recording star, having sold over 56 million albums worldwide. The son of the Spanish vocalist Luisito Rey and the Italian-born actress Marcella Basteri, he started his career with his first musical appearance in Costa Rica at the age of four. He made his first record in 1981 and he began to appear throughout Latin America several years later.

In 1991 his recording *Romance* became the best-selling Spanish language album of all time. In 1993 his recording *Aries* won the Grammy Award for the Best Latin Pop Album at the same time that he became the first Latin American performer to sell out New York City's Madison Square Garden.

Later in 2003, Prince Felipe of Spain presented him with an award for being the best-selling foreign artist in his country's history. His most recent recordings have sold internationally in the millions and he continues to tour worldwide.[16]

SHAKIRA

This Colombian singer, born Shakira Isabel Mebarak Ripoli, of a Colombian mother and an American-born father of Lebanese ancestry, is named for her grandmother with the Arabic name Shakira, which means "grateful." Having begun to write musical compositions at the early age of 8, her first album, *Magia*, was made for Sony in 1991. Her real fame in Latin America did not begin until after the release of her *Pies descalzos*, which sold more than 5 million copies. This was followed by other multi-million selling albums, which opened up many international markets and brought her to the attention of worldwide audiences. In 2000 she was awarded an MTV Video Music Award in the category of Favorite International Artist.[17]

XII

Medicine and Healing

Latin America has what are without doubt some of the finest medical specialist and surgeons in the world. Nevertheless Latin America also has a long and illustrious history of local or native healers known as *curanderos/as*, or people who cure; *hierberos/as*, healers who use medicinal plants, and more mysteriously perhaps, *chamanes*, shamans, and even *brujos/as* or witches.

To make it more confusing, many such native or traditional healers use more than one medicinal vehicle to achieve healing, so the definition and description of any practitioner is unclear to say the least. To put such activities in proper perspective, however, it is best to remember that they in no way represent a strange aberration in human history. On the contrary, healing by herbs and altered shamanistic states of consciousness was generally mankind's only form of healing for millions of years of pre-history. Since the advent of civilization it still constitutes an important approach to medicine and healing on just about every continent from Siberia to Africa, to the United States and then to Latin America and Asia.

In Latin America many people, especially those living in isolated rural areas, have little or no access to modern medicine or they are unable to pay for such services. As a result, they traditionally seek the help of native healers of various types and descriptions.

What herbs and plants do these healers use? The list is endless for there are thousands of plants in the Amazonian rain forest alone which have traditionally been used for medical treatments. The study of which herbs to use and how to prescribe them is hardly a hit-or-miss operation. On the contrary herbalists may spend the better part of lifetime in a study of the healing effects of certain plants. Such knowledge is often passed on from one native healer to another, from one generation to another, and this knowledge has almost certainly been accumulated over thousands if not millions of years that human beings have lived in the Amazon.

Nor is such knowledge mere superstition. One estimate is that a good 60 percent of the chemicals found in plants in the rain forest form the basis for drugs sold by gigantic drug companies. The difference is that one can't patent a plant in the wild, but a company can add another element to this naturally occurring plant, give it a scientific name that few people can pronounce, and then call it a proprietary drug. Then they can apply for a patent, at which point the cost of this natural substance, the original basis for such a prescription drug, may rise astronomically. Of course not all modern medicines come from native plants, but it is safe to conclude that many do.

A cursory overview of just some of the plants which have been used by native healers in the Amazon region would include aripari, the mastreco, tatuyaa and the jurubeba.[1]

Readers may wish to consider that prior to the twentieth century a druggist usually did just what these native healers did. Before the advent of the gigantic pharmaceutical companies, the local pharmacist would sell herbs for their medicinal value, often using the proverbial bowl and pestle, which can still be seen as a professional symbol for a drug store, to crush the herbs individually in a combination of healing remedies.

Among Latin Americans of indigenous background it is still difficult to separate religion from medicine, since *brujos* and shamans use spiritual traditions to effect healing. One of the basic differences between modern and indigenous cultures both in and outside of Latin America is the concept of progress. As the scholar of comparative religions, Mircea Eliade, has noted, "Any meaningful act performed by archaic man ... suspends duration, abolishes profane time, and participates in mythical time." Eliade also says, "Archaic man, acknowledges no act which has not been previously ... lived by someone else, some other being who was not a man."[3] So it may be logical to conclude that the healing act, viewed as a religious or transcendent experience, is often considered to be an imitation of similar acts performed by gods or superheroes in the past. Such actions are often dramatic presentations. As anthropologist Claude Levi Strauss has put it, "In treating his patient the shaman also offers his audience a performance."[4]

In addition to the *brujo* and *curandero*, in Mexico you find the *nagual*, or witch, from the Aztec word for "transforming witch." Some indigenous groups see this as a kind of companion spirit while others conceive of the *nagual* as he or she was seen in the pre–Hispanic era, as a transforming witch.[5] Though the term is used differently by different indigenous peoples, its original meaning obviously implies that the witch may change into the body and spirit of animals in order to achieve healing power. The *nagual* is supposed to have the ability to sense the affinity that an individual, supposedly the person that is sick, has to the healing spirit of a certain animal.

The term is vague and it changes from one society to another. In some Indian societies the *nagual* may refer to a person's sign in the zodiac or even the date in which a person was born in the Maya-quiché calendar of 260 days. Among the Nahuatl Indians of Tepoztlan, the *nagual* is supposed to be an individual who can change into an animal. Also in many societies the person whose *nagual* become a certain animal is often considered to be able to acquire the characteristics of that animal which will help him to be strong and healthy. For example if a person should be a *balam* or tiger, that person is supposed to be bold and strong.[6]

In other communities the *nawal* or *nagual* is an animal counterpart that helps a person to be healed. He is often believed to reveal himself to that person in a dream. Among tribes that believe in the existence of malevolent beings or witches, it may be admissible to try to kill a witch who has put an evil spell on a person, while it is believed that a sick person may be the victim of a curse brought by such a witch.

The person casting the spell may actually send his *nawal* or animal spirit to converse with the *nawal* of the person who is affected by an illness. Such witches may use a number of means to cast these spells including the use of dolls and items that may belong to the person to be cursed. Indeed since illness are sometimes believed to be caused by witchcraft and spells, or what are frequently called *trabajitos*, shamans are often called on to remove a curse from a sick person by means of what is known as a *limpia* or cleansing.

The spiritual center at Nanclyaga, Mexico, routinely performs such cleansing by thousands of seers, shamans and other assorted native healers.[7] Such procedures are common in Latin America and are not restricted to rural or purely indigenous groups of people. In fact they are quite common in Latin American communities in the United States, where *brujos*, shamans and *curanderos* can be found just as they are found south of the border.[8]

It is important to remember that the line between healers who use herbs and other natural substances to cure and healers that use magic or shamanistic practices is not absolute at all. On the contrary many native healers tend to blend both manners of healing to achieve the progress that they and their patients look for.

Basic to this kind of healing process is the tradition by which the shaman goes into a higher state of consciousness and communicates with beings in another dimension of life that tell him how to effect a cure for the illness that besets the victim. These beings in another dimension may take many forms, however they frequently are believed to be spirits of the animals that protect and guide the sick person. They are believed to know best what the sick person's condition is and what is the best manner to heal him.

Such practices may also include the use of power objects. As anthropologist Michael Harner notes in his book, *Way of the Shaman*, "a shaman may group such objects together in a power or medicine bundle. He especially includes objects encountered during powerful personal experiences connected with shamanic work. If you have a visionary experience or sense power at a particular location, look about you and see if something distinctive is lying there."[9]

In his *Autobiography of a Runaway Slave*, Esteban Montejo tells of religious ceremonies in Cuba based on a game called *mayombé*, in which a pot was placed on a patio. Local people believed that the power of the saints that they worshiped were contained in that pot, so if they wanted to make someone ill or even kill him all they had to do was bring offerings to that place by way of earth from the four corners of the cemetery. These corners represented the four corners of the universe. If a master harmed a slave, people could make that master ill by way of such incantations.

Although the most common explanation for the effect of such spells is the unknown power of the mind, or the power of suggestion, spells are usually cast in secret and the victims of such spells, real or imagined, are rarely if ever informed.[10]

Speaking of two African religions in Cuba during his lifetime, the Lucumi and the Congolese, Esteban notes that "the Congolese worked magic with the sun almost every day. When they had trouble with a particular person they would follow him along a path, collect up some of the dust he walked upon and put it in the *nganga* or in some little secret place. As the sun went down that person's life would begin to ebb away, and at sunset he would be dying."[11]

Nevertheless it would be a mistake to believe that herbal cures, plant-based medicines and medicinal teas such as manzanilla and annisette teas are used only in indigenous societies. They are utilized by millions of people throughout all of Latin America.

In addition Latin Americans are in the habit of believing in what some may call "folk illness," or maladies which are the product of traditional beliefs that are not necessarily recognized or not fully recognized by modern medicine.

The *Mal de Ojo* or the Evil Eye is believed by some Latin Americans to be a spell or a malevolent influence that can very easily make people sick. As a remedy, a raw egg is often rubbed on the forehead of the victim to effect a cleansing or *limpia*.[12]

Another supposed illness is the *recargo de estomago*, which is the common belief that stomach ailments are not caused by an actual stomach infection but simply by having over loaded one's stomach with too much food. This includes the famous tourist sickness which afflicts countless visitors to locales south of the border and the *venganza de Montezuma*, better known as Montezuma's revenge.

Another folk belief is called *susto*. This is the idea that because of traumatic or overwhelming events a person can suddenly become very ill or the human spirit may actually leave the body and thus cause death.

Hot and cold imbalance is supposedly based on the classical belief in the "humors" of the body. In Hispanic homes, particularly in Mexico and Puerto Rico, there exists a belief that a lack of balance between supposedly cold and hot parts of the body can cause illness. Foods and liquids can have a cold or hot effect on the body, thus potentially throwing it out of balance. Certain herbs and medicines are used to restore balance. The difference between hot and cold is not necessarily based on temperature. Ice is "hot" because it has an intense effect on the body while Linden tea, while served hot, is considered to be cold.

Homeopathy

Homeopathic medicine is not too well known in the United States, but it is well known throughout many other parts of the world. It is not what might be called "folk medicine" but rather it is often referred to as an alternative form of modern medicine. Along with acupuncture, Reiki and other forms of the healing process which have a long history of success in other parts of the world and in other cultures, it may be considered an alternative form of healing.

Originating in Europe centuries ago, this school of medicine is based on the principle that very small amounts of certain substances are able to counteract the negative effects of illness. As with the vaccination process, practitioners of this form of medicine believe that tiny substances provoke a reaction within the body which neutralizes the negative effects of bacteria or other harmful substances which cause illness.

Homeopathy is very popular in Latin America, where homeopathic hospitals and homeopathic pharmacies can easily be found. Homeopathy is consistent with the practice of modern medicine. Some M.D.s practice this form of healing. In France for example, there are said to be at least ten thousand M.D.s who use homeopathy as an adjunct to other forms of modern medicine.

Today some 400 million people in the world use homeopathic medicine. In the United States in the nineteenth century, magazines dealing with homeopathic cures were very popular and very well known. Since homeopathic medicines are natural substances and homeopathy does without expensive technology and expensive, mass produced drugs, it has been in the interest of some sectors of society to diminish the reliance on homeopathic medicine. Right now, few Americans are aware that such a school of healing actually exists.[14]

However, there is a National School of Homeopathic Medicine in Mexico City and a U.S. charity, A Promise of Health, has set up a homeopathic clinic in poor rural areas of Mexico's Yucatan Peninsula that has taken care of 22,000 patients and has prescribed 44,000 homeopathic medicines.[15]

In Latin America as elsewhere there are health-giving practices which are designed to enhanced the flow of the body's energies. The study of Chinese Ti Chi is popular, as is the study of Feng Shui, the oriental art of placing objects in the home or office in such a way as to increase the natural flow of energy. This is in order to not only improve the energy level of the body and therefore increase basic health, but also to improve the mental processes of those who practice such procedures and therefore improve their personal and family relations.

Another way of increasing the flow of the body's natural energy relates to the traditional practice of the *sobadores* or massage therapists who use their skills to relieve muscular aches and pains.[16]

Along these lines, spas offering such procedures as mud baths and massages are also designed to increase the natural flow of energy in the body. In Mexico participants in the annual ritual of the solar equinox connected with the ancient Aztec Pyramids of the Sun and the Moon believe that these ancient constructions also give off healing energies which may be associated with what has for centuries been considered to be a holy place or because, as some believe, there is a mystical power in the pyramid structure itself.

We have already mentioned that the Buenos Aires area of Argentina is noted for having more psychotherapists per capita than any other place in the world, and it is often claimed that the main reason that so many people there seek out therapy is to help define their personal and national identity. For this reason it is interesting to note that in recent years a new approach to therapy has been developed. This is called ethnopsychopharmacology, an approach to therapy that emphasizes the effect that a patient's ethnic background has on his or her mental condition.[17]

Notable Healers

ARIGÓ

Although there are and have been many folk saints and popular healers who have claimed to be able to heal the sick by extraordinary means, it would be impossible to mention them all. However we can make note of some of the more well known of such healers. Indeed some of the healers of Latin America who have earned wide reputations in spite of their lack of real medical training have gained national and sometimes international fame. Perhaps the foremost of these is the Brazilian "doctor" known as Arigó.

In his biography of this healer, *Arigó, the Surgeon with the Rusty Knife*, John Fuller relates his amazing medical exploits. Arigó had no formal medical training when he decided to take an interest in politics. He accompanied a politician on an ambitious campaign for public office. This official had been diagnosed with chest cancer yet his doctor told him that it would be all right for him to take such a campaign trip. One night he saw his hotel door open as Arigó walked into his room holding a large knife. That was the last thing that he remembered. When he returned home he went to his doctor, who told him that his cancer was cured. Subsequently many people came to believe that Arigó had opened up this man's chest with a knife, he had operated on him without any bleeding and thereupon the politician became cancer free.

After that Arigó began a healing practice that became internationally famous. He would take patient after patient all day long. If an operation was necessary he would use what has been described as a rusty penknife and would operate without doing any formal diagnosis or even asking the patient to describe his or her symptoms. The reports of his healing activities went into the hundreds and thousands of cases, including a reported healing of the daughter of the then-president of Brazil, who had visited specialists in many countries unsuccessfully before she was cured by Arigó.

More unbelievable was the report that Arigó spoke Portuguese with a German accent even though he never went to Germany and he never studied the German language. Even more incredible was Arigó's reaction when medical personnel from the United States filmed his healings. It is said that he nearly fainted or actually did faint, explaining that all of his healing was done in a trance without him really being aware of his own medical activities; he claimed that he literally did not know what he was doing.

When asked how he could possibly be effecting all of those reported cures, he said that he had been contacted by the spirit of a doctor who had died prematurely in Germany many years before, at a time when he believed that he could have helped many more people if he had lived longer. Therefore he took over the body of the Brazilian to continue his healing activities through the body of a surrogate who happened to live in Brazil — our folk healer Arigó.

Claims of similar types of healing have been made elsewhere. In the movie *Man on the Moon*, the film biography of an eccentric U.S. comedian, the subject of the film went to the Philippines to seek out the curative powers of folk healers who supposedly operated without anesthesia and without causing any bleeding to their patients. However in that and in other cases that have been reported, little or no healing actually has taken place.

Arigó's international reputation rests on the numerous claims that he healed people. In fact, Arigó did get into trouble for practicing medicine without a license and he did spend some time in jail, but it was often rumored that he avoided more possible legal troubles because of the tacit backing of the then-president of Brazil, who believed that his daughter had been cured by the famed healer.[18]

THE MEXICAN HEALER "EL SANTO TATITA"

This healer, known as "Saint Tatita" or "*El santo Tatita*," was a well-known healer in Mier Tamaulipas. He gained a reputation as a saint who used divine power to heal and to foretell the future. A Catholic priest, Father Parisot, a French oblate missionary in Brownsville, Texas, during the 1860s, claims to have visited the supposed saint and to have attended his celebration of the mass in the main plaza. During this visit he said that this Catholic "saint" indulged himself in his own version of theology, stating that Almighty God had revealed to him that the faithful should adore God, say the rosary, and attend confession and mass, however all other religious practices in the church should be abolished.

Not surprisingly, this same Father Parisot declared that this renowned healer was nothing but a charlatan, stating that "the hand of God will someday smite him," to which the healer supposedly replied that he was going to amend his life and really dedicate it to God.[19]

EL NIÑO FIDENCIO

El Niño Fidencio was the name of a popular Mexican folk healer of the early years of the twentieth century. His reputation at that time exceeded that of "El santo Tatita." Born José Fidencio in 1898 in the northern Mexican state of Nuevo León, he led a conventional life until his talents as a healer began to receive notoriety. He apparently started working as a local *curandero*. Having gained the reputation of being very skilled in animal medicine, he assisted farm animals in giving birth and then he moved on to assist in human births. But Fidencio claimed to be much more than just a person who had the innate gift of healing. He stated that he had undergone a number of supernatural experiences in which Christ himself had appeared to him, and he had another supernatural visitation by a bearded man who imbued him with a great knowledge of healing plants as well as the spiritual gift or *don* of healing.

In addition Fidencio claimed that the divine providence visited him a second time in 1927 and told him to prepare for a large gathering of people who desired healing. Fidencio held such a meeting without those present apparently believing his claim that God had been reborn in the person of Fidencio himself. From that time on, Fidencio presented himself to the masses as a holy man capable of working supernaturally based cures.

By the late 1920s thousands of people seeking cures descended on Fidencio's town of Espinazo, building a so-called Camp of Pain (*Campo de Dolor*) or a settlement providing accommodations for the numerous visitors who put their hopes for a miraculous cure in this well-known healer. Whatever his real abilities may have been, he was credited with curing the blind and those suffering from paralysis among many other illnesses. According to reports in the Mexico City newspapers, Fidencio made the dumb speak and he even cured leprosy. As a result it is reported that his reputation extended not only throughout Mexico but to the United States and Europe as well.[20]

JUAN DE DIOS

Another world-famous Brazilian healer known as Juan de Dios (John of God) has held healing ceremonies in his remote village in the interior of Brazil for visitors from all over the world.[21]

A VENEZUELAN HEALER

Dr. José Gregorio Hernández studied medicine in France and returned to Venezuela in 1891. He then became professor of medicine at the Central University of Venezuela. Although a doctor trained in Western medicine, he was and is revered in Venezuela because of his charity work for indigenous patients. Although a traditionally trained doctor and not really what might be called a folk-healer, stories of this doctor's supernatural healing ability do exist in Latin America. Some believe that even after he was killed in an auto accident in 1919 he was seen delivering healing procedures to those that needed them.[21]

Peruvian Healing

In the ancient traditions of the Andes mountains, folk healers were and still are referred to as *kallawayas*. During the Inca empire, which stretched through large sections of the western mountains of South America, such healers worked from Panama in Central America down to the southern tip of Latin America using hundreds of native plants in the healing process. These remedies were supported by elaborate ceremonies and prayers to native gods.

As in other parts of Latin America, folk remedies in the form of herbs are sold publicly in open air markets. Coca leaves, for example have been chewed by native peoples in Peru and Bolivia for centuries to provide relief from a number of maladies, especially what is called *soroche* or altitude sickness.

Many local shamans and folk healers still live in mountain towns as they have for countless years dating back before the arrival of European settlers. Many of these are known mostly to local people, such as the popular healers Papá Pablo and Mamita Carolina, a healer who came from a small Peruvian village to the capital of Lima.[22]

Diagnosis for such healers may come from the interpretation of dreams, from hallucinatory states and through clairvoyance arising from the casting of coca leaves, which can be read like tea leaves and which are said to predict future events.[23]

Contemporary Perspectives of Folk Healing

Those who become familiar with the traditions of folk healing for the first time are likely to reject the claims of healing from *curanderos* and other local practitioners of traditional medicine as simply being nonsense. Or they may chalk up such real or supposed healing practices to the power of suggestion, similar to what is known as the placebo effect. Whether this is really the cause of the curative powers of such individuals, however, would have to be determined by direct investigation rather than by broad generalizations, usually made from afar, as is often the case with those who claim that their approach to understanding such phenomena is "scientific."

At the same time medical personnel trained in the Western tradition are beginning to take a new look at the placebo effect, this time applying what might be called a renewed dose of common sense to this concept, realizing that if it is true that the human mind can cure illness that defies contemporary medicine through the power of suggestion, then this must suggest that the curative powers of the mind are or can be much greater than was believed heretofore. It suggests that research in the future should center on this untapped power of the human mind and spirit rather than dismissing it as a mere curiosity or superstition.

Certainly strides have been made in recent years in the attempt to link modern medicine with schools of therapy from other cultures such as acupuncture and acupressure to mention only a few. This is done in the name of holistic healing, which tries to look at the patient in terms of his culture and his condition, as well as the possibility of curing him or her by way of alternative therapies like oriental Reiki. This includes the mind-body intelligence approach to healing which combines meditation techniques with Western and Buddhist psychology.[24]

But holistic medicine has another meaning. It can also refer to the attempt to see a patient in terms of his role in the total cosmos. Here, we approach once again an appreciation of the indigenous mind as it exists today in Latin America and in other parts of the world. One scientist has gone as far as to say that, "for most of us our basis for accepting the models and theories of our scientists is no more solid or objective than that of the voodooist who accepts the metaphysical theology of the hougan ... we scientists work under the constraints of our own illusions."[25]

Shamanism, after all, attempts to bring the body and the human spirit in balance with the rest of creation. It attempts to achieve a harmony with the natural world which has largely been lost in the highly industrialized world. Speaking of traditional healing, author Tom Crockett states, "We know what it feels like to live out of balance. It may begin as a nagging sense of dis-ease or discomfort — a lack of energy or enthusiasm for life. We should be happy but we don't feel happy.... We've lost the sense of the world as a living, animate web of relationships, and it is this fundamental imbalance that is fueling our search for meaning through healing therapies."[26]

Such interpretations of the way towards better health are controversial since they delve into our basic vision of what reality is and what it could be and what its limits may be. Readers may disagree with interpretations of the possible value of native healing, but what is certain is that our understanding of the popular mind and the popular culture of an area of the world as important as Latin America will never be complete unless we widen our own vision to at least try to understand an alternative view of the world and of our place in it.

XIII

Film

The cinema in Latin America has produced few works which have reached a worldwide audience although this is changing rapidly as actors and directors from that part of the world are now beginning to produce works which are commanding the attention of filmgoers everywhere. It may come as a surprise therefore to learn that although the cinema has long been a struggling industry in most of Latin America with the possible exception of certain nations such as Mexico, Argentina and Brazil, Latin American movies date back in some cases to the very beginning of the film era, including many works of silent film.

In the 1940s there was talk of a golden age of cinema in countries such as Mexico and Argentina, while certain film critics and historians began to speak of "The New Cinema of Latin America" in the 1960s. Whether this really was the beginning of a new wave in the history of Latin American film is still debatable, especially since any adoption of avant-garde themes and techniques was at best spotty and irregular. It would be difficult to define all of the film industry since that time in the same way.

Even in the most developed Latin American film traditions many difficulties have arisen for filmmakers which are perhaps particular to Latin America. In the case of Argentine director Carlos Sorín's *A King and His Movie* (*La película del rey*, 1986), the remarkable story of a Frenchman who tried to make himself king of Patagonia in nineteenth-century Argentina, British film critic Michael Chanan has commented that "it's a very good demonstration of why the epic is not a well-developed genre in Latin American cinema." The final irony is that despite winning an award at the Venice Film Festival, the film failed to cover its costs.[1]

The opposite has occurred in the case of television films known as *telenovelas*, which are a mainstay of Latin American visual entertainment. Beyond their large audiences in Latin America and the rest of the North American continent, these programs are routinely broadcast to upwards of one hundred countries throughout the world, thus bringing the collective audiences for these stories into the hundreds of millions if not billions of viewers. As a result, the performers gain an international reputation.[2] As an example, one U.S. tourist in the Middle East recently attended a religious ceremony in a Muslin mosque, and found that the clergyman who was conducting the ceremony looked at his watch towards the end of the proceedings. He told the faithful in attendance that he was cutting short the religious service so that he and his whole congregation could rush home to watch the latest part of a popular Latin American soap opera that was being shown in translation.

Argentina

Without question Argentina has one of the oldest and most productive cinematic traditions in Latin America. The first Argentine to make a film was an expatriate Frenchman by the name of Eugene Py whose short film *The Argentina Flag* (*La bandera argentina*) was shown in 1896. A surgeon, Dr. Alejandro Posadas, began to film his own surgeries in 1898. By 1900 the first movie theaters began to appear in Argentina. The first movie camera in Latin America was developed in Argentina while Mario Gallo made the film *The Shooting of Dorrego* (*Fusilamiento de Dorrego*) in 1896. This was the first film using a written script. In 1915 Humberto Cairo wrote and directed *Gaucho Nobility* (*Nobleza gaucha*), the first big box office hit in that nation.[3] Early silent films included *Amalia*, based on a classic Argentine novel of the same name, which was filmed in 1914, and *Gaucho Nobility*, completed in 1915.

Sound movies began in 1933. Important film stars in that era were the singer Libertad Lamarque and the comedian Luís Sandrini, whose works remained favorites of Latin American audiences for many decades to come. Soon as many as thirty films were produced in Argentina each year, and these films had enthusiastic audiences throughout the rest of Latin America, including as many as 200 silent films produced in Argentina alone.[4] Notable films of the 1930s included such works as *The Return to the Nest* (*La vuelta al nido*), by the gifted director Leopoldo Torres Ríos, whose work also included *Those Which We Love* (*Aquellos que amamos*).

In the subsequent decades various forms of censorship began to appear in the national cinema, however movie production continued to grow, especially due to the work of such talents as the singer, actor and filmmaker Hugo del Carril. He produced such works as *The Quintrala* (*La Quintrala*), based on the life of a notorious woman of colonial times, as well as the film *The Turbulent Waters* (*Las aguas turbulentas*).

In the 1950s, director Leopoldo Torres Nilsson achieved international fame for such works as *The House of the Angel* (*La casa del angel*), and *The Hand in the Trap* (*La mano en la trampa*). Also popular was the actor, singer and director Leonardo Favio, especially in his film *Chronicle of a Lonely Boy* (*Crónica de un niño solo*), while experimental cinema, often shown in quasi secret performances, included works like *The Time of Furnaces* (*La hora de los hornos*) and other films by such directors as Pino Solanas and Octavio Getino.

After a brutal military dictatorship, Argentine cinema has acquired new worldwide audiences with works such as the gaucho drama *Juan Moreira*, and *Rebellious Patagonia* (*Patagonia rebelde*). Recently *La tregua* (*The Truce*) based on a novel by Mario Bendetti was nominated for an Oscar. After the military dictatorship came films by the Oscar-nominated director María Luisa Bemberg, *Gardel's Exile* (*El exilio de Gardel*) and *The Internal Debt* (*La deuda interna*) along with other works by a new generation of filmmakers who quickly formed international reputations.[5]

Argentine Directors

Among the many notable and talented directors who have developed the Argentine cinema we might mention the following.

MARÍA LUISA BEMBERG

She wrote and directed *Camila* (1984), which deals with the era of the nineteenth century Argentine dictator Juan Manuel de Rosas, a film nominated for the Academy Award as the Best Foreign Language film. She also presented *The Worst of All* (*La peor de todas*, 1990), based on the life of the great Mexican poet Sor Juan Inés de la Cruz. She received many international awards, and her last film *You Don't Speak of That* (*De eso no se habla*), starred the famous Italian Marcello Mastroianni.[6]

ARMANDO BO

He enjoyed a long career in Argentine films, starring in *Ambition* (*Ambición*) in 1939, then going on to become a producer, screenwriter and score composer. Having had a hand in the completion of some 100 films, he was married to the internationally known actress Isabel Sarli, who starred in a number of his films.[7]

LEOPOLDO TORRES NILSSON

He was internationally known in his capacity as a director, producer and writer. The son of the early film director Leopoldo Torres Ríos, had began his career in 1947 with *The Wall* (*El muro*). He is known for his film adaptations of the works of classic Argentine authors such as Adolfo Bio y Cásares and Jorge Luís Borges. Perhaps he is best remembered for his film version of the national epic of Argentine literature, *Martín Fierro*, by the nineteenth century poet José Hernández. Many have regarded him as the first Argentine director to have achieved an international reputation.[8]

CARLOS SCHLIEPER

He worked as a director in what has been considered to be the classic era of the Argentine cinema, the 1940s and '50s. He wrote and directed some forty films, including *Alejandra* in 1956.[9]

MARIO SOFFICI

He was born in Italy, but he developed a career in the cinema of Argentina in the 1930s as an actor, then as a director. He directed *The Soul of the Bandoneon* (*El alma del bandoneón*) in 1935. He made many tango-based films with stars such as Libertad Lamarque, and he worked as an actor, director and screenwriter on such works as *Lost Kisses* (*Besos perdidos*, 1945), *Julia's Sin* (*El pecado de Julia*, 1947), and *Three Men from the River* (*Tres hombres del río*, 1943). He is also remembered for later films such as *The Folk Healer* (*El curandero*) made in 1955.[10]

LEOPOLDO TORRES RÍOS

Born in 1899 he produced over forty films working also as a director and writer between 1920 and 1959.[11]

KURT LAND

Kurt Land, originally Kurt Landesberger, was born in Vienna, Austria, yet he developed his film career in Argentina, having moved to the country in the 1930s. He edited at least 20 films in the era which has been called the golden age of Latin American cinema, before moving into the field of directing with such works as *Goodbye to Problems* (*Adios problemas*) in 1955 and *Alfonso* in 1957, starring Amelia Bence. His career in the Argentine film industry lasted until 1970, and it included his well-known works with popular Argentine actress Olga Zubarry.[12]

Mexico

According to film historian Carl J. Mora, what were called moving pictures were introduced into Mexico in 1895 by way of Thomas Edison's kinetoscope. In 1986 French pioneers of the film industry Louis and Auguste Lumière arrived in Mexico with their cinematographe, the first movie projector in Mexico, at 9 Platero Street in Mexico City. Viewers delighted to see such films as *The Magic Hat* and *The Card Players*.

In 1898 Salvador Toscano Barragán opened Mexico's first movie house, which was really a generic movie hall where he showed, among other productions, Mexico's first non-documentary film, *Don Juan Tenorio*, featuring the actor Paco Gavilanes.[7]

By 1908 movie houses had spread to the provinces, and Mexico watched its first major film made from a prepared script, which was entitled *The Cry of Dolores* (*El grito de Dolores*), which was a re-creation of Mexico's famous declaration of independence from Spain almost one hundred years before.

Much of pre-revolutionary Mexican cinema up to 1910 appears today to be propagandistic, designed mainly to glorify the administration of President Porfirio Díaz, and much of the heritage of the silent film era in Mexico is either lost or difficult to find.

According to Carl Mora, the first sound movie made in Mexico was *Stronger than Duty* (*Más fuerte que el deber*) in 1930, although many other film scholars date the first talking movie back to *The Saint* (*Santa*), based on the classic Mexican novel of the same name.

Starting with talking movies, a number of Mexican superstars began to appear, such as the luminary in the history of the Mexican cinema, María Félix. She is better known even today as "La Doña," a title with a double meaning referring to her eminence in the Mexican film industry and her starring role of the classic movie *Doña Bárbara*. It was a much-beloved film version of the classic Latin American novel *Doña Bárbara* (a play on words meaning "Miss Barbara" and "Miss Barbarian") by former president of Venezuela, Rómulo Gallegos.

María Félix performed other memorable roles in works such as *The Other Woman* (*La otra*) and *María Candelaria*, which also featured the international star Pedro Armendariz.

During the 1940s and '50s, often considered to be the golden age of Mexican cinema, many films offered now legendary stars the opportunity to gain international reputations. This certainly would include Mario Moreno, better known as "Cantinflas," who made dozens of comedies now considered to be classics in the Spanish-speaking world. Often referred to as the Mexican Charlie Chaplin, he was the creator of a beloved comic character whose pants perennially looked like they were about to fall down, while his face was adorned with cat-like moustache that sported an extra wide separation between both its left and right sides.

He starred in *There Is the Detail* (*Ahí está el detalle*), his first feature-length presentation, as well as *Neither Blood Nor Sand* (*Ni sangre ni arena*), a satire on the then-popular American movie based on the novel of the same name by the Spanish writer Blasco Ibáñez.

This was followed by many other hits such as *The Unknown Policeman*, (*El gendarme desconocido*), also starring Mapy Cortés and Gloria Marín, and *The Extra* (*El extra*) among many other popular works. Later, Cantinflas costarred with David Niven in Mike Todd's ambitious Hollywood version of Jules Verne's *Around the World in 80 Days*.

Closely following Cantiflas in popularity was comic actor Germán "Tin-Tan" Valdés, whose efforts included *Three Love Lessons* (*Tres lecciones de amor*) in 1959 and *There Are Dead People Who Make No Noise* (*Hay muertos que no hacen ruido*) in 1946. To this day, this popular entertainer is immortalized by a statue in his honor which stands in a park in one of Mexico's major cities, Ciudad Juárez.[14]

Also much-beloved are the films of another classic performer, Jorge Negrete. Well-known as a singing idol as well as for his work as an actor, he made many highly popular films including *The Devil's Godmother* (*La madrina del diablo*).[15]

The well-known Mexican Hollywood star Dolores del Río at first expressed her reluctance to work in the film industry of her own country, claiming that it had not reached a sufficient level of maturity to produce serious works. She later reversed herself as she went on to star in such works as *María Candelaria* (1943) and *Wild Flower* (*Flor silvestre*), which also premiered in 1943. Brazilian film historian Silvia Oroz considers that the support of the administration of President Miguel Alemán was instrumental in the development of Mexican cinema during this era.[16]

By the 1960s the varied themes of Mexican films included traditional cowboy dramas, better known to national audiences as *dramas rancheros* featuring the adventures of charros or Mexican cowboys; historic dramas: crime and horror tales and a series of comedies. These featured such stars as Sasha Montenegro, Pedro Weber (better known simply as "Chattanooga"), Lyn May, Maribel Guardia and Alfonso Zayas, among many others.

Some of these blended with the subgenre of *cabaretera*, films that took place in night clubs, dance halls or burlesque theaters. Perhaps the best known of these was director Alberto Bout's *Aventurera* (1952), starring Ninón Sevilla, a melodramatic opus about a young woman who is lured into the underworld of vice and corruption in Ciudad Juárez.

By the 1970s, Mexico was producing hundreds of films per year, including works by the internationally acclaimed director Alejandro Jodorowski, whose film *The Mole* (*El topo*) became synonymous with his shockingly surrealistic mode of creation. One other popular figure of the day was a wrestler named "Santo" (Saint), who performed in an endless series of dramas whose very titles would lead us to believe that they were intended for a popular or mass audience. These included such works as *Santo against the Diabolical Brain* (*Santo contra el cerebro diabólico*) in 1961, and *Santo v. Frankenstein's Daughter* (*Santo vs la hija de Frankenstein*), which must have delighted his loyal fans when it was presented in 1971.[17]

Mexican New Wave Cinema

The appearance of *Amores perros* (*Dog Love*), directed by Alejandro González Iñárritu caused him to receive international acclaim after its *estreno* or opening presentation in 2000. This film, which was nominated for an Oscar, is one of an increasing number of Mexican films that have gone on to receive international attention. Recently Mexican cinema has begun to delve into controversial subjects never presented before to a national mass audience. This was certainly true of *The Crime of Father Amaro* (*El crimen del Padre Amaro*), and *My Brother's Wife* (*La mujer de mi hermano*), which displayed the international dimension of the Mexican film industry, as it showed the collaboration of Peruvian director Roberto de Montreuil and the Uruguayan-born actress Barbara Mori. This movie, which also was released in the United States, was reported to have earned one million dollars in its first few days of presentation.

Perhaps the most impressive success that a Mexican film has had in the international arena has been *Like Water for Chocolate* (*Agua para chocolate*), based on a traditional Mexican expression indicating boiling anger. This film definitely showed international audiences the growing sophistication of the modern Mexican cinema.[18]

Mexican Directors

Among the many important directors in the history of the development of the Mexican cinema, the following are certainly worthy of attention.

ALFONSO CUARÓN

He is a Mexican director and writer as well as a producer who has been nominated for the Academy Award. His comedy, *Only with Your Partner* (*Sólo con tu pareja*) made an impact on national audiences. In 1995 he worked on the American film, *A Little Princess* as well as a film version of the classic by Charles Dickens, *Great Expectations* before returning to Mexico where he made *And Your Mother Also* (*Tu mamá también*), which became a favorite with international film fans. It earned him an Academy Award nomination for best original screenplay.[19]

EMILIO "EL INDIO" FERNÁNDEZ

Truly a classic name in Mexican cinema, Emilio Fernández received a long prison sentence during the Mexican revolution of 1910, however he managed to escape to the United States. Eventually receiving a pardon from President Lázaro Cárdenas, he returned to Mexico where he acted in *The Heart of a Robber* (*Corazón bandolero*) in 1934. After making *The Island of Passion* (*La isla de la pasión*) in 1942, he went on to direct two classics of Mexican film, *María Candelaria* (1943) and *Flor silvestre*, also made in 1943.[20]

ANTONIO SERRANO

He studied film internationally in Denmark and England as well as in Mexico. Starting his work in the Mexican television industry, he directed such stars as Salma Hayek and Gael García Bernal in Mexican soap operas. Working in the theater as well, he adapted the play *Sex, Shame and Tears* (*Sexo, pudor y lágrimas*) into a movie that won the Ariel Award from the Mexican Academy of Film. He was nominated again for the Ariel Award in 2004 for his work *Lucy, Lucy* (*Lucía, Lucía*).[21]

GUILLERMO DEL TORRE

He is another Academy Award nominee. His works include historical dramas and horror films. Two of his films, *The Devil's Backbone* (*El espinazo del diablo*) and *Pan's Labyrinth* (*El laberinto del fauno*), have received international attention. Del Torre wrote the screenplay for the latter work, which received six Academy Award nominations including Best Foreign Language Film.[22]

ALEJANDRO GONZÁLEZ IÑÁRRITU

Working initially in radio and television, his first film works included many short productions that led up to *Dog Love* (*Amores perros*) in 2000, an Academy Award-nominated film which starred Gael García Bernal. On the heels of this success he moved to Hollywood, where his film *21 Grams* earned Academy Award nominations for its lead actors, Benicio del Toro and Sean Penn. His latest film, *Babel*, received no less than seven Academy Award nominations.[23]

Cinema in Other Nations

Bolivia has produced such films as *Written in the Water* (*Escrito en el agua*) in 1997. *A Question of Faith* (*Cuestión de fe*), premiered in 1995, and *The Triangle in the Lake* (*Triángulo en el lago*) was filmed in 1999.

The cinema tradition in Uruguay goes back to 1896, however only recently have Uruguayan films begun to gain international attention with works like *Whiskey*, which won the Goya Prize at the Spanish Huelva film festival. Also winning prizes at Huelva was the *The Trip to the Sea* (*El viaje al mar*), while *The Wait* (*La espera*), directed by Aldo Garay, won an award at the seventh Festival of Latin American Film as well as the Latin American OCIC Award, announced at the Mar del Plata Film Festival in Argentina.

Paraguay's comparatively small cinema industry goes back to a short film in 1905, Hipólito Carrón's *Paraguayan Soul* (*Alma paraguaya*). Nevertheless, production has been slow and unsteady until recent decades, with such movies as *María Escobar* in 2002. Notable also was *Cora Hill* (*Cerro Cora*) in 1978, *The Woman's Secret* (*El secreto de la señora*) in 1989 and *The Land Was Burning* (*La tierra ardía*), which was filmed in 2005.

In Peru, director Francisco Lombardi made his first feature-length film, *Dead at Dawn* (*Muerte al amanecer*), in 1974. This story of a man condemned to death for a crime that he did not commit was followed by *The Wolf's Mouth* (*La boca del lobo*) in 1988. He is also known for his adaptations of the works of his countryman, the novelist Mario Vargas Llosa, such as *The City and the Dogs* (*La ciudad y los perros*) and *Pantaleon and the Visiters* (*Pantaleón y las visitadoras*) in 1999.

Recently the novels of Jaime Bayly, including *My Brother's Wife* (*La mujer de mi hermano*), have been made into movies, while Peru has the honor of having made the first 3-D animated film in Latin America, *The Pirates of Callao* (*Los piratas del Callao*).

In 2006, the film *Madeinusa*, a combined venture made by artists from Peru and Spain, won an award at the Rotterdam Film Festival. Other Peruvian films include *Anaconda* in 1997, *Anniversary* (*Aniversario*) made in 1992 and *In the Shade of the Sun* (*A la sombra del sol*) in 1967, which continued the tradition of pioneering Peruvian film efforts dating back to *Peruvian Soul* (*Alma peruana*) made in 1930.

In recent years Luís Llosa, the cousin of noted Peruvian author Mario Vargas Llosa, has been active in films that have garnered international attention.

Outstanding Chilean directors at the present time include Jorge Olguín, who specializes in horror and terror films like *Eternal Blood* (*Sangre eternal*, 2002), and *Black Angel* (*Angel negro*).

Outstanding is the word often used to describe the artistry of Chilean director Gustavo Graef-Marino, who has worked in Germany, Chile and in the United States. His film *One Hundred Dollar Johnny* (*Johnny Cien Pesos*, 1993), is a thriller that has been compared with the American movie *Dog Day Afternoon*. Subsequently he directed *Diplomatic Siege* in 1999 as well as *Instinct to Kill*.

Raúl Ruiz is the distinguished Chilean director of such films as *White Pigeon* (*Palomita blanca*, 1973). Working in France he made *Comedy of Innocence* (*Comedie de l'innocence* in 2000, and *Time Regained* (*Le temps retrouvé*) in 1999.

In Cuba, early versions of films were being shown as early as 1987. The first film actually made in that country was a documentary, *Imitation of a Fire* (*Simulacro de incendio*). From then until the Cuban revolution, some 80 films were produced. These included musicals which featured the talents of important musicians such as Bola de Nieve and Ernesto Lecuona.

In recent decades notable works have included *Memories of Underdevelopment* (*Memorias de subdesarrollo*), named by the International Federation of Film Clubs as one of the 100 best films of all time. Also popular was *Strawberries and Chocolate* (*Fresas y chocolate*) made in 1993 by Tomás Gutiérrez Alea and Juan Carlos Tabio.

The cinema of Venezuela is distinguished by the work of such directors as José Ramón Novoa, whose work includes *El Don* in 2004, *Devil's Gold* (*Oro diablo*) in 2000 and *Hired Assassin* (*Sicario*) made in 1994. Since the 1970s the national government has begun to support the film industry, which produced 29 movies between 1975 and 1980. Margot Benacerraf is a noted filmmaker with such works as the documentary *Reverón*, about the life of the Venezuelan artist Armando Reverón.

Mariana Fuentes has a resume which includes such films as *Lupe's Café* (*El café de Lupe,* 2007), and *Before the Scene* (*Antes de la escena*), made in 2004.

Fina Torres became internationally known after winning the Camera d'Or prize at the Cannes Film Festival in 1985. Her credits also include director's honors for *Oriana* in 1985 and *Celestial Clockwork.*[24]

Brazil

By all accounts the golden age of the Brazilian cinema has long passed. Yet there are strong indications that the largest country by far in Latin America is undergoing a cinematic renaissance, with more than 50 films in various stage of production. This will round out a history of some 2,000 films in that geographically and culturally diverse country over the past one hundred years. Indeed the film tradition started early in Brazil. In 1896 citizens in Río de Janeiro were treated to a presentation of visual images on what was called an omniograph machine. As early as 1908, when land in Hollywood was still described as real estate with "great potential" that sold for as little as forty dollars an acre, Brazil had already started its own film industry. Humberto Mauro has been considered the real pioneer of Brazil's movie tradition, with the release in 1933 of *Rough Gang* (*Ganga bruta*), while another early filmmaker had made a reputation for himself with silent films even before that with *Limit* (*Limite*) in 1929. A work which showed the influence of the European avant-garde, it is the moving story of three men adrift in a boat who tell their dramatic life stories.[25]

Later, classic names in comedy included Oscarito and Grande Otelo in the 1940 and '50s. Starring in works which have been called examples of the *chanchada,* a style of comedy unique to Brazil which includes farce combined with elements of a musical review, these films made by the classic Atlantida studio were supplemented by works of Brasil Filmes such as the hit *The Bandit* (*O cangaceiro*) in 1953. Post-war Italian neo-realism as seen in such classics as *The Bicycle Thief* influenced the movies of Glauber Rocha, a participant in what has been called "the aesthetics of hunger," a movement which also included works like Nelson Pereia dos Santo's *Dried Up Lives* (*Vidas secas*). In 1969 his *The Dragon of Evil Against the Warrior Saint* (*O dragão da maldad contra o santo guerreiro*) earned him the Cannes Festival award for the best director of a foreign film. The Museum of Modern Art in New York has included others of his films in its collection of the best films of all times.

Brazil's film heritage includes the movie version of works of some of its most renowned authors such as *Family Ties* (*Laços de família*, 1960), a film version of Clarice Lispector's earliest short stories, as well as that author's *The Hour of the Star* (*A hora da estrela*, 1986). This list would also include *Dona Flor and Her Two Husbands* (*Dona Flor e seus doîs maridos*) by Jorge De Amado and *Love Relations* (*Lição de amor*) by the classic Brazilian author Machado de Assis.[26]

Brazilian Directors

Foremost among Brazil's distinguished directors are the following.

WALTER SALLES

He is director of the Brazilian classic *Central Station* (*Central do Brasil*) which won awards at festivals in Venice, Cannes and Berlin. As the driving power behind the success of Video Filmes, he made his first work in 1991, *The Great Art* (*A grande arte*) and went on to make *Foreign Land* (*Terra estrangeira*) in 1995, a film about an expatriate Brazilian couple. His creativity is highly visible in this work, which won him prizes at the Paris International Film Festival. It was also shown at a dozen other international film festivals. One of his most recent films is *Countdown* (*Contagem regressiva*).

BRUNO BARRETO

He shot his first film *Tati, the Girl* (*Tati, a garota*) at age 17. Barreto, who has made more than a dozen films, has worked in Hollywood and other parts of the United States. He is perhaps best known for having made the popular Brazilian movie version of the novel *Dona Flor and Her Two Husbands* (*Dona Flor e seus dois maridos*) based on the novel of the same name by the internationally known writer, Jorge Amado. His work *What Is This Brother?* (*O que é isso, companheiro?*) ranks third in popularity in the history of Brazilian films. In the U.S. he has become well known for his work on films like *Show of Force*, a political thriller.

The work of other popular Brazilian directors includes Carla Camurati's *Carlota Joaquina Princess of Brazil* (*Carlota Joaquina princeza do Brazil*) and Tizuca Yamazaki's *The New Rebel*, which drew an audience of more than one million viewers on its first showing in the major urban centers of Brazil alone. Héctor Babenco's *The Kiss of the Spider Woman*, based on the novel by the Argentine author Manuel Puig, was nominated for an Oscar.[27]

A close view of the Latin American cinematic tradition indicates that it is much older and much richer than many international audiences and critics may believe at first glance. It is only recently that actors and directors from many Latin American countries are beginning to appear frequently in the international film arena, which garners the attention of countless hundreds of millions of filmgoers outside of Latin America. In addition it may surprise many film buffs outside of that part of the world to learn that what has been considered the golden age of movie production in a number of countries, we have seen, lies decades in the past, not necessarily in the present.

In the meantime many Latin American films have been international hits within Latin America itself, supplying entertainment for countless millions of viewers. They presented the great talents of legendary performers such as the Mexican comedic actor Cantinflas and the Argentine singer-actor Carlos Gardel, considered to have been one of the greatest matinee idols of the twentieth century, not just in Latin America, but in the entire world. Not to mention the names of actors who went on to gain fame in Hollywood, such as the Brazilian actress Carmen Miranda and the Mexican star Dolores del Río.

Still, in considering the history of this important aspect of popular culture, it would be hard to overestimate the impact of American movies, especially the popularity of major stars as reflected in the recent novel *The Betrayal of Rita Hayworth* (*La traición de Rita Hayworth*) by Manuel Puig. The Argentine novelist gives ample and vital testimony to the great impact made upon him and his contemporaries by Hayworth and other major American celebrities during what has been called the golden age of American movie-making.

XIV

Popular Literature

The first records of literature in Latin America go back literally thousands of years to poems, both oral and written, sacred books such as the *Popol Vuh*, the sacred book of the Mayas in Mexico, and dramas that formed part of religious ceremonies among pre–Hispanic peoples.

Texts of such theatrical works still exist and they include *Ollantay*, a work of mysterious origin which has been pegged by some scholars as a product of the ancient Inca culture of the Andean mountains of South America.[1]

In Mexico and Central America the drama *Rabinal Achí*, is likewise attributed to the early Mayan culture as are a vast store of thousands of largely unknown literary works which have become part of the oral tradition of indigenous people in such places as the Yucatan Peninsula in Mexico. There, the Cultural Institute of the Yucatan has been assiduously collecting these works and putting them in written form.[2]

Since native people carry their religious beliefs and legends from one generation to another by means of the oral tradition, it has sometimes been claimed that mankind has lost a great part of its memory bank with the invention of writing and mass communication. Native peoples around the world who do not read or write have been found to posses an astounding memory with the ability to remember literally hundreds if not thousands of literary works in their heads. Indeed an indigenous poet of the modern era was asked how she created her works. She answered that her people invented them long ago, and she was only the "secretary" that put the words down on paper. Of course in Latin America some of the popular pre–Hispanic literary traditions are still preserved in inscriptions, which archeologists and historians are still struggling to decipher. At the same time we must realize that the artifacts are only a small fraction of the archeological treasures that still await discovery. In Mexico alone there are an estimated tens of thousands of archeological sites. At any given moment it is likely that no more than a relative handful of these are being investigated by experts. In Bolivia an estimated thirty thousand such sites are believed to exist while only a relatively small number are being studied by qualified researchers.

At the same time local robbers and grave diggers, known in some areas as *huaqueros*, routinely excavate pre–European artifacts to sell them illegally on the international market.

Hispanic Popular Traditions

During the colonial period, much of Latin American literature, including works destined for *el pueblo* or the common person, were imitations of literary productions in Spain. For example, medieval religious dramas based on the story of the nativity were performed in Latin American countries. They still are today, not only in Latin America, at the Christmas season but also in areas of the United States where there is a high concentration of speakers of Spanish. These plays, commonly known as *pastorelas*, are part of a tradition which goes back many hundreds of years to medieval Spain.

Catholic missionaries in Latin America tried to teach Catholic doctrine to the Indians by way of morality plays known as *el teatro catequista*. Since many native people could not read or write the Spanish language, a visual and oral presentation of doctrine was considered the best way to reach the local population. Similarly, churches in medieval Europe had three entrances which symbolize the three persons of the Holy Trinity — a lesson in faith for people who generally did not read or write.

In the baroque colonial period, especially in the important cultural centers of early Latin America such as Mexico City and Lima, Peru, poetry contests took place as well as theatrical works that catered to popular tastes. These plays were often presented in the open air in public places such as the *corrales de comedia*, which basically meant anywhere the average person in the street congregated.[3]

Scholars often state that the beginning of popular satiric themes in Latin American drama dates from the comic works of the Peruvian dramatist Juan del Valle Caviedes. These skits were short comedies presented between the acts of the ponderous, serious dramas of the colonial era which often dealt with the vicissitudes of ancient gods and goddesses amidst the flowery trapping of the overly pompous theatrical styles of the day.[4]

Comedic plays must have been enjoyed as a breath of fresh air for the

Latin American audiences of that time, in contrast to the dramatic works which appear to have been second- or third-rate imitations of theatrical offerings presented at that time in Europe.

Indeed it has been said that the works of Caviedes mark the beginning of the Latin American theater, since they depict everyday life in situations which could be understood by the common man or woman.

Latin America continues its popular dramatic tradition until today in plays and skits presented in *carpas* or some other type of hastily assembled theatrical stage.

In Argentina the cowboy or gaucho literary tradition was for years a mainstay of that country's traditional literature, dating back before the publication of Argentina's most famous epic poem, *Martín Fierro*. This is the story of a wandering cowboy in the pampas of Argentina in the nineteenth century.

Dramatic presentations of the popular gaucho figure appeared in novels, poems and dramas dating back to the role of gauchos in circus performances. Indeed one such performer, known as Pepino el 88, was a clown working in the circus of Humberto I when he received an invitation to give a pantomime version of the legendary cowboy Juan Moreira, thus opening the gaucho tradition in Argentina and Uruguayan theater.

Through the centuries, many Latin American dramatists have dealt with the problems and conflicts of the everyday life of their countrymen and women without resorting to the extreme of what has been called expressionistic theater or the theater of the absurd.[5] These include Florencio Sánchez (Argentina),[6] Sebastián Salazar Bondy (Peru), Samuel Eichelbaum (Argentina), René Marqués (Puerto Rico), and Rodolfo Usigli (Mexico), to mention only a handful of the hundreds if not thousands of writers who have contributed to the Latin American dramatic tradition in modern times.

This includes such works as *Collacocha* by the Peruvian author Enrique Solari Swayne, which dramatizes the perennial Latin American theme affecting the lives of millions of people — the struggle of man versus nature. This play also introduced one of the most memorable characters of modern Latin American literature, the larger-than-life engineer named Echecopar.

Also we might mention the powerful plays of another Peruvian author, César Vallejo, better known as one of Latin America's most outstanding poets, who captured the concerns of the working masses in his dramas denouncing the injustices inflicted on them.[7]

As noted before, the soap opera remains the most popular form of drama in Latin America as a vehicle for dramatic expression for the mainstream of society. Singers and actors who take part in these works often have a worldwide following.

Fiction

The Latin American novel was a latecomer to literary expression in the Americas, with the first novel in Spanish, *El periquillo sarniento* (*The Mangy Parrot*) published in 1816. Prior to that the novel had not been an expression of popular tastes since it was actually prohibited or highly discouraged by local authorities, who brought the strict policies of the Spanish inquisition to Latin America.

From the earliest days of long fiction in Latin America, however, popular types began to appear in print. First and foremost is the *pícaro* or rogue, a type of anti-hero descended from older models in Spanish peninsular literature — a figure that some literary critics assert gave birth to modern literary realism.

Throughout the nineteenth century and the first half of the twentieth, Latin American fiction was generally concerned with the problems of the common man by way of themes such as man against nature, as seen in the classic Colombian novel of the jungle, *La vorágine* (*The Vortex*) by José Eustacio Rivera.[7]

The grim stories of the Uruguayan Horacio Quiroga as well as novels protesting social injustice toward workers and peasant farmers would fit into this category, as would gaucho novels such as the Argentine classic, *Don segundo sombra*, by Ricardo Güiraldes. Well known also is the Brazilian class novel *The Devil to Pay in the Backlands* by Guimãres Rosa.

Common also were indigenous figures of the so-called *Indianista* and *indigenista* novels, as well as the peasant soldiers of the novels of the Mexican Revolution. The most famous of them was *Los de abajo* (*The Underdogs*) by Mariano Azuela. Colorful also are the depictions of the *llaneros* or rural cowboys of Venezuela. A story by the former president of Venezuela, Rómulo Gallegos, featured them and was immortalized in the well-known classic of Latin American cinema, *Doña Bárbara* (Miss Barbara), starring the great Mexican film star María Félix.

An important aspect of fiction works of this period is *costumbrismo*, the use of local color such as names of exotic flora and fauna as well as popular types such as gauchos and Indians in picturesque locations. Popular dialectical speech also fills these works to the point that all of this "scenery" comes to be the soul of the narratives themselves with the plot developments often appearing almost as window dressing. In such works it is not uncommon for an author to interrupt the basic conflicts that form the plot in order to dedicate a chapter or two to the description of a rodeo or other ranch-based activities with the colorful cowboy dress and rural language taking precedence over the basic plot development.

More recent developments have included the trend towards experimental works which are supposedly not for mass consumption such as *Rayuela* (*Hopscotch*), by the Argentine Julio Cortázar.[8] In this category we would have to include the stories of Jorge Luís Borges, arguably the most complicated writer of the twentieth century in the Spanish language, as well as the novel by the Novel Prize–winning Colombian writer Gabriel García Márquez, *Cien años de soledad* (*One Hundred Years of Solitude*).[8]

Although not really designed for the mass-market reader as mentioned, amazingly, many of these books are read or at least known by millions of Latin Americans. It would be difficult to speak with an Argentine citizen with even a smattering of education who is not familiar with the works of Jorge Luís Borges, and just about any Latin American reader has read or at least heard of *One Hundred Years of Solitude*.

Here, as in the case of language, national pride is an important factor. Latin Americans take great interest in their national writers even though they may not write on a level that might be traditionally called "popular taste." If a visitor were to disparage Argentine writer Jorge Luis Borges in comparison with other internationally known literary figures, the average citizen of Argentina would take umbrage.

In addition, many so-called literary novels have a strong basis in popular beliefs.[11] A good example is the classic of modern Mexican literature, *Pedro Páramo* (*Peter Páramo*), by Juan Rulfo, which represents a fragile demarcation between the living and the dead that reflects age-old Mexican beliefs in *ánimas en pena* or souls in torment in the next world that return in daily life to ask us to pray for them so that they may rest in peace. The same may be said of the play *Los fantoches* (*The Puppets*) by the Mexican dramatist Carlos Solórzano, the fantasy of a group of puppet figures who wait for their eventual destruction. The author has stated that the premise for this work is the Mexican popular custom of the *quema de Judas* or the burning of puppet-like figures of Judas at the celebration of the Easter season.

Many popular modern novels in Latin America often lack traditional plot development, which has been called the Latin American "anti-novel." Critics have noted that this is not only a reflection of avant-garde literary styles coming from Europe and North America. It also shows the influence of pre–Hispanic popular cultures that did not believe in chronological time but rather in cyclical time. For indigenous cultures, progress often did not exist in the future but rather in imitating the epic achievements of gods or traditional heroes in the past. In the destruction of plot or chronological time such novels have also been compared to pre–Hispanic mosaic art as well as to musical works that repeat certain melodies and themes in thematic importance rather than logical order.

Popular Genres

A number of observations can be made about the genres of Latin American popular fiction designed for the masses. Certain types of fiction which are popular in the Anglo-Saxon world do not appear to be as popular south of the border.

For example, mystery fiction, which is written by certain authors such as Jorge Luis Borges. He admits his fondness for English authors of detective stories such as G.K. Chesterton, but his stories reach a profundity of meaning and philosophical analysis which far transcend this well known popular genre.[11]

Of course there are writers of mystery fiction, most especially in Argentina, including such authors as Bioy Cásares, Mempo Giardinelli, Ricardo Piglia, Marco Denevi, Sergio Olguín, Manuel Puig and Jerónimo del Rey, better known as Leonardo Castellani. Less known are the stories of Chilean creator Alberto Edwards, the inventor of a Chilean Sherlock Holmes type of detective, Julio Téllez.[12] Also worthy of note are the excellent Inspector Espinosa novels, *December Heat*, *The Silence of the Rain* and *Southwesterly Wind*, by the Brazilian author Luis Alfredo García-Roza.

Still the vast number of mysteries which have been written in the English language during the twentieth century is not equaled in the Spanish language.

Romance

Romance novels also fall into this category of less-popular genres. The Spanish author Corín Tellado has acquired a large following in Latin America but it would appear that few mass-market authors, such as a Latin American Danielle Steele or Barbara Cartland, have yet to come forth. Although there are some works of romance fiction available on the shelves of Latin American bookstores, up to recently they have mostly been translations of novels published originally in other languages. This contrasts with the estimate that the best-selling works of fiction in the United States today are romance novels, with women constituting the largest segment of the fiction-reading public.

Science Fiction

Although the tradition of literary fantasy is well developed in Latin America, it does not generally include works of medieval fantasy nor science fiction. Stories of trips to other planets, visits by aliens or even about alternate futures do not seem to have a great place in the repertoire of Latin American fiction in the past or present. Nevertheless some works of science fiction do exist such as a short story by Marco Denevi, in which he conjectures about the world of the twenty-third century in which machines dominate the world and people no longer exist. Likewise, Peruvian author Clemente Palma wrote a novel, *XYZ*. We might also mention *El libro de la tierra negra* (*The Book of the Black Earth*) by Argentine novelist Gilberto Guardini, considered to have been Argentina's first real science fiction novel.[13]

We would have to also add the little-known story by Mexican author Martín Luis Guzmán, *Como acabó la guerra en 1917* (*How the War Ended in 1917*), which has been considered the first real science fiction narrative in Mexican literature, as well as the stories in the book *Cuentos de magia, de misterio y horror* (*Stories of Magic and Mystery and Horror*), by the Costa Rican writer with long residence in Mexico, Cardona Peña.[14]

Political Espionage Thrillers

As popular as this genre is in novels, movies and television drama in other parts of the world, the political or espionage thriller also fails to stand out as an important home-grown product of Latin American literature, even in a very popular sense of the word, with the exception of foreign works that are translated or subtitled in the movies or on television. The most notable genres or themes that come close, however, are the dictator novels, with the best-known being *Mr. President* (*El señor presidente*) by the Nobel Prize-winning author from Guatemala Miguel Asturias, as well as *Yo supremo* (*I the Supreme One*) by the Paraguayan author Augusto Roa Bastos and *La hidra* (*The Hydra*) by Carlos Fuentes.

Related genres, however, may be found in the historical and political conflict in many novels of the Mexican revolution, its most notable example being *Los de abajo* (*The Underdogs*) by the Mexican author Mariano Azuela.

Although such works do deal with political events, they rarely show conflict unfolding as a result of spycraft or unexpected political conspiracy, as in the espionage thriller. Furthermore the hero rarely if ever has the responsibility of saving the entire world, as is often the task of the familiar James Bond-type character.

Strangely, traditional histories of Latin American literature never comment on the lack of popularity of such genres as the political or espionage thriller. Perhaps this is because of the overly popular orientation of these genres. Still, the reason for this difference in taste is not generally recognized nor explained.

Perhaps the key may be found in the statement of a Latin American who once hosted the author and his family at a ranch in a very isolated area of Central America during a period of dictatorship. She commented that she had read a popular thriller that was a worldwide bestseller, but said she found it to be of little interest. She said living in a country such as hers with the volatile political developments that occurred on a frequent basis, she did not have to reach for a book to look for excitement. It was always present.

Westerns

Even though we may realize already that Latin Americans do not share the U.S. fascination with historical events in the western parts of their countries as more violent or more colorful aspects of their cultures, we have noted before that traditional works of Latin American fiction frequently deal with rural areas replete with characters which represent *el pueblo* or the common man, such as the Argentine Gaucho cowboy.

The differences with the traditional American western are notable in that the Latin American cowboy or rural novel rarely dwells on violence for the sake of violence. It tends to shy away from presenting characters that go around with loaded guns looking for a fight; nor does it usually present hard-bitten characters who claim to make their living as gunslingers.

Nevertheless most U.S. readers may not realize that the American cowboy tradition actually started with the Mexican cowboy, simply because a large part of the western United States belonged to Mexico for more years than it has been a part of the United States. As a result, much of the western ranch life actually harks back to the Mexican cowboy or *charro*.

The first rodeos took place on Mexican ranches, with the word "rodeo" itself, as well as many other cowboy terms such as "palaver," "hombre," "calaboose," "corral," and "lasso," actually coming from the Spanish language.

The Essay

Latin America is a place where the essay is alive and well. It is an area where a multitude of issues applying to the whole spectrum of human life such as are discussed by the common man or woman on a daily basis are commented on in written form.

Among some of the most important essay writers of modern times in

Latin America are Octavio Paz (Mexico), Germán Arciniegas (Colombia), José Enrique Rodó (Uruguay), Osvaldo de Andrade (Brazil), and Jorge Luis Borges (Argentina) among many others.

While in other societies life appears to be increasingly considered as a quasi legal-governmental affair, with the majority of essays that the public reads perhaps being political columns in newspapers and magazines, in Latin America essays are still being written on general questions such as the search for Latin American identity.

One of the most famous early essays in Latin America, "Facundo," by the Argentine author Domingo Faustino Sarmiento, compares nineteenth-century Argentina with the United States, finding the former to be a country symbolized by the political strongman Facundo, while the U.S. boasts of a more democratic society.

While these speculations may appear to be the province solely of intellectuals, they express issues of immediate concern to the mass of the inhabitants of the lands south of the United States. During the Sandinista war in Nicaragua, for example, one report indicated that young Nicaraguans were reading the anti–American thoughts of one of the influential essay writers, José Enrique Rodó, such as in his well-known work, *Ariel*.

Indeed much of Latin speculation about identity centers around the search for personal as well as the national identity. Many Latin Americans wonder if they are indigenous people with only an overlay of European culture or if they are an extension of European culture with only some vestiges of Indian and African cultures?

Poetry

Latin American poetry is truly a form of direct and popular communication, not just an expression of emotion in a book for scholars and literary critics. It is a living, breathing part of everyday life which remains in the mainstream of culture. Cigar workers used to hire poetry readers to recite poems as they wrapped tobacco leaves. It might be hard indeed to conceive of assembly line workers in other cultures doing the same.

Likewise student demonstrators in Mexico City in 1968 marched in the thousands as they recited the moving words of the gifted Chilean writer Violeta Parra.

In Brazil the tradition of chants and poetic choruses sung aloud goes back for centuries.[15] Mexico has the tradition of popular ballads or *corridos* which number literally in the thousands. These popular poetic works recall the heroic deeds of the Mexican revolution of 1910 among many other themes.

Today Mexican movie actor Eric del Castillo has recorded some of these ballads, making them available to millions of listeners by way of the modern CD.

These songs are so up-to-date that there are even *corridos* recalling the illegal activities of drug dealers or *narcotraficantes*, anti-heroes to be sure, whose lyrics have caused a national furor to the point that many Mexicans have called for these recordings to be declared illegal.

A curious popular poetry tradition in Mexico is the one in which short poems known as *calaveras* or "skulls" are exchanged on the Mexican Day of the Dead, when Mexicans celebrate the memory of departed loved ones with altars decked out with skulls, food and mementoes. Bakers prepare cookies in the shape of a human skull and these cookies are given to others as sincere tokens of friendship, and a gesture of warmth and affection. These baked goods come with poetic inscriptions dedicated to the recipient, describing what type of person they were when they were alive, even though, of course, they are not dead.

What is most surprising to visitors from other countries is that Mexicans are pleased to receive such gifts as they are a measure of their popularity with friends and co-workers. It must be understood that in Mexico the symbol of death is an ancient one that has long been an important part of popular culture. Indeed skulls and skeleton figures appear frequently not only in Mexican poetry, but also in the art of such creators as José Guadalupe Posada and Diego Rivera as well as in Mexican handicrafts.

Indeed the theme of death in works of Mexican literature reflects the whole popular cultural perspective of that country. One of the foremost Mexican authors of modern times, Salvador Novo, writes in his poem, "Renewed Death," that "We have all been arriving at our tombs/ at a good hour/ at the right time/ In ambulances that charge reasonable prices/ either from suicide or from natural causes."[16]

In these and so many other customs, both in Mexico and in other parts of Latin America, we find a link to an ancient, mythically abundant past where the forces of life are celebrated and brought into daily life by way of poetry which repeats and recalls age-old customs that have emerged from the popular mind ever since time immemorial. For, as the great scholar of comparative religions Mircea Eliade has stated so well, "Archaic man acknowledges no act which has not been previously posited and lived by someone else.... His life is the ceaseless repetition of gestures initiated by others." He goes on to say that "any meaningful act performed by archaic man ... suspends duration, abolishes profane time and participates in mythical time."[17]

XV

Food

The cuisine of any country or any part of the world is a basic and important part of the culture of that area at both a high cultural level, if you include haute cuisine, and a popular cultural level, if you include the tastes of the masses.

Food does much to establish the cultural identity of a people, and it often is what we might called the best ambassador to the rest of the world, especially in terms of internationally famous cuisines such as Chinese, Italian and French. Still the majority of Latin American cooking remains unknown to most people in the U.S. and many people will go to a Mexican restaurant to order tacos and burritos and then come away thinking that Mexican food consists only of these two food items and nothing more.

This unfortunate stereotype extends to much of Latin America, as many consumers don't know about home-grown cuisine in countries like Peru or Chile simply because they have never encountered a Chilean or Peruvian restaurant, nor have they ever seen a cookbook with recipes from those or many other Latin American nations.

Perhaps it is a tendency of human nature to confuse our ignorance with reality. If we don't know about it, it doesn't exist. The same tendency can be observed in relation to other aspects of life south of the U.S. border. Some people say Latin Americans have no literature because everyone lives in abject poverty and no one can read or write. This is despite the extremely high level of literacy in such countries as Mexico and Costa Rica, to mention only two examples, and despite the title of one reference book on Latin American literature which claims to list ten thousand Latin American authors.

The same lack of awareness pertains to the cosmopolitan nature of urban life in Latin America. A person once said that he didn't want to go to Mexico because he didn't like Mexican food. Given the vast richness of Mexican cuisine, with literally thousands and thousands of recipes, one would have to wonder exactly what kind of food he was referring to.

Even more shocking in terms of negative stereotypes is the lack of awareness that Latin American cities are as international in terms of food as any U.S., European or Canadian city, where just about any type of national cuisine can be found. In a metropolis like Mexico City, which boasts a population of some thirty five million people including the suburbs, the number of restaurants and types of food available is almost endless. For someone to say they don't want to go to Mexico because they don't like Mexican food would be tantamount to a traveler in another country saying that he didn't want to go to New York City because he didn't like hot dogs or hamburgers, as if no other food choices were available.

Not only is the study of Latin American food a complicated matter, but it is often the case that food styles will vary from one section of a country to another. One time while visiting Peru we came upon a book of recipes from the provincial city of Arequipa. We were amazed that this reference work appeared to be as thick as the phone book of any major city in the United States.

Because of the vast complexity and richness of Latin American food traditions it would be beyond the scope of this book to mention each and every variety of food and its style of preparation, let alone the complete list of ingredients in all the cuisines, however we can get some idea of the richness of these traditions by focusing on a number of the best-known and most popular cuisines of that vast part of the world.

Chile

One of the most famous products of Chile is wine. In Europe during the nineteenth century, a plague killed many varieties of grape including the Carmenere grape, which was exported to Chile, and which still survives and is cultivated as a staple in Chilean wine making. Other Chilean drinks include *pisco*, a type of brandy liquor popular both in Peru and Chile which is frequently made into *pisco sour*, a cocktail made of such elements as lemon, sugar and egg whites. *Piscola* is *pisco* with cola, and *navegao* is warm red wine served with oranges and sugar. *Vaina* is a cocktail made up of port wine, sugar and cinnamon.

Typical Chilean entrees include *empanada de pino*— an empanada filled with meat, onions, raisins and olives along with an egg.

Bistec a lo pobre combines steak and French fries with onions and fried eggs.

Cazuela de ave is a local variety of chicken soup that includes potatoes and green beans or peas along with meat.

Charquicán consists of meat combined with spices such as garlic, onions and pumpkin.

Pernil is a salted hock of ham.

Costillas de chancho is a Chilean variety of spare ribs.

Parrillada combines varieties of meats that are grilled then put on a plate along with such items as rice or potato salad.

Porotos granados is a serving of beans with corn and pumpkin.

Given the importance of Chile's port cities such as Valparaíso, and its extensive coastline that hugs the edge of the Pacific Ocean, seafood forms an important part of Chilean cuisine. Typical local dishes include:

Almejas con limón— clams with lemon.

Empanada de marisco— sandwich-style empanadas filled with seafood, onions and assorted other spices.

Seviche or *ceviche*—raw fish marinated in lemon or lime.

Mariscal is a soup served cold, combined with uncooked seafood.

Typical Chilean sandwiches include different types of *churrasco*, which is the generic Latin American name for beef, often found in the simple beef sandwich or *churrasco* sandwich.

Churrasco con palta is meat mixed with avocado while *churrasco con tomates especiales* and *Italianos* are varieties of hotdog. *Lomito completo* is made of pork along with sauerkraut and other types of dressings such as mustard and ketchup.

Among popular Chilean desserts are the *alfajor*, a pastry topped off with chocolate; *kuchen*, a type of flan; *berlín*, a tasty donut loaded with a sugary filling; and *papaya con crema*, which is simply a papaya topped off with cream.

In recent years the Chilean wine industry has grown by leaps and bounds to the point that it is now one of that country's leading exports. At the same time the fishing industry remains extremely important, and the importance of seafood as a basic staple can easily be seen in the list of national specialties above. The important Germanic influence in the country, which is part of the southern cone of Latin America including Argentina as well as Chile, can also easily be seen in the above list, especially in terms of Chile's tempting dessert specialties.

Like Latin Americans in general, Chileans like to take time with their meals since food is not simply a physical need. It is the setting for a social exchange of ideas ranging perhaps from the ridiculous to the sublime. That is to say that conversation is enjoyed for the pure sake of conversation, without many limits put on the pragmatic value of the topics under discussion.

As a country in which the indigenous population has not had a cultural influence as decisive as those in Mexico, Ecuador and Peru, the heritage of the specialties from the native palate may not be as visible here as it may be in some other areas of Latin America, nor is the famed spicy nature of Latin American foods as much in evidence as it might be in a country like Mexico. Again, stereotypes can be misleading as much in the area of food as in any other aspect of life, and what is true for one country may not be true for another, for food reflects not only native plants and soil but also the heritage of those who settled in a particular nation, the climate and the proximity to the sea as well as other features of the natural world.[1]

Argentina

Just to say the name Argentina (which comes from the Spanish word for silver, or being covered with silver) brings to mind an immediate association with beef and cattle-raising. It is true that the varied geographical features of this large Latin American country include vast prairie lands better known as *las pampas*, ideal for cattle ranches and the production of meat products. Indeed not only in Argentina itself but just about anywhere in Latin America a restaurant advertising itself as an Argentine food establishment probably prides itself on its meat dishes, especially charcoal-broiled steaks.

To some, Argentina is synonymous with the pampas, and some years ago a well-known Argentine prize fighter by the name of Luís Firpo was nicknamed "The Wild Bull of the Pampas." The gauchos or Argentine cowboys celebrated in film, fiction, drama and such poetical works as the national epic poem of Argentina *Martín Fierro*, are a colorful group of individuals that have always possessed a popular culture of their own. This encompasses the *boleadoras*, their own type of lasso; the *facón* knife, which some believe may have been an inspiration for the North American "Bowie knife"; as well as other aspects of their way of life which has been commemorated and celebrated both in and out of Argentina.

Nevertheless as we have already noted, the foreign influences in Argentina have been strong, especially the influence of Italian culture, and perhaps nowhere is this more obvious than in the specialties which appeal to the Argentine palate. This would include various types of pizza such as *pizza por metro*, *pizza a la parrilla*, and *pizza canchera*.

Of Italian origin also are *tallarines* (fettucini) or *ravioles* (ravioli), *noquis* (gnocchi) and *canelones* (cannelloni). Also Italian polenta is popular as is *sorrentino*, which did not actually originate in Italy but rather in Argentina as a kind of large ravioli with cheese, topped off with tomato sauce.

Empanadas are popular, as they are in many parts of Latin America, and the Spanish influence in food can be found in the popularity of *churros*, which are long pieces of pastry; flan or custard and *tortillas*.

Popular pastries include *medialunas* as well as rolls known as *piononos* and *alfajores*, which are cookies combined with what is called *dulce de leche*, all of which are known to tempt the Argentine taste buds, especially at dessert time.

Northwestern Argentina boasts of the production of such delicacies as *dulce de batata* and *Dulce de membrillo*. Southern Argentina can count on such dessert items as *chocantes*, *rosa mosqueta* and *zarzaparrilla* (sarsaparilla).

Argentina has a coastline, however the consumption of fish has been relatively low while wine production, both domestic and for export, has formed a notable part of the Argentine economy for many years. *Quilmes* is national beer named after its place of origin in the town of Quilmes.

With the coming of English settlers to Argentina in the nineteenth century, tea became a popular drink as well. Most notable is a well-known Argentine brand of tea know as *mate* or more familiarly as *yerba mate*. This is a variety of tea which is drunk from a small, hand-held container, usually a gourd or some item with a similar shape. The tea sipped through a *bombilla* or long straw. As with other types of tea, *mate* may be drunk as is or it may be sweetened with sugar or some other substance to suit one's taste.

Of course the consumption of beef is a mainstay of the Argentine diet and grilled meat said to be cooked *a la parilla* is highly popular. *Bifes* and *churrasco* are highly popular as are different types of sausages such as *chorizo*, which are consumed in large quantities as well. In the southern part of Argentina, lamb and goat meat is popular along with *sanwiches de miga* which are combinations of meat, cheese and lettuce.

The cuisine of Argentina is truly then a mixture of the various cultures which have come to that fascinating country. Perhaps little is left over from the traditional dishes of the early settlers of the pampas, the gauchos, yet they too have left their imprint on the culture of this country in many important ways, as have successive waves of immigrants from Germany, Italy, Spain and just about any part of the world that we might wish to consider. The flavor of this society is rich and varied, just as rich and varied as is its cuisine, which beckons to the visitor to give it a try, tasting its complexity and its sophistication.[2]

Colombia

The cuisine of Colombia varies greatly depending on the climate of each region. For example in Medellin, a popular dish is *bandeja paisa*, made up of ground meat, sausage, eggs, *arepas* or flour tortillas and rice. In Bogota and other mountainous areas, *ajiaco* is a popular item. This is a soup composed of potatoes and chicken seasoned with an herb known as *guasca*.

In the Caribbean section of the country, seafood is very popular. Frequently it is prepared with hot spices and coconut rice, while in the Amazonian region cooking often takes on the tastes which are most popular in the tropical area of neighboring Peru. Staple foods in Colombia also include *sancocho* soup, *arepas*, and tamales, which are frequently wrapped up in plantain leaves, as well as the soup known as *cuchuco*, which is often composed of beans, wheat, potatoes and peas.

Popular desserts include *algodón de azúcar*, which is really cotton candy; *dulce de maduro, dulce de papaya* or *dulce de las tres leches*, which combines three different types of milk; *cocadas*, which combine fruits such as coconuts and sugar; and *bocadillo*, which is guava paste.

In terms of drinks, Columbia's best known product is coffee, which is ground in areas of the country where the climate is especially suited for it. *Aguardiente* (literally *agua ardiente* or burning water) is a common alcoholic drink as is *guarapo*. *Chicha* is a popular alcoholic drink among native peoples of the Andean region, and is found in Peru and Ecuador as well. It is made of fermented corn or other similar food products. *Canelazo* is a drink made by combining *aguardiente* or a similar beverage with cinnamon and sugar. Its power punch is reflected in its name, since the suffix "azo" in Spanish often refers to a blow or direct hit of some kind or other.

Colombian fruits come in endless varieties including many which are all but unknown in non-tropical climates such as *mamey, chontaduro, coroso, zapote, mamoncillo* and *chirimoya* among others.

Colombia is a great producer of bananas, including plantain bananas which are often fried then served with sugar or some other condiment.[3]

Brazil

The cuisine of Brazil is divided by region.

The north includes the huge tropical rain forest where native people consume a diet of basic foods consisting mostly of fish and local plants including tropical fruits. Typical recipes from this region are *picadinho de jacaré*, which is made from alligator meat.

The northeast has areas which show a marked influence of African culture, including such specialties as *vatapá* and *moqueca*, which is seafood seasoned with palm oil, and *acarajé*, which is a type of muffin. Various types of rice and beans are also popular.

Contrary to popular opinion, Argentina is not the only Latin American country that has a well developed cattle-raising industry. Brazil boasts of numerous ranches, perhaps more than can be found in Argentina itself, and of course meats such as beef and pork form an important part of the national menu along with other foods which are grown in the region such as corn, rice and manioc.

In the southeast, including Minas Gerais, Rio de Janeiro and São Paulo, Brazil's principal urban centers, variations on staples like rice and beans are found in such dishes as *virado a paulista, arroz e feijão, rajadinho* and *carioguinha*. In addition, numerous types of meat dishes, often accompanied by such favorites as fried bananas and manioc flour, are traditional favorites.

In the major urban areas as anywhere in large cities in Latin America, food influences from just about every part of the world are prevalent. Preferred is the dish called *moqueca capixaba* composed of fish, tomatoes and a perennial favorite in the Hispanic world, *chourizo*, a sausage found here in its Brazilian variety or *chouriço*.

In addition, tropical fruits such as *açai* and *cupuacú* are used as a basis for various different dessert specialties. Also popular are *salgadinhos* and *pão de queijo*, a type of bread, as well as *pasteis*, pastries whose very name is similar to its Spanish language counterpart, *pasteles*.

Among its other products, Brazil is a cheese-producing nation with pizza, as in so many countries, being a perennial favorite for vast numbers of Brazilians. A liquor known as *cachaça* is popular, while the most famous national drink is probably what is known as *caipirinha*. When vodka is the basis for this drink rather than the aforementioned *cachaça*, the result is a drink commonly known as *caipirosca*, while rum is sometimes used a basic ingredient as well.

Brazil is known far and wide as a coffee-producing country and coffee is served under a variety of names including *café duplo*, double espresso; *café com pingo*, coffee with milk; and *café glacê*, or iced coffee.[4]

Peru

The geography of Peru is amazingly varied, contrasting between the coastal area, the Andes mountains, which include some of the highest mountain peaks in the world, and the dense jungles which form a part of the Amazonian rain forest. Given that country's long sea coasts it is little wonder that seafood is an important part of the national cuisine. Prominent among popular Peruvian foods is *ceviche*, which is often considered to be Peru's national dish. This is prepared with corbina fish, lemons and garlic. In addition, many other types of seafood are popular in Peru, including *chupe de camarones* (shrimp soup), *sopa de choro* (green mussel soup), *chupe de cangrejo* (crab soup), *parihuela* (fisherman's soup or stew), *milanesa de pescado* (fish fillets served in an Italian style) and *pescado con salsa tamarindo* (fish fillets with tamarind sauce).

Among an almost endless number of other seafood specialties are *aji de langostinos*, shrimps in aji cream sauce; *cau cau de mariscos*, scallop and octopus stew; *chita refrita*, the local fried fish with Creole sauce; and last but not least *lenguado a lo macho*, which in spite of its forbidding name is simply grilled flounder in a so-called macho-style spicy sauce.

The many salads that enrich the Peruvian palate include such delicacies as *saltero de queso zarza*, fresh cheese salad; *ensalada mixita*, mixed vegetable salad; and *ensalada de pulpo*, octopus salad. Other recipes include *causa limena*, and *arroz con pato*, or duck with rice.

Cacerola de cholco, the latter word being the local Quechuan word for corn, is a mixture of ground chicken and corn.

Potatoes are also a staple of the Peruvian table, and a favorite is called *papas a la huancaína* or potatoes *a la huancaína*, prepared with boiled potatoes topped off with a sauce made out of cream and different types of cheese.

In the interior of the country, especially in the mountainous areas, *pachamanca*, a local type of barbecue, is highly popular. This is barbecued meat cooked in the ground, often for many hours. *Chicharrones* or pork is also popular with corn tamales.

Peru enjoys a variety of fruits which complement a wide variety of local recipes. These include *chirimoya*, *guanábana*, *tuna*, papaya and mango.

Among a wide number of regional dishes we might mention *timpo* or *puchero*, which is a combination of lamb, bacon, potatoes, chickpeas and rice, as well as *chuño cola*, a broth mixed with sausage, rice, chickpeas and potatoes combined with a local food item called *chuño*.

A popular Peruvian drink is *pisco*, often enjoyed in the form of a cocktail know as *pisco sour*.

Like other Latin American countries, Peru enjoys a wide selection of cuisines served in restaurants with an international flavor. Perhaps most notable among these are Chinese restaurants called *chifas*, which are known for their beauty, size and landscaping as well as the richness and variety of their food. Peru also enjoys a variety of less-known regional foods waiting to temp the tourist who ventures into the hinterland of this fascinating Latin American nation.[5]

Mexico

Mexico is a country with a wide variety of climatic regions and a wide variety of geographical settings. Accordingly there are variations of cuisine in each part of this important country. Staple food products are corn, commonly called *elote*, beans or *frijoles* and tomatoes or *jitomates*. Contrary to popular opinion, Mexican food is not uniformly hot or spicy, and the variety of popular plates not to mention the basic ingredients that go into typical Mexican recipes is vastly complicated. Sausages, *salchichas* or *chorizo*, which are found in one uniform size in many other countries, hang in Mexican supermarkets and meat markets in dozens of sizes and varieties.

The well known chile, famous in its red and green varieties, actually comes in more than forty different types, and a good Mexican cook would have to know when to use each one. Popular also are *fajitas*, which are made with chopped onions, molasses, lime juice, garlic and other assorted spices mixed with sirloin steak cut into strips. Add a cup of salsa and cream and tomatoes and cheese while all of this is folded into a tortilla and the result is tempting to the taste buds.[6]

Mexican food is prepared traditionally with age-old cooking utensils including a *molcajete*, a mortar and pestle used for onions and tomatoes, as well as a *comal*, or cast iron griddle used for heating up tortillas (not to be confused with the same word in Spain to refer to omelets), which are pieces of dough that serve the same function as bread as the basis for a sandwich. They are filled with various kinds of meats, cheeses, vegetables and spices.

Guacamole is a highly popular dip made of ground up avocados spiced with lemons, onions and chopped garlic. Mexican Salsas come in many varieties, all combining tomatoes with chopped vegetables and such flavorings as onion, chilies and garlic among others.

Other basic staples of the Mexican table are beans, or *frijoles*, and cheese; *enchiladas*, which are tortillas rolled around meat or cheese cooked in a casserole; and *empanadas*, turnovers either served either with meat or dessert-like fillings.

Very basic to Mexican cuisine also is *mole*, which is a thick sauce made of onion, garlic, sesame or pumpkin seeds and chocolate.

Mexico is an important producer of chocolate. The English word is derived from the Spanish word which is spelled the same. It was enjoyed by native Mexicans long before the arrival of Spanish settlers.

Other Mexican desserts include Flan or custard, Mexican wedding cookers, honey *sopaipillas*, and Mexican sugar cookies or *polvorones*.

The variety of Mexican candies is so great that they are commonly sold in special stores known as *dulcerias*, while Mexican bakeries offer a bewildering variety of cookies and pastries each with their own separate name, so that even a casual visit to a typical Mexican bakery can be a time-consuming affair.

Mexico produces a wide selection of brands of beer and it is also a wine-producing country. Mexican liquors include kahlúa and the popular drink *rompope*, which has a flavor similar to holiday eggnog. Very well known is Mexican tequila, a potent concoction derived from the agave plant found in the state of Jalisco, where this drink is distilled according to age-old methods, some of which actually go back to pre–Hispanic times.

Although not as well known as Colombia or Brazil as a coffee-growing country, Mexico produces some varieties which are sought after by gourmet coffee lovers throughout the world.

Mexico has many coastlines and seafood plays an important role in the national diet, with *huachinango* or red snapper being one of the most highly prized delicacies of traditional cuisine. At the same time many Mexican meals would not be considered complete without some serving of soup such as *pozole* or *sopa de tortillas*, or tortilla soup.

Truly Mexican cuisine comes in an almost dizzying variety, with something to suit just about every tastebud. One of the reasons Mexican and other Latin American cuisines are so good is because cooks to use fresh ingredients available from a local market on a daily basis, while the animals who graze on Latin American farms and ranches eat organic food or feed with fewer additives, hormones and colorants. This benefits locals as well as tourists.[6]

The Caribbean

The tropical climate of the Caribbean produces a large number of fruits as well as many other agricultural products which have found their way into the cuisine of this part of the world. This includes such items as rice, yucca, papaya, chile, corn, *guayabas*, and sugar, among many other products. Seafood is also a staple of many countries in this region. The influence of traditional meals of Spain can be found in *caldo gallego* (Galician style soup), *arroz con habichelas* and *moros y cristianos*, the black beans and rice of Cuba, called *moro* in the Dominican Republic.

Above all, bananas shine in Caribbean cuisine. Fried bananas are a perennial favorite, cooked in oil and sweetened to taste with sugar. The coast of Venezuela and part of the coast of Colombia border on the Caribbean, showing its influence in music as well as cuisine. Popular in Venezuela is what has been called the national dish, *el pabellón criollo*, which is meat fillet cooked with cumin and served with black beans and rice. In fact, beans are such a staple in the Venezuelan diet that they have been called the *criollo* caviar.

Another dish which is almost synonymous with Colombia and is consumed in great quantities on its Caribbean coast as well as in other parts of that country is *sancocho*, a soup which is also popular in Panama and Venezuela. This is composed of sweet potato, chicken, onion, garlic, oregano, chilies, yucca and corn, boiled in a large pot or *olla*.[7]

XVI

High Culture —
Popular Culture

Given the strong connection between the popular culture that has been the subject of this volume and "high culture," namely symphonic or classical music, artwork important enough to be shown in museums and works of literature as opposed to popular genres, it is worth recalling the statements that we have already made about the popular nature of much of the culture in the part of the world under study.

This trait, which holds true in almost all of this area, is to a large extent a result of the modern or twentieth-century tendency to reevaluate indigenous and African cultures.

In the field of music we may note popular influences in the themes of notable composers such as Heitor Villa-Lobos, who formed part of a group of composers who used Brazilian folk music in their modernistic compositions in the important Week of Modern Art celebrated in Brazil in 1922. Perhaps his best-known compositions outside of Brazil are his *Bachianas Brasileiras*, which combine the counterpoint style of Bach with traditional local melodies.[1] However, even before that, another Brazilian composer, Brasilio Itibere, showed the influence of the folk music of his nation in his composition *Sertaneja* (1869).[2]

In Puerto Rico, Juan Morel Campos adapted the European minuet, combining it with popular Caribbean rhythms.[3] In Mexico, Juan Manuel Ponce utilized traditional melodies in his brilliant piano pieces at the same time that Carlos Chávez wrote his *Sinfonía India* (*Indian Symphony*) that requires the use of indigenous instruments. Notable also is the brilliant

Huapango, a symphonic piece by Mexican José Pablo Moncayo, who found his inspiration in the native sounds, rhythms and sound patterns of the music of Veracruz, Mexico.[4]

Most recently in Mexico the very gifted young composer Mauricio Vázquez has revived indigenous melodies in his celebrated *Sinfonía Azteca* (*Aztec Symphony*).

In the field of literature, the melding of African-American and Indian elements into what have often become classics of Latin America are legion. To mention only a few important works we might refer to *El Indio*, by the Mexican author Gregorio López y Fuentes; the novels of the Peruvian José María Argüedas, as well as those of another Peruvian author, Ciro Alegría, creator of such novels as *El mundo es ancho y ajeno* (*The World Is Wide and Alien*); the Bolivian Alcides Argüedas, author of *Raza de bronce* (*Bronze Race*) and the *Leyendas de Guatemala* (*Guatemalan Legends*) by the Nobel Prize-winning Miguel Angel Asturias.[5]

The world of artistic creation likewise shows the very same indigenous influence. We have already noted the importance of Indian subjects and themes in the murals of the Mexican artist Diego Rivera, however it is worthwhile to also mention the native-based elements in the paintings of the Cuban artist Wifredo Lam, who even went so far as to find inspiration in the native Santería religion for his work *La jungle* (*The Jungle*).

Osvaldo Viterini of Ecuador was a member of a whole school of indigenous or *indigenista*-inspired painters. His compatriot Camilo Egas did a mural entitled *Festival Indio Ecuatoriano* in 1932 while other Ecuatorians like Estuardo Martínez and Aníbal Villacis composed a series of artworks called *Precolombinos*, thus making them part of a generation of creators that looked for inspiration in age-old traditions.

The Brazilian painter Cándido Portinari broke with traditional European-inspired art by featuring blacks and mulattos as prominent figures in his art.[6] Likewise Joaquín Torres-García, a pioneering Uruguayan modernist, went back to ancient cultural roots for the inspiration for his painting *Pachamama* or *Mother Heart*. In Peru, José Sabogal sought inspiration in the native cultural traditions, and his woodcut of an Indian face became famous when it was displayed on the cover of the first issue of the influential cultural and literary journal *Amauta*.[6]

The above are only a handful of serious artists who have delved into their national backgrounds to do homage to their important cultural heritage. This acceptance of ancient forms of expression should be seen as a great movement towards Latin America's acceptance and reevaluation of its formative roots as well as a realization of what traditional popular culture can and still is contributing to us today. Times have indeed changed, for in colonial Peru, at one time the Spanish government actually forbade the wearing of Inca costumes and the use or teaching of the native Quechua language.[7]

Any absolute division between the different spheres of social and artistic patterns in this, as in many parts of the world, would have to appear artificial. Yet in light of the studies of high culture and its value to human society, a greater appreciation of the profundity, pervasiveness, and richness of Latin American popular culture will complete our understanding of this increasingly vital section of the Western Hemisphere.

XVII

Conclusion

Our study of Latin America shows us that the popular culture of this part of the world is indeed popular. This is to say that the roots of social patterns and traditions not only reflect tastes and tendencies which enjoy popularity in today's world, they literally reflect what the people or the *pópulo* (or the *pueblo* in the Spanish sense of the word, meaning the common man) have felt, lived and enjoyed for centuries if not for thousands of years.

Popular culture then refers not only to what enjoys mass appeal today in terms of marketing and commercial success. It goes right to the heart of our existence. In terms of Latin America it includes, in addition to the European traditions brought by the Spanish and Portuguese, the African and Indian ways of life. An awareness of the vibrancy of these diverse sensibilities has much to do with a basic issue — the search for national and hemispheric identity which has marked Latin American thought patterns, especially in the essay, for centuries. The basic question therefore may be, is Latin America, or at least most of it, a continuation of indigenous Indian and African cultures with a layer of European culture added as a kind of icing on the cake, or did the European mind alter the native societies to the point that this part of the world is basically European in its social orientation with small, and relatively unimportant vestiges of native cultures hanging on as a reminder of the past without any real legitimacy in the modern world?

On the basis of our study alone we can conclude that the indigenous elements in the ethos of Latin America are still alive and well, and they have had a decisive influence on what has characterized much of the social and artistic heritage of this area of the globe for centuries. Nevertheless it is to be hoped that a study such as this one will also put us on guard against making sweeping generalizations, as many do, to the effect that all nations of the southern part of this hemisphere are alike, and therefore they all march in lock step with each other. Such is not the case nor has it ever been the case. Just as an example, the indigenous traditions in some Latin American countries are obviously much stronger and more influential than they have been in others. This heritage may allow us to see, perhaps for the first time, a unity between Latin and North American sensibilities, since just as in the case of music alone, many of the popular traditions of the United States in terms of jazz, blues, rhythm and blues and rock and roll, come generically from deep African roots, as does much of the popular music of Latin America.[1]

No one volume can hope to solve this monumental question of national and hemispheric identity to everyone's satisfaction, but a study of patterns of living such as is presented in this work may help the outside observer to make some enlightened judgments. Still, a study of popular culture must make an author as well as his readers aware that the vastness of the traditions in question makes it impossible to form a comprehensive or all-inclusive catalogue of the endless variations of popular tastes in art and in life in such a complex group of republics.

This is also significant not only to bring to the fore an awareness of the richness of Latin American popular culture, but also to help the casual observer define his or her terms. Frequently people say they like or don't like "Spanish music." The phrase must most directly refer to the music of Spain, however that country also has rich and varied artistic traditions including many forms of music, ranging from classic to highly popular music, and music and dance which characterize the multiple diverse regions of that complex nation.

The music of each country of Latin America as well as the various regions each country and the types of musical instruments used are different. To talk about "Latin American music" as good or bad is akin to saying you don't like the music of the U.S. after hearing a jazz recording. The musical heritage of the United States is also, of course, incredibly rich and varied. Music in the U.S. ranges from classical and operatic traditions to country and western music, Tex-Mex, new age, blues, pop ballads and a whole host of other genres.

Although we have often emphasized the sub-strata or indigenous and highly traditional aspects of Latin American culture there may still be those that believe that these aspects of society and art are the *only* bases for the Latin American tradition. For that reason it is important to mention that as we look at what might be called high as well as popular culture, to the surprise of many perhaps, there does exist a tradition of classic and operatic music native to Latin America. As a matter of fact it is a documented reality that the first opera written and performed in the Western Hemisphere was *La púrpura y la rosa*, composed by the Peruvian Tomás de Torrejón y Velasco, which was performed in Lima in 1701. Also the first symphonic orchestra in this hemisphere began performing in Caracas, Venezuela, in 1750.[3] In more modern times, the youngest classical composer to have a work premiered by the prestigious Milan Conservatory in Italy, the training ground of some of the greatest composers of the classical tradition, was the superbly gifted Mexican Mauricio Vázquez.

In today's world, art and architecture in Latin America are definitely as avant-garde and experimental as any other artistic forms in any other part of the world. And Latin American artists and intellectuals are as globalized in their thinking and in their awareness of worldwide trends in their fields as anyone else; they frequently study internationally and they know of artistic developments in every part of the globe.

But our awareness of the living patterns of millions of persons in the Spanish and Portuguese-speaking parts of our hemisphere goes beyond a study of artistic traditions to include attitudes and actions which form an intimately basic aspect of daily life, including the conduct of business on all levels and in many forms, all levels of education, home and family life and many other topics. Above all, we have begun to investigate the way in which Latin Americans see themselves and their nations, and how they look at government and law as basic parts of their lives. Of course when dealing with hundreds of millions of people we have had to make broad generalizations which should make us pause to realize that these are, after all, just that, generalizations, and there must always exist numerous exceptions to any abstraction that we might wish to conceive in our minds.

In the last analysis perhaps any study of culture must remain incomplete, since this is a study of patterns of human life, and human life and human nature, in spite of innumerable studies in the field of psychology, still defy complete understanding. As St. Augustine is supposed to have said about one person talking to another person about the nature of God, this is a situation in which one mystery speaks to another mystery about an even greater mystery.

To the extent that this is true, the study of culture, especially comparative culture, is a study of life itself, and such a study is never complete, nor can the last word ever be spoken or written. Accordingly then, we are left with a challenge as well as an opportunity for further learning throughout our lifetimes.

After all, the open road to greater understanding stretches out, right there in front of our eyes. It beckons to us to travel through its highways and byways for the rest of our lives.

Chapter Notes

Preface

1. See for example Robin Varnum and Christina Gibbons, eds., *The Language of Comics* (Jackson: University of Mississippi Press, 2001).

Chapter 1

1. Alex Bradbury, *Belize: The Bradt Travel Guide* (Guilford, Conn: The Globe Pequot Press, 2000).

2. Geoffrey Fox, *Hispanic Nation, Culture, Politics, and the Constructing of Identity* (Secaucus, N.J.: The Carol Press, 1996); Himilce Novás, *Everything You Need to Know about Latino History* (New York: Penguin Putnam, 1998); Jaime Eyzaguirre, "Promise and Prejudice in Spanish America," in R.A. Humphreys and John Lynch, eds., *The Origins of the Latin American Revolutions, 1808–1826* (New York: Alfred A. Knopf, 1969), 256–261.

3. Hubert Herring, *A History of Latin America from the Beginning to the Present* (New York: Alfred A. Knopf, 1959); Frank Tannenbaum, *Ten Keys to Latin America* (New York: Alfred A. Knopf, 1962).

4. Leopoldo Castedo, *A History of Latin American Art and Architecture from Pre-Columbian Times to the Present* (New York and Washington: Frederick A. Praeger, 1969).

5. Liliana Najdorf, *Mashimón* (Buenos Aires: Editorial Galerna, 2001), 30, author's translation.

6. Angel del Río, *Historia de la literatura Española* (New York: Holt, Rinehart Winston, 1961) vol. 1, 206–246.

7. Dámaso Alonso, "La novela española y su contribución a la novela realista moderna," *Cuadernos del idioma* (Buenos Aires), Ano 1, num. 1, 17–43.

8. Himilce Novás, *Everything,* p.175. Remember that Mexico City was the largest city in the world even as far back as the days when the Spanish first came to Mexico in the sixteenth century. See Charles C. Mann, *1491: New Revelations of the Americas Before Columbus* (New York: Vintage Books, 2006).

9. Mário de Andrade, *Macunaíma,* trans. E.A. Goodland (New York: Random House, 1985).

10. Enrique Anderson Imbert and Lawrence Kiddle, *Diez cuentos latinoamericanos* (New York: Appleton Century Crofts, 1960).

11. Carlos Castañeda, *Journey to Ixtlán, The Lessons of Don Juan* (New York: Simon & Schuster, 1972), 8.

Chapter 2

1. Alejo Carpentier, "Prologue: The Kingdom of This World," in Ilan Stavans, ed., *The Oxford Book of Latin American Essays*

(New York: Oxford University Press, 1997), 197.

2. Irving A. Leonard, introduction to Mariano Picón-Salas, *A Cultural History of Latin America*, trans. Irving A. Leonard (Berkeley and Los Angeles: University of California Press, 1968), ix.

3. Mariano Picón-Salas, *ibid.*, 24.

4. For more information on this topic see Pablo E. Pérez-Mallaina, *Spain's Men of the Sea*, trans. Carla Rahn Phillips (Baltimore and London: Johns Hopkins University Press, 1998), 243.

5. Randall Peffer, "The Powerful Magic of Comandatuba," *Fate* (January 1994), 54–58.

6. Scott Corales, "Santería: A Belief for Our Times?" *Fate* (January 1994), 48–53.

7. Himilce Novás, *Everything You Need to Know about Latino History* (New York: Plume Books–The Penguin Group, 1994), 212.

8. Interview with Mexican artist and writer Yolanda Salido Arriola.

9. For more information about an historically influential Mexican psychic see William Curry Holden, *Teresita* (Owings Mills, Md.: Stemmer House Publishing, 1978).

10. David St. Clair, *Pagans, Priests and Prophets* (Englewood Cliffs, N.J.: Prentice Hall, 1976), 24, 177, 178.

11. Antonio Vázquez Alba, *Experiencias insólitas del brujo mayor* (México City: Futorología Editores, 1999), author's translation.

12. Leopoldo Zea "Concerning an American Philosophy," Stavans, *Oxford Book*, 266; Alfonso Reyes, "Notes on the American Mind," Stavans, *Oxford Book*, 88.

13. Stavans, 88.

14. Jorge Luis Borges, *Other Inquisitions, 1937–1952*, trans. Ruth L.C. Simms (New York: Simon and Schuster, 1968), 33.

15. Luis Rafael Sánchez, "Caribbeanness" in Stavans, *Oxford Book*, 418, 419.

16. José Luis Martínez, *Unidad y diversidad de la literatura latinoamericana* (Mexico City: Joaquín Mortiz, 1979), 22, author's translation.

17. Stephen Tapscott, *Twentieth-Century Latin American Poetry: A Bilingual Anthology* (Austin: University of Texas Press, 1996), 19.

18. No Yong-Park, "A Chinese View of the American Character," *America in Perspective*, ed. Henry Steele Commager (New York: Random House/The New American Library, 1962), 291.

19. Osvaldo de Andrade, "Anthropophagite Manifesto," Stavans, *Oxford Book*, 97.

20. A talk given at the American International College, Springfield, Mass., April 14, 2005.

Chapter 3

1. Ana C. Jarvis and Luís Lebredo, *Spanish for Business and Finance* (Boston and New York: Houghton Mifflin, 2000); Donna Reseigh Long and Janice Lynn Macian, *De paseo* (Boston: Heinle & Heinle, 2005), 63–87.

2. Arturo A. Fox, *Latinoamérica presente y pasado* (Upper Saddle River, N.J.: Prentice Hall, 2003), 313–330; Germán Arciniegas, *El continente de siete colores* (Buenos Aires: Editorial Sudamericana, 1965).

3. Candace McKinniss and A. A. Natella, *Business in Mexico* (New York: Haworth Press, 1993).

4. Carlos Fuentes, *Tiempo mexicano* (México: Joaquín Mortiz, 1971), 26; Mariano Velázquez de la Cadena et al., *The Velázquez Dictionary of the Spanish and English Language* (El Monte, Calif.: The Velazquez Press, 2003).

5. "Professor Sees Our Future in Soaps," *Boston Globe* (February 11, 2001), C 21; Ibsen Martínez, "Romancing the Globe," *Foreign Policy* (November-December, 2005), 48–57.

6. Don Richardson, "Communication, Culture and Hegemony: From the Media to the Mediations," *Canadian Journal of Communication* (Jan. 1, 1994), quoted in http://www.cjc.online.ca/viewarticle.php?id=260.

7. Héctor René Lafleur and Sergio D. Provenzano, *Las revistas literarias* (Buenos Aires: Centro Editor de América Latina, 1968), 64–70.

8. For more information about the Caribbean aspects of the Spanish language see Augusto Malacret, *Vocabulario de Puerto Rico* (New York: Las Américas, 1955). This author deals with local terms found in many parts of the Caribbean, not just in Puerto Rico. He lists such local terms as *chiquear*, "to spoil" (Cuba); *ojanco*, a fish found in that area and *nanguería*, a joke or jest, among many other local terms.

9. Fox, *Latinoamérica*, 17–28.

10. For more information about the Spanish spoken in border regions and in the southwest in general, see the excellent work by Roberto A. Galvan and Richard Teschner, *El diccionario del español chicano* (Lincolnwood, Illinois: National Textbook Co., 1986).

11. Velázquez de la Cadena, *The Velázquez Dictionary*; Martha Olivella de Castells et al., *Mosaicos* (Upper Saddle River, N.J.: Prentice Hall, 2001). Note the words of the Colombian scholar Rufino Cuervo, "Nothing in our opinion, symbolizes our country as well as our language, in it is symbolized what is most cherished by the individual and by the family" (author's translation). Rufino Cuervo, "Apuntaciones críticas sobre el lenguaje bogotano," *Cuadernos del idioma* (Buenos Aires), Ano 1, numero 1, 143.

12. Miguel de Cervantes, *Don Quixote de la Mancha*, trans. Peter Motteux (New York: Random House, 1941), 212.

13. Ramon Saldivar, *Chicano Narrative: The Dialectics of Differences*, ed. Frank Lentricchia (Madison: University of Wisconsin Press, 1990).

14. Luigi Barzini, *The Italians* (New York: Bantam Books, 1968).

15. Raymond L. Gordon, *Living in Latin America: A Case Study in Cross-Cultural Communication* (Lincolnwood, Illinois: The National Textbook Company, 1990).

Chapter 4

1. L.A. Wilkens, *A Spanish Reference Grammar* (New York: Henry Holt and Co., 1923), 49.

2. Hygino Aliandro, *The Portuguese-English Dictionary* (New York: Pocket Books, 1965), 276, 109.

3. Ana C. Jarvis and Luis Lebredo, *Spanish for Business and Finance* (Boston and New York: Houghton Mifflin, 2000), 135–140.

4. Eugenio Chang-Rodríguez, *Latinoamérica: su civilización y su cultura* (Boston: Heinle & Heinle, 2000), 27.

5. Enrique Anderson Imbert and Lawrence Kiddle, *XX cuentos latinoamericanos* (New York: Appleton-Century-Crofts, 1960).

6. J. García López, *Historia de la literatura española* (New York: Las Américas Publishing Co., 1964), 325–336.

7. Poem quoted in Eduardo Gudiño Kieffer, *Será por eso que la quiero tanto* (Buenos Aires: Editorial Emecé, 1975), 5.

8. J.M. Stewart, *American Cultural Patterns* (Camden, Maine: Intercultural Press 1976).

Chapter 5

1. Edward C. Stewart, *American Cultural Patterns: A Cross-Cultural Perspective* (Yarmouth, Maine: The Intercultural Press, 1972), 53.

2. Eric Lawlor, *Bolivia* (New York: Vintage Books, 1989), 139.

3. For a study of this concept see Philip K. Howard, *The Death of Common Sense: How Law Is Suffocating America* (New York: Random House, 1994).

4. Steve Scott, "Jury Acquits ex-Dallas Officer of Theft," *The Dallas Morning News*, (Nov. 9, 1995), 38A.

5. "The Battle for Latin America's Soul," *The Economist* (May 20, 2006), 11.

6. *Costa Rica, Land of Pure Life*, Video Visits World Travel Library, 1992, videocassette.

7. *The Boston Globe*, (Aug. 1, 2006): A1.

8. Ramón Menéndez Pidal, *The Spaniards in Their History*, trans. Walter Starkie (New York: W.W. Norton and Co., 1966), 44–74.

9. Quoted in Bill Richardson, *Spanish Studies: An Introduction* (London: Arnold Publishing, 2001), 38; *Spanish Culture and Society: The Essential Glossary*, ed. Barry Jordan (London: Arnold and Co., 2002).

10. Julián Marías, *Meditaciones sobre la sociedad española* (Madrid: Editorial Alianza, 2005), 17. For more on this subject see Uslar Pietri, "The Other America," *The Oxford Book of Latin American Essays*, ed. Ilan Stavans (New York: Oxford University Press, 1997), 207–215.

11. Burton Bollac, "Bolivia's Indian Majority Goes to College," *Chronicle of Higher Education*, vol. L11, No. 45 (July 14, 2006): A36.

12. Unpublished monograph by Eve Taylor.

13. Eugenio Chang-Rodríguez, *Latinoamérica: su civilización y su cultura* (Boston: Heinle & Heinle, 2000), 81.

14. Burton Bollac, "Bolivia's Indian Majority," A36.

Chapter 6

1. Edward T. Hall and Mildred Reed Hall, *Hidden Differences: Doing Business with the Japanese* (Garden City, N.Y.: Doubleday Books, 1987).

2. James Surowiecki, "Punctuality Pays," *The New Yorker* (April 5, 2004), 31.

3. Neil Chesanow, *The World-Class Executive: How to Do Business Like a Pro Around the World* (New York: Rawson Associates, 1985), 268–272.

4. Candace McKinniss and A. Natella, *Business in Mexico* (New York: Haworth Press, 1991); Gus Gordon and Thurmon Williams, *Doing Business in Mexico: A Practical Guide* (New York: Haworth Press, 2002).

5. Chesanov, 27.

6. Sandra Snowdon, *The Global Edge: How Your Company Can Win in the International Marketplace* (New York: Simon & Schuster, 1986), 293–366.

7. Albert Koopman, *Transcultural Management: How to Unlock Global Resources* (Cambridge, Mass.: Basil Blackwell,1991); Alfred M. Jaeger and Rabindra N. Kanungo, eds., *Management in Developing Countries* (London and New York: Routledge Publishers, 1990), 193–222.

Chapter 7

1. Sheryl Lindley, "U.S. Americans and Mexicans Working Together: Five Core Mexican Concepts for Enhancing Effectiveness," in Larry A. Samovar and Richard E. Porter, *Intercultural Communication*, (Belmont, Calif.: Wadsworth Publishing Company, 1999), 335–341.

2. E.S. Kras, *Management in Two Cultures* (Yarmouth, Maine: The Intercultural Press, 1989).

3. Robert T. Moran et al., *International Business Case Studies for the Multicultural Marketplace* (Houston, London: Gulf Publishing, 1994), 267–278, 285–300; Larry Hirschhorn, *Managing in the New Team Environment: Skills, Tools and Methods* (Reading, Mass.: Addison Wesley, 1991); Roy W. Poe, Rosemary T. Fruehling, *Business Communication: A Case Method Approach* (St. Paul, Minn.: Paradigm Publishing, 1995).

Chapter 8

1. Leopoldo Castedo, *A History of Latin American Art and Architecture from Pre-Columbian Times to the Present*, trans. and ed. Phyllis Freeman (New York: Praeger Books, 1969), 116–181.

2. Raymond L. Gordon, *Living in Latin America*, ed. H. Ned Seelye (Lincolnwood, Illinois: National Textbook Co., 1974), 16.

3. *Ibid.*

4. *Ibid.*, 68–71.

5. Charles H. Harris III, *A Mexican Family Empire: The Latifundio of the Sánchez Navarro Family, 1765–1867* (Austin: University of Texas Press, 1975).

6. Eugenio Chang-Rodríguez, *Latinoamérica: su civilización y su cultura* (Boston: Heinle & Heinle, 2000), 118–135.

7. Leopoldo Castedo, *A History of Latin American Art and Architecture,* trans. Phyllis Freeman (New York and Washington: Frederick A. Praeger Publishers, 1969), 222–228. See also Moisés González Navarro, "Mestizaje in Mexico During the National Period," *Race and Class in Latin America*, ed. Magnus Morner (New York: Columbia University Press, 1970), 145–169.

8. Arthur Natella, *The New Theatre of Peru* (New York: Senda Nueva de Ediciones, 1983), 21.

9. Hubert Herring, *A History of Latin America from the Beginning to the Present* (New York: Alfred A. Knopf, 1959), 211.

10. Simon Schwartzman, "Prospects for Higher Education in Latin America," http://www.be.edu/bc/-org/avp/soe/cihe/newsletter/News 17test 5.html.

11. Burton Bollac, "Bolivia's Indian Majority Goes to College," *Chronicle of Higher Education,* L11, No. 45 (July 14, 2006), A36–37.

12. *Ibid.*, 2.

13. Rodolfo Usigli, *El gesticulador,* ed. Rex Ballinger (New York: Appleton-Century-Crofts, 1961).

14. Thomas Merton, "Conquistador, Tourist, Indian," *A Thomas Merton Reader,* ed. Thomas P. McDonnell (Garden City, N.Y.: Doubleday Books, 1974), 309.

15. Comment made by Mexican writer Octavio Paz in a television drama about the life of Sor Juana Inés de la Cruz, Mexico City, 1991; Irving A. Leonard, "Sor Juana Inés de la Cruz, the Supreme Poet of Her Time in Castilian" in Lewis Hanke, *Latin America: A Historical Reader* (Boston: Little, Brown and Co., 1967), 136–144.

16. Marian Lloyd, "Slowly Enabling the Disabled," *Chronicle of Higher Education,* L11, No 49 (Aug., 11, 2006).

Chapter 9

1. Dominique Aubier and Manuel Tuñón de Lara, *Spain*, trans. Neline C. Clegg (New York: Viking Press, 1968), 5; Francisco Ugarte, Michael Ugarte, Kathleen McNerney, *España y su civilización* (Boston: McGraw-Hill, 2005).

2. Joan Connelly Ullman, *A Study of Anticlericalism in Spain, 1871–1912* (Cambridge, Mass.: Harvard University Press, 1968).

3. Arthur Natella, "St. Theresa and Unamuno's San Manuel Bueno, Mártir," *Papers on Language and Literature* (Fall, 1969): 458–464.

4. Wade Davis, *The Serpent and the Rainbow* (New York: Simon & Schuster, 1985), 174.

5. Alejo Carpentier, *The Lost Steps*, trans. Harriet De Onís (New York: Avon Books, 1967).

6. Enrique Anderson Imbert, *A History of Latin American Literature*, trans. John V. Falconieri (Detroit: Wayne State University Press, 1963), 146–149.

7. Lesley Byrd Simpson, *Many Mexicos* (Berkeley and Los Angeles: University of California Press, 1959), 280–295.

8. Interview by the author of Ernesto Cardenal on the island of Solentiname, Nicaragua, July, 1972.

9. Thomas Merton, *Thomas Merton in Alaska* (New York.: New Directions Books, 1988).

10. Lecture given by Manuel Puig, College Park, Md., April, 1971.

11. Arturo A. Fox, *España: Ida y vuelta* (San Diego, Calif.: Harcourt Brace Jovanovich, 1981), 19.

12. Philippe Thoby-Marcelin and Pierre Marcelin, *The Beast of the Haitian Hills*, trans. Peter C. Rhodes (San Francisco: City Lights Books, 1986).

Chapter 10

1. Octavio Paz, *El laberinto de la soledad* (Mexico: Fondo de Cultura Económica, 1999).

2. Conversation with the author. See Neglia's excellent study, *Aspectos del teatro moderno de Hispanoamérica* (Bogotá, Colombia: Editorial Stella, 1975).

3. Unpublished study from the office of Colombian holiday festivals by Colombian researcher Jennifer Cardozo, 6, 7.

4. www.fromers.com/destinations/south america.html; E-mail from São Paulo, Brazil, resident Ana Paula Trulín.

5. Matilde Olivella de Castells, *Mosaicos*, (Englewood Cliffs, N.J.: Prentice Hall, 2001).

6. Review by Raymond Boisvert of Mary Jane Gagnier de Mendoza, *Oaxaca Celebration: Family, Food and Fiestas in Teotitlan* (Santa Fe: Museum of New Mexico Press, 2005) in *Multicultural Review* 15, no. 2 (Summer, 2006): 92.

7. http://gosouthamerica.about.com/od/culfiestas/aSemSantaColVen.html.

8. Alex Bradbury, *Belize: The Bradt Travel Guide* (Guilford, Conn: The Globe Pequot Press, 2000), 19.

9. J.-M.G. Le Clézio and Geoff Winningham, *In the Eye of the Sun: Mexican Fiestas* (New York: W.W. Norton, 1997), 36.

10. Michael Coe, Dean Snow, Elizabeth Benson, *Atlas of Ancient America* (New York: Facts on File, 1990), 223.

11. Michael E. Garrett, "La Ruta Maya," *National Geographic*, vol. 176, no. 4 (October, 1989): 473.

12. Nathaniel Bishop, *The Pampas and Andes, A Thousand Miles' Walk Across South America* (Boston: Lee and Shepard Publishers, 1872), 205–207.

13. www.joeskitchen.com/Chile/fiestas-patrias.html.

14. Bradbury, *Belize*, 19; Television news report broadcast on the UNIVISION network Oct. 24, 2006.

15. David Nelson Blair, *The Land and People of Bolivia* (New York: Lippincott, 1990), 2, 128.

16. www.topics.mag.com/international/customs/venez-yare-masks.html.

17. Mary McVey Gill et al., *En Contacto* (Boston: Heinle & Heinle Publishers, 2007), 3.

18. Bill VanPatten et al., *Sol y viento* (New York: McGraw-Hill, 2004), 217.

19. www.pulseplanet.com/archive/june 98/1647.html.

20. Esteban Montejo, *The Autobiography of a Runaway Slave*, ed. Miguel Barnet, trans. Jocasta Innes (New York: Vintage Books, 1973), 75–76.

21. Alfonsina Barrionuevo, *Cuzco mágico* (Lima: Editorial Universo, no date), 132, 133; www.fromers.com/destinations and celebrations.html.

22. Le Clezio and Winningham, *In the Eye of the Sun*, 31, 34, 47.

23. Michael Coe, Dean Snow, Elizabeth Benson, *Atlas*, 223.

24. Bradbury, *Belize*, 166.

25. Garrett, "La Ruta Maya," p. 473.

26. Barrionuevo, *Cuzco mágico*, 31, author's translation.

27. G.M. Foster, *Tzintzuntzán: Mexican Peasants in a Changing World* (Boston: Little, Brown and Co. 1967), 168,184–185; quoted in Robert Anderson, *Magic, Science and Health* (New York: Harcourt Brace, 1996), 130–131.

Chapter 11

1. Tim Weinter, "Duke Jordan, 84, Jazz Pianist Who Helped to Build Bebop," *New York Times* (Aug. 17, 2006); Michael Cuscuna, liner notes, *Hampton Hawes Live at the Montmarte*, Arista Records; James Gavin, *Deep in a Dream, the Long Night of Chet Baker* (New York: Alfred A. Knopf, 2002); Ted Gioia, *West Coast Jazz* (New York: Oxford University Press, 2002).

2. http://welcometopuertorico.org/culture/music/html.

3. Unpublished monograph by Colombian researcher Jennifer Cardozo, p.7.

4. Liner notes from *Salsa Hits*, Sony Discos Inc. 2004, compact disc; http://welcome topuertorico.org/culture/music/html.

5. Cardozo, 5–6.

6. http://www.lafi.org/magazinersarticles.ven-music.html.

7. http://lre.salemstate.edu/aske/latmusic.htm.

8. Cardozo, 2, 3, 7, 8.

9. Eugenio Chang-Rodríguez, *Latinoamérica: su civilización y su cultura* (Boston: Heinle & Heinle, 2000), 176,177; Liner notes for *Inkuya, Land of the Incas* (Tucson, Arizona: Fortuna One Records), compact disc.

10. http://en.wikipedia.org/wiki/Music_of_Chile; liner notes for *Galería de Recuerdos*, vol. 2, Fabricantes Técnicos Asociados S.A. Lima, Peru; Gina Canepa-Hurtado, "La canción de Violeta Parra y su ubicación en el complejo cultural chileno entre los años 1960 a 1972. Esbozo de sus antecedentes socio-históricos y categorización de los fenómenos culturales antigentes," *Revista de crítica de literatura latinoamericana* (Lima, Peru), año 9, no. 17, 117–147.

11. http://en.wikipedia.org/wiki/music_of_Paraguay.

12. http://www.Mafusa.Ufse.br/BT.173 0002.html.

13. http://en.wikipedia.org/wiki/Luis_Miguel.

14. http://www.class.ufl.edu/users/cap/chiclete/dunn.html; *Arquitetura da alegría*, Manchete (São Paulo, Brazil), no. 2535 (Marco, 2006), 47.

15. http://wikipedia.org/wiki/Celia_Cruz; Himilce Novás, *Everything You Need to Know about Latino History* (New York: The Penguin Group, 1998), 294–296.

16. http://wolo/edoa/.Prg/wiki/Luis Miguel.

17. http://en.wikipedia.org/wiki/Luis_Miguel.

Chapter 12

1. Chris Kilham, *Tales from the Medicine Trail* (Emmaus, Penn.: Rodale Books, 2000).

2. Mircea Eliade, *Cosmos and History: The Myth of the Eternal Return*, trans. Willard R. Trask (New York: Harper & Row, 1959), 36.

3. *Ibid.*, 5

4. John Middletown, ed., *Magic Witchcraft and Curing* (New York: The Natural History Press, 1967), 37.

5. *Ibid.*, 71–75.

6. Eliade, *Cosmos and History*, 71–75.

7. Brad and Sherry Steiger, *Conspiracies and Secret Societies: The Complete Dossier* (Detroit: The Visible Ink Press, 2006), 501.

8. Manning Nash, "Witchcraft as a Social Power in a Tzetzal Community" in Middletown, *Magic Witchcraft*, 150–130.

9. Michael Harner, *The Way of the Shaman* (New York: Bantam Books, 1982), 138.

10. Esteban Montejo, *The Autobiography of a Runaway Slave*, ed. Miguel Barnet, trans. Jocasta Innes, (New York: Vintage Books, 1973), 26, 73.

11. *Ibid.*, 34.

12. http://www.banderasnews.com/0608/hb-curanderos.htm.

13. Susane Salimbene, *What Language Does Your Patient Hurt In?* (St. Paul, Minn.: EMC Paradigm, 2000), 33–36.

14. Liz Charles, *A Practical Introduction to Homeopathy* (London: Caxton Editions, 2002), 12–19.

15. William Grannell, "A Promise of Health," *Homeopathy Today* (March/April, 2006): 24–25.

16. Ilan Stavans, ed., *Encyclopedia Latina* (Danbury, Conn.: Scholastic Library Publishing, 2005), vol. 3, 94–101.

17. *Ibid.*, 101.

18. John G. Fuller, *Arigó, Surgeon of the Rusty Knife* (New York: Bantam Books, 1975), 228.

19. http://vpea.utb.edu/elnino/research articles/historicfolksainthood.html.

20. *Ibid.*; David St. Clair, *Pagans, Priests and Prophets* (Englewood Cliffs, N.J.: Prentice Hall, 1976).

21. http://luckymojo.com/drhernandez. html.

22. http://xploreheartlinks.com.

23. http://www.sacredheritage.com.

24. Ellen M. Adelman, "Mind-Body Intelligence, Mindfulness Meditation Psychoneuroimmunology, Qigong," *Holistic Nursing Practice* 20 (2006):147–151.

25. Wade Davis, *The Serpent and The Rainbow* (New York: Simon & Schuster, 1985), 175.

26. Tom Crockett, *Stone Age Wisdom: The Healing Principles of Shamanism* (Gloucester, Mass.: Fair Winds Press, 2003), 16–17.

Chapter 13

1. http://www.tau.ac.il/eial/IX-1/chanan.html.

2. Ibsen Martínez, "Romancing the Globe," *Foreign Policy* (November/December, 2005): 48–57.

3. Carl J. Mora, *Mexican Cinema: Reflections of a Society 1896–1980* (Berkeley: University of California Press, 1982), 242.

4. www.surdelsur.com/cine/cinein/cin inl.html

5. www.travelsur.net/facts104.html; Roger Manvell, ed., *The International Encyclopedia of Film* (New York: Crown Books, 1972), 328–333.

6. http://en.wikipedia.org/wiki/Mar%C3%Ada_Luisa_Bemberg.

7. http://en.wikipedia.org/wiki/Armando_Bo.

8. http://en.wikipedia.org/wiki/Leopoldo_Torre_Nilsson.

9. http://en.wikipedia.org/wiki/Carlos_Schlieper.

10. http://en.wikipedia.org/wiki/Mario_Soffici.

11. http://en.wikipedia.org/wiki/Leopoldo_Torres-R%C3%ADos.

12. http://en.wikipedia.org/wiki/Kurt_Land.

13. Mora, *Mexican Cinema*, 6–10.

14. *Ibid.*, 52–55; Carlos Monsivais, "Laughing Through One's Tears," *Literary Culture of Latin America: A Comparative History*, trans. Suzanne D. Stevens, eds. Mario J. Valdés and Djelal Kadir (Oxford: Oxford University Press, 2004), vol. 1, 591–297; Andrea Noble, *Mexican National Cinema* (London: Taylor & Francis, 2005).

15. Mora, *Mexican Cinema*, 52–55, 80–84, 245.

16. *Ibid.*, 48, 61–67. Sylvia Oroz states, "Between 1946 and 1950 there were stimulating developments in Mexican cinema, and that period saw a 'spectacular growth' [It was] "part of the policies of President Miguel Aleman" (author's translation). "Entre 1946 and 1950 no Mexico acentuouse o incentivo a indústria cinematográfica, e esse período e conhecido como o de 'crescimento espetacular' ... parte da política do presidente Miguel Alemán." Sylvia Oroz, *Melodrama: O Cinema de Lágrimas da América Latina* (Rio de Janeiro: Rio Fundo Editora, 1992), 161.

17. *Ibid.*, 22, 85–88, 101–102, 155–117.

18. http://www.topix.net/content/kri/3663181247415033903809912068 8

19. http://en.wikipedia.org/wiki/Alfonso_Cura%C3%B3n.

20. http://en.wikipedia.org/wiki/Emilio_Fernandez.

21. http://en.wikipedia.org/wiki/Antonio_Serrano.

22. http://en.wikipedia.org/wiki/Guillermo_del_Torre.

23. http://wikipedia.org/wiki/Alejandro_Gonz%C3%ALLEZ_1%C3%b

24. http://amautaspanish.com/amauta spanish/culture/cinema/movies-by-country.asp?Co; Fabiana Sacchi, Silvia Pessoa, Luís Martín-Cabrera, *Más allá de la pantalla* (Boston: Heinle & Heinle, 2005) 46; http://en.wikipedia.org/wiki/cinema_of_Peru; http://en.wikipedia.org/wiki/Luis_Llosa; http://en.wikipedia.org/wiki/Jorge_Olgu%C3%ADn_28director%29; Sacchi, Pessoa and Martín-Cabrera, *Más allá*, 184; http://en.wikipedia.org/wiki/Lautaro_Mur%CS%BAa; http://en.wikipedia.org/wiki/Ra%C3

%BAI_Ruiz.; http://en.wikipedia.org/wiki/Cinema_of_Cuba; http://en.wikipedia.org./wiki/María_Fuentes; http://en.wikipedia.org/wiki/Fina_Torres; http://en.wikipedia.org/wiki/Margot_Benacerraf; http://faculty-staff.on.edu/L/A-Robert.R.Lauer-I/NovoSicario.html; http://en.wikipedia.org/wiki/Cinema_of_Paraguay; http://cineuruguayo.cinecin.com/main.html; Randall Johnson and Robert Stam, eds., *Brazilian Cinema* (New York: Columbia University Press, 1982) 307; Lucia Helena, Sylvia Oroz and Sylvia Paixao, "Brazilian Women: Literature From the Nineteenth to the Twentieth Centuries," *Literary Cultures of Latin America A Comparative History,* ed. Mario J. Valdés and Djelal Kadir (Oxford: Oxford University Press, 2004), 328–335.

25. http://209.85.165.104/search?q=cache:aC4kUzbltfoJ:www.brazil.com.

26. http://209.85.165.104/search?q=cache:aC4kUzbltfoJ:www.brazil.com. Johnson and Stam, *Brazilian Cinema,* 214.

27. http://209.85.165.104/search?q=cache:aC4kUzbltfoJ:www.Brazil.com; Sylvia Oroz, *Melodrama,* op.cit.

Chapter 14

1. José Cid Pérez and Dolores Marti de Cid, *Teatro indio precolombino* (Madrid: Editorial Aguilar, 1964); Rubén Vargas Ugarte, *De nuestro antiguo teatro* (Lima: Editorial de la Universidad Católica, 1943).

2. William Brito Sansores, *La escritura de los Mayas* (Merida: Editorial Dante, 1986); Danauiek G., Brinton, ed., *El macho ratón o el güegüence* (Managua: Papelera Industrial de Nicaragua, 1974); conversation by the author with William Brito Sansores, president of the Yucatan Institute of Culture in Mexico City, August, 1988.

3. Willis Knapp Jones, *Behind Spanish-American Footlights* (Austin: University of Texas Press, 1966) 248; José Juan Arrom, *El teatro de Hispanoamérica en la época colonial* (Habana: Anuario Bibliográfico Cubano, 1956), 29–30.

4. Daniel Reedy, *The Poetic Art of Juan del Valle Caviedes* (Chapel Hill: University of North Carolina Press, 1964); Daniel Reedy, "Signs and Symbols of Doctors in *Diente del Parnaso,*" *Hispanic* 47, No. 4 (December, 1964): 705.

5. Carlos Solórzano, *El teatro latino-americano del siglo XX* (Mexico: Editorial Pormaca, 1964); Frank Dauster, *Ensayos sobre el teatro hispanoaméricano* (Mexico: Editorial Sepsetentas, 1975).

6. "El teatro en la vuelta del siglo: Florencio Sánchez," *Capítulo: la historia de la literatura Argentina* (Buenos Aires: Centro Editor de América Latina, 1962); Angela Blanco Amores de Pagella, *Nuevos temas en el teatro argentino* (Buenos Aires: Editorial Huemel, 1965).

7. Enrique Anderson-Imbert, *Spanish-American Literature: A History,* trans. John V. Falconieri (Detroit: Wayne State University Press, 1963), 146–148.

8. Pedro Simón Martínez, ed., *Sobre García Márquez* (Montevideo: Biblioteca de Marcha, 1971); M. Ian Adams, *Three Authors of Alienation* (Austin: University of Texas Press, 1975).

9. Ronald Christ, *The Narrow Act: Borges' Art of Allusion* (New York: New York University Press, 1969).

10. Enrique Anderson-Imbert, "Literatura fantástica," "Realismo mágico," and "Lo real maravilloso," *Actas del XVI Congress of Iberoamerican Literature* (Michigan State University, August, 1973).

11. For example see the works of Carlos Castañeda such as *The Teachings of Don Juan: A Yaqui Way of Knowledge* (New York: Pocket Books, 1975).

12. John E. Englekirk et al., *An Outline History of Spanish-American Literature* (New York: Appleton-Century-Crofts, 1965); Alberto Edwards, *Cuentos fantásticos* (Santiago, Chile: Editorial Zig-Zag, 1957).

13. Anderson-Imbert, *Spanish-American Literature,* 297.

14. René Rebetez, "Lo fantástico en la literatura mexicana contemporánea," *Espejo* (Mexico) no. 2, segundo trimestre, 1967: 23–50.

15. Claudia Neiva de Matos, "Brazil's Indigenous Textualities," *Literary Cultures of Latin America: A Comparative History,* ed. Mario J. Valdés and Dejlal Kadir, (Oxford: Oxford University Press, 2004), vol. 1, 234–237.

16. Octavio Paz et al., *Poesía en movimiento* (Mexico: Siglo XXI Editores, 1970), 329.

17. Mircea Eliade, *Cosmos and History: The Myth of the Eternal Return,* trans. William R. Trask (New York: Harper & Row, 1959), 5, 36.

Chapter 15

1. http://www.woodward.cl/chilefood.htm.

2. Magdalena Andrade et al. *Cocina y comidas Hispanas* (Boston: McGraw-Hill, 1998); http://en.wikipedia.org/wiki/Cuisine_of_Argentina.

3. http://en.wikipedia.org/wiki/Colombian_cuisine; http://en.wikipedia.org/wiki/Latin_American_cuisine.

4. http://en.wikipedia.org/wiki/Cuisine_of_Brazil; http://gosouthamerica.about.com/od/cuisine/aEcuBrazil.htm

5. Mark Copeland, *The Exotic Kitchens of Peru, the Land of the Inca* (New York: M. Evans and Co., 1999); Gloria Hinostroza, *Cocina Limeña* (Lima: San Martín de Porres University, 1999); http://travel.peru.com/travel/idocs/2002/11/23/DetailDocumento_571.

6. No author given, *Mexican Fiesta!* (Lincolnwood, Illinois: Publications International Ltd, 2004); http://www.targetwoman.com/articles/mexican-food.html; Susan Feniger and Mary Sue Milliken with Helene Siegel, *Mexican Cooking for Dummies* (Foster City, Calif.: IDG Books, 1999).

7. Andrade et al., *Cocina*, 9–13; no author given, *1,000 Low Fat, Salt, Sugar, & Cholesterol Recipes to Tempt Your Tastebuds* (Bath, U.K.: Parragon Publishing, 2003); http://en.Wikipedia.org/wiki/Cuban_cuisine; Jinx and Jefferson Morgan, *The Sugar Mill Caribbean Cookbook: Casual and Elegant Recipes Inspired by the Islands* (Boston: The Harvard Common Press, 1996); Andrade et al., *Cocina*, 10–13.

Chapter 16

1. http://en.Wikipedia.org/wiki/Music_of_Brazil.

2. Eugenio Chang-Rodríguez, *Latinoamérica: su civilización y su cultura* (Boston: Heinle & Heinle, 2000), 371.

3. http://welcometopuertorico.org/culture/music.shtml.

4. Chang-Rodríguez, *Latinoamérica,* 375; http://Jalisco/gov.mx/nuestroedo/muro/Moncayo.html.

5. John S. Brushwood, *The Spanish-American Novel: A Twentieth-Century Survey* (Austin: University of Texas Press, 1978).

6. Jacqueline Barnitz, *Twentieth-Century Latin American Art* (Austin: University of Texas Press, 2001) 57, 86, 87, 89, 94, 134, 135, 154, 155.

7. Jane Turner, ed., *Encyclopedia of Latin American & Caribbean Art* (London: Macmillan Reference Library, 2000), 538.

Chapter 17

1. Andre Hodeir, *Jazz Is Evolution and Essence*, trans. David Noakes (New York: Grove Press, 1956).

2. Eugenio Chang-Rodríguez, *Latinoamérica: su civilización y su cultura* (Boston: Heinle & Heinle, 2000), 369, 381.

Index

193